International Relations:
PEACE or WAR?

International Relations:

PEACE or WAR?

Richard Rosecrance
Cornell University

McGraw-Hill Book Company

New York   St. Louis   San Francisco   Düsseldorf   Johannesburg
Kuala Lumpur   London   Mexico   Montreal   New Delhi   Panama
Rio de Janeiro   Singapore   Sydney   Toronto

For Barbara

sine quo non

International Relations: Peace or War?

1 2 3 4 5 6 7 8 9 0 DODO 7 9 8 7 6 5 4 3 2

Library of Congress Cataloging in Publication Data

Rosecrance, Richard N
    International relations: peace or war?

    1. International relations. I. Title.
JX1315.R62   327   72-2686
ISBN 0-07-053697-X
ISBN 0-07-053698-8 (pbk.)

This book was set in Press Roman by Creative Book Services, division of McGregor & Werner, Incorporated. The editor was Robert P. Rainier; the designer was Creative Book Services, division of McGregor & Werner, Incorporated; and the production supervisor was Sally Ellyson.
The printer and binder was R. R. Donnelley & Sons Company.

Preface

The focus of international relations studies has always been on the prevention of war. Throughout history men have speculated on the causes of war and have striven to stop it or to reduce its incidence. Broad historical or philosophic approaches have suggested remedies such as the elimination of the nation-state. More recently, and on a less grandiose basis, various other means of war prevention or reduction have been offered. Some of these could be implemented by individual states without a wholesale reform or recasting of the international system. Quantitative analyses have been performed which indicate the need for changes in specific international instrumentalities, such as the need to find different patterns of alliance or perhaps even to avoid alliances. Yet there has been little effort at stocktaking, little effort to draw together the various approaches and propositions into a single analysis which might summarize existing research.

This book seeks to perform this function for the undergraduate student. However, it is not confined merely to repeating the "conventional wisdom" of past practitioners. In several respects, where research is vague or contradictory, it strives to break new ground. In this process and in that of seeking to summarize the conflicting tendencies of international relations research, the author is only too conscious that a satisfactory unification of theory and practice has not been fully achieved. Some of the trends of international political research emphasize continuing nationalism in world politics. Others note a trend toward internationalism or regionalism. Some studies emphasize power or military measures of political reality; others point to an emergence of economic strength as a primary measure. These differences are not merely disagreements among international relations theorists; they lie in the data themselves. There *are* contradictions in international politics. We cannot know the final result of the various forces operating today.

Given this, I have still tried to press the argument further, to seek modest reconciliations between apparently contradictory viewpoints. In this effort, I have greatly benefited from the work of my coworkers in the field. Those familiar with the literature will note the great debt to Karl Deutsch, Ernst

Haas, Kenneth Waltz, Thomas Schelling, John Harsanyi, Daniel Ellsberg, Kenneth Boulding, Arthur Lee Burns, J. David Singer, and a host of other theorists. But the indebtedness does not end there. A wide variety of students and colleagues have made important contributions to this work, so much so that it is hard to say where their contribution begins and my own ends. Three of my colleagues who wish to remain anonymous did major criticisms of the original manuscript. Their comments have greatly improved it in both focus and style of presentation. Three coworkers, Jeffrey Hart, Brian Healy, and Arthur Stein went far beyond the bounds of friendship in laboring over an obdurate manuscript. Their contributions to the substantial argument have been immense, and I am deeply grateful to them. I also have an unacknowledged debt to a generation of students at UCLA, Berkeley, and Cornell. Most students are not aware of the influence they have upon their teachers. I am sure I have learned more from them than I have taught. Mrs. Barbara Stephens spent endless hours typing and retyping successive drafts and in drawing the innumerable diagrams. If they convey meaning, it is because of her inexhaustible patience. My greatest debt, however, is to Barbara Benjamin Rosecrance, who not only read and caviled over every word, but exposed the inaccuracies and shoddy reasoning which I had employed. I am the more conscious of the book's deficiencies because I know I have not satisfied her. Dedicating the book to her is small recompense for all she has done.

Richard Rosecrance

Contents

PART

1

Introduction

Perhaps a special justification has to be made for studying international relations today. For too many people, international relations provides such a record of duplicity and wanton violence that its very contemplation is offensive. Yet the nation-state system is with us. It will not be eradicated by a magic formula or by a return to isolationism. National interests often conflict; when they do, war is always a possibility. If war is to be limited or prevented, leaders and peoples must have a far clearer awareness of the vital principles and facts of international relations than they do at the moment.

This book seeks to make a contribution to that awareness. The first chapters deal with the need to study relations among nations and with the origins and essentials of the state system. International history of the past two hundred years is then briefly surveyed. The fourth chapter offers an introduction to three basic determinants of war: *systems, objectives,* and *techniques.* These three theoretical notions are the central explanatory concepts which will be examined and developed in the rest of the book.

CHAPTER ONE

Why Study
International Relations?

The study of international relations is of fundamental importance today, for the problem of war has not been solved. Although all-out war has not occurred recently, there has been a rising number of limited wars since World War II. Violence is on the increase. And while the Vietnam war may be winding down in terms of American participation, its scope and destructiveness have not abated.[1] The problem of unlimited war, moreover, has not been eliminated. People may be deluded into thinking that while limited war is horrible, all dangers of nuclear war have disappeared. In fact, nuclear weapons, rockets, and other delivery capabilities are rapidly spreading to major areas of conflict such as the Middle East and Southeast Asia. It is not inconceivable that resort to these weapons may take place, if there is a renewal of fighting in these areas. As nuclear weapons spread, moreover, they are likely to pass to states which are much more dissatisfied with the existing system than the present possessors—China, the Soviet Union, France, Britain, and the United States. Unless we find some means for moderating or eliminating international conflicts, we can anticipate further and perhaps even larger scale violence on the international scene.

The elimination or moderation of conflict has in fact become the predominant goal of the international relations field.[2] The solutions offered by academic practitioners, however, have not resolved the issue of war. We still have too little understanding of the basic processes and too little knowledge of relevant theory to offer a solution. In short, one cannot merely put one's head in the sand and hope that war will go away. Nor can its effects be ignored. Why should we study international relations?

DOMESTIC PRIORITIES

The first argument is that war and continuing military involvement have caused a major derangement of domestic politics. Often, when unpopular wars persist, governments dissemble. They seek to hide the real objective of their policies and to pursue them by partly covert means. Publics gradually realize that they cannot trust their governments. Their opposition to policy extends to governmental institutions themselves, and the domestic fabric of society is partially unravelled.

Equally important, with major military involvement there is an enormous wastage of human life and world resources. In addition to the human costs of war, each year arms expenditure in the world exceeds $200 billion. If these resources, or even a part of them, could be turned to the solution of such problems as population control, education, urban rehabilitation, ecology, and welfare, the lives of the world's inhabitants could be greatly improved. If we are not able to divert our resources to constructive ends our very survival may be threatened. As long as wars occur or threaten, however, this necessary diversion to social tasks will not take place. Domestic societies will be beset by cynicism and hypocrisy. Governments will systematically mislead their publics. Until we know how to prevent war, we will not be able to solve other critical social and political problems.

REPETITIVE WAR

A second point is that it is by no means clear that the problem of all-out war has been solved, no matter how confident we are about the impossibility of nuclear conflict. Actually, the theories of peace which leaders have used in the past have usually been out of date by the time they were tried. Today we have no theory of war prevention which actually comes to grips with the contemporary situation. Throughout history men have developed theories which were designed to prevent the last war, but which had little application to a future war. International change has chronically outrun man's perception of events. After a major conflict leaders resolve to take those actions which will prevent that conflict from recurring. But the international system does not stand still—the specific causes of one war are not the specific causes of another. The means used to prevent one may actually make another more likely. Let us cite a few examples:

1. After the Revolutionary and Napoleonic Wars of 1792 to 1815 the leaders of Europe agreed that domestic revolution was the likely cause of war. They set up a system of international conferences, called the Concert of Europe, that were designed to prevent revolution within the body politic of

Europe. Without revolution, there would be no war. If such a system had been in existence in 1789 it might have averted the revolutionary and Napoleonic conflicts which ensued. But domestic revolution was not the cause of war after 1815. By 1850 leaders had become so concerned with maintaining their own power positions that they could not have cared less about the prevention of war. They were even willing to use war to reinsure their own positions domestically. Instead of suppressing revolution to prevent war, they were willing to use war to prevent revolution. The Concert of Europe could not help with the latter task.

2. After World War I, the diplomats decided that the absence of a regular international conference system had allowed war to occur. (The Concert of Europe had lapsed in the interim and had held only two general meetings: on the Near East in 1878 and on Morocco in 1906.) If all European nations had been required to come and sit at a common table to discuss their differences in July 1914, war might have been prevented. So the peacemakers created the League of Nations, which was supposed to be a standing international conference. Henceforth all states would be forced to discuss their disputes before the bar of the League Council or Assembly and to present their arguments in the glare of world publicity. Open covenants were to be openly arrived at. If aggression were intended, not only world opinion, but also opinion within the potential aggressor's own territory would rally against a breach of the peace and prevent war. Had such a system been in effect before 1914, World War I might not have occurred. None of the leaders of Europe in July 1914 wanted a general war, but they all thought that by committing themselves to action they could face down an adversary and either prevent war or ensure that it would be local. Had they been able to see the results of their actions, all would have hesitated, and a conference on the eve of war might have produced general understanding.

3. Such a system, however, could not have prevented war in 1939. The League probably would have been able to cope with misunderstandings among statesmen who held a common aversion to war. German Chancellor Adolf Hitler did not share these views; he wished to humiliate his opponents by military force. Thus, no matter how hard the British and French strived to meet his demands and to settle differences, meetings and conferences could not guarantee peace.

Another difficulty was that the British had concluded that their advance understandings with France as well as the general system of European alliances had brought on war in 1914. If they refused to commit themselves to any power or to join any alliance, they reasoned, Britain would not be drawn into a second conflict. Noncommitment and a readiness to use the League machinery was the British prescription for peace.

The British theory did not prevent war; it made the task of stopping Hitler even more difficult. Since Britain did not support France, Paris was afraid to make a strong stand against Berlin. Hitler was led to believe that both the

French and the British would back down in a crisis. Oddly enough, World War II occurred partly because the lessons of World War I had been learned too well.

4. Today we are in danger of repeating similar mistakes. After World War II the United States helped to devise an international system based upon commitment and deterrence. If commitments were made to other nations, if alliances were contracted, then those commitments and those allies would not be challenged. Solemnly promising to support an ally, we would deter an adversary's attack upon him.

Again we succeeded in devising a means of preventing the last war. Since the British and French failure to commit themselves in advance led to the appeasement of Nazi Germany, the post-World War II system would not make the same mistake; we would make commitments and would back them with military force. We would resolutely foreswear appeasement. We seemed to believe that the more alliances and commitments we made, the more surely would our foe be contained and deterred, hemmed in by a network of United States military alliances.

We have since found, however, that commitments in themselves do not produce deterrence. Pledges are not self-enforcing and are sometimes challenged. When they are, a nation is forced to ask how much expenditure in resources and manpower deterrence obligations are worth. How much risk of nuclear war should one willingly tolerate?

In one sense it is difficult to understand how we could have embraced such a limited theory. How could we assume that we could make commitments to more than forty nations without being called upon to honor them? Or if called to honor them, that we could carry them out with little cost and minor risk? Once again we seem to have been over-influenced by erroneous "lessons of history." Our interpretation of the 1930s was that the British and French could have resisted Hitler in 1935 or 1936 with little cost to themselves or to Europe. If commitments had been made and honored, either World War II would not have occurred, or it would have been decided as a minor skirmish in 1936 resulting in German defeat. Hitler would have been dispatched before he had time to build a major military machine. Thus it seemed possible to conclude that the policy of making commitments was not only a correct strategy, it was not a costly strategy. Commitments then would offer deterrent benefits without countervailing costs.

These notions have now been put to test as a result of United States participation in a large number of limited conflicts since World War II culminating in Vietnam, Laos, and Cambodia. We have been forced to reconsider the costs and benefits of the commitment strategy, to ask whether the gains justify the costs. The old strategy is inadequate, but we have yet to find a new one. Once again operative theories remain behind the march of events. War has not been ruled out. Peace cannot be taken for granted.

Nor should one have faith in the rationality of decision makers. Under conditions of stress and in circumstances of crisis, decisions can be made which overlook crucial pieces of information or fail to foresee the ultimate outcome of a chain of events. The Austrian role in 1914 appears to suggest that Vienna engaged in criminal wishful thinking in hoping that Serbia could be defeated without the intervention of other powers. Austrian leaders stopped receiving information which was contrary to their fixed beliefs, thereby precipitating war. In 1941 the Japanese had neither a plan for victory over the United States if the war went beyond 1942, nor a plan to bring United States capitulation during 1942—yet they still attacked. Germany also had no concrete plan for victory over the United States, yet she declared war after the Japanese attack on Pearl Harbor. These and other cases raise the prospect of future irrationality of decision makers in a crisis in which nuclear weapons might be used. If one answers that all statesmen will be rational in the face of nuclear deterrence, we could respond by asking whether nuclear threats would have deterred the Japanese in 1941 or whether Hitler would not have used nuclear weapons (if he had had them) against the nuclear-armed United States. It may even be that the world has been incredibly lucky in the past twenty-five years in avoiding reckless decision makers at the helm of major world powers. But this luck cannot be counted on forever.

THEORY AND THE STUDY OF INTERNATIONAL RELATIONS

Political leaders have been at a loss to find the right path to peace. But academic practitioners have not come up with more consistent or correct notions. The systematic empirical study of international politics has proceeded for more than a generation, at least since the work of L.F. Richardson and Quincy Wright.[3] Yet we are still at a loss to know certainly what factors are correlated with peace, which with war. At various times we have been told that war is a function of internal conflict, and that if we manage to prevent domestic strife and insecurity we will avoid international conflict.[4] On the other hand, we have been informed that for certain periods in international history there is no correlation, or only a very low correlation, between domestic and international conflict.[5] Eliminating the former, then, could not be expected to prevent the latter.

It has been argued that international conflict is more likely in a bipolar world than in a multipolar order.[6] However, various empirical studies seem to show that multipolar systems evince more conflict in operation than bipolar systems.[7]

Some theorists have contended that war is a function of the level of economic development and that developed states manifest far less violent behavior than those in more primitive economic circumstances.[8] We are also told, however, that rapid economic development is destabilizing and is likely to be the cause of political extremism on both internal and external levels.[9]

On a historical basis it has been asserted that peace tends to prevail where there is an even distribution of power among major states, and that war occurs when an imbalance develops.[10] But the obverse has also been claimed. Some theorists argue that an exact balance of power is the most dangerous international situation; neither protagonist is thereby deterred from attacking. World War I occurred, it is asserted, precisely because of an emergent balance of power between Triple Alliance and Triple Entente. But, in conditions of imbalance, with one bloc at the top and another in a subordinate position, the first has no incentive to attack, and the second cannot hope to succeed in doing so.[11]

Confusion also exists on the precise role of communications among nations in fostering peace. One venerable strand of analysis claims that as communications links between countries intensify and deepen, nationalist or conflictual attitudes recede.[12] Clearly, however, there are crucial thresholds in this process. Up to a certain point an increase in the communications links between two states may actually foster conflict, particularly if there is no background compatibility of main values.[13] Initial communications links may actually show states how different they are. Increasing communication between Germany and Britain prior to World War I was not stabilizing. Increasing communication between Germany and the outside world in the 1930s did not foster a harmony of points of view. Gross communications theories stated in quantitative fashion obscure the point that some kinds of communications are much more important than others in assuring a peaceful relationship among states.

We are also uncertain what type of alliance networks to recommend for the international system. We are told that alliance may be likely to reduce the number of interaction opportunities and therefore may be a factor for war.[14] Empirical studies, however, have tended to show that while alliance aggregation may be a factor for war in the twentieth century, it was not a factor in the nineteenth century.[15] World War II emerged out of a context in which major states were not rigidly bound in alliance commitments.

The entire argument concerning the desirability of participation in alliances remains ambiguous. It would seem that alliances represent a cooperative element in the system; if all powers could participate in like-minded alliances, the amount of cooperation in the system would increase. Yet alliances between two states may increase the hostility between them and some third nation.[16] Thus we are not sure whether the amount of cooperation in the system can be indefinitely increased or whether cooperation in one part of the system engenders conflict in another part. Reacting to this possibility, some theorists have prescribed nonalignment as an alternative.[17] But this concept, if extended to the limits of the system, would recommend cooperation with no one.

Nor is there consensus on the desirability of a world government which would control the international activities of member states. Certain theorists appear to believe that such a world governmental system would break down in feuding among component parts in the same way in which colonial or imperial systems have disintegrated.[18] Oddly enough, the attempt to set up a world government, if opposed by major states, could actually increase the amount of violent conflict. Even those theorists who are sure that a world government is the answer to our problems are pessimistic that it actually can be created.[19] Academic practitioners and theorists obviously do not have the answer to the cause of war. They do not know how to give us peace.

EFFORTS TO PREVENT WAR

The problem of finding a correct theory of war prevention, however, is not the only difficulty in assuring peace. Not only do leaders and theorists often suggest incorrect or contradictory means of preserving peace, nations and peoples often waver in their pursuit of peace. As we look at history, it appears that every period of major conflict gave rise to energetic efforts to prevent that conflict from recurring. The major achievements of peacemakers have always followed a catastrophic war: The Concert of Europe grew out of the Napoleonic Wars; the League of Nations out of World War I; the United Nations out of World War II. Leaders try to avoid the repetition of chaos. Even where a full agreement between victors cannot be achieved, they initially tend to follow policies which avoid large-scale war.

Then something happens. The quest for peace loses its old urgency. The structure of international cooperation begins to deteriorate. Separate national objectives begin to take precedence over the general objective of avoiding war. To be sure, leaders have operated on incorrect theories; therefore it is perhaps desirable that they lose the public support necessary to carry them out. But no new urgency, no new mandate is given to leaders offering new theories. The need to secure peace seems less. Nationalism reasserts itself. Once peace has been temporarily established people come to think of it as a permanent condition. They depart from previous convictions that war can be prevented only by persistent effort and are deluded into the belief that major war is unthinkable. Alternatively, and even worse, they may convince themselves that war can be risked because its consequences are no longer disastrous. In the latter part of the nineteenth century, some historians even glorified war.

In part, the maintenance of peace is made more difficult by the rise of a new political generation. New leaders may not remember the previous conflict vividly enough. They seek new national objectives. If peace requires cooperation among states, some new leaders may find that this cooperation restricts their national ambitions. If peace requires a primary attention to international interests, the new leaders may stress a greater attention to national interests. Not accidentally perhaps, in the history of international relations since 1820, periods of warfare have tended to be concentrated at roughly twenty-five year intervals.[20] War occurs partly because of the regular cycle of forgetting. The lessons of one generation are not effectively transmitted to the next.

If we consider the errors that nations and peoples may make in pursuing the quest for peace, it is even possible that we are in danger of having the worst of both worlds. The theories devised after World War II to prevent future conflict have not worked: in Vietnam they have involved us in a war which has little relationship to United States national interests and which has had deplorable human consequences for all involved. The academic practitioners of international relations have not come up with a set of theories which will solve our problems: their recommendations are inconsistent. Finally, not only are the theories which policy makers operate on based on a rather gross attempt to apply the lessons of Munich, but nations and peoples everywhere seem to have lost interest in international cooperation. Major war is perhaps becoming more and more unthinkable only because it is not being thought about. It is within the realm of possibility that we will glide from one international dispute to another without realizing that we are on a slide whose ultimate end is the abyss of World War III. Today we employ World War II theories and convince ourselves that no great effort is needed to prevent war.

Given the dangers of repetitive war, the need to understand its causes and possible remedies is obvious. The study of international relations may even be more crucial today than it was immediately after World War II. In the aftermath of that disastrous war leaders and peoples were convinced that future war could only be avoided by a single-minded concentration upon preventing it. Even in the context of cold war this resolve was uppermost in the minds of national leaders. Today the need for a similar effort to rule out future war is not taken as seriously by statesmen and publics. Unfortunately, it is precisely in those periods in which peace is taken for granted that the seeds of the next war are sown. When nations are confident that major war cannot occur—that all see its futility and unacceptability—that is when it may begin. We may now be in such a period. Events of the 1970s may well determine for good or ill, the fate of mankind.

HOW SHOULD WE STUDY INTERNATIONAL RELATIONS?

If war is to be avoided in the future, we must have a better knowledge of two realms of inquiry: (1) history and (2) theory. The two must be studied together. History cannot be studied without theory. Merely searching historical accounts for the causes of war will not help unless we have theory to guide us. What, after all, should we look for? If, on the other hand, we have theoretical hypotheses to use in studying the historical record, we can strive to see whether history bears out or refutes the hypotheses. Among hypotheses that have been advanced by international relations theorists through the ages are the following:

1. That war is caused by an imbalance of power. (Thus, if a balance of power could be maintained, there would be peace.)

2. That war is caused by a balance of power. (Hence, if an imbalance of power could be established, war would be ruled out.)

3. That war can only be generated under circumstances where the multiplicity and balance of transactions among states (migration, tourism, trade, political interchange, communications, and so on) is below some level. (Thus, if states had higher levels of transaction, war could be prevented.)

4. That war is the result of having separate state units. (Hence, if state units were abolished, and a world government set up, peace would reign.)

5. That war is related to the amount of internal conflict in society. (Thus, if internal conflict could be reduced, war would be reduced.)

6. That war is a function of the type of polarity in the system. (Some theorists assert that bipolarity helps to cause war; others that multi-polarity makes war more likely.)

7. That war is a function of exclusive alliance patterns. (Thus, the more alliances of this type, the more war.)

8. That war is the result of a failure of deterrence. (Thus, if general deterrent conditions could be established and maintained, there would be no war.)

9. That war is the result of certain types of decision-making practices among major states. (Hence, if these practices could be changed, war could be prevented.)

10. That war or conflict is a function of the bargaining position of states. (Thus, if the structure of the game could be changed, more cooperation would result.)

11. That war is a function of a particular form of the internal polity. (Hence, if that form could be changed, there would be peace.)

12. That war is the outcome of certain patterns of the arms race. (If those patterns could be changed, war might be avoided.)

When we look at historical documents and accounts, we can seek to discover whether any of these propositions are supported. If they are not, we can then try to modify the hypotheses, or to generate new ones.

But if theory or theoretical hypotheses are required to illuminate the study of international history, the validation of theory also requires historical testing. Hypotheses or generalizations cannot be tested in the abstract; we must find some data against which they can be validated or discredited. Thus, the historical record is crucial for an informed study of international relations. History requires theory, and theory requires history.

THE PURPOSE OF THIS BOOK

This book seeks to take some of the leading hypotheses in the field of international relations and to apply them to historical contexts, and to see if and in what degree they can be confirmed. In some cases we do not have enough historical information to know whether the theories are true or not. When this is the case, the hypotheses will be stated in theoretical terms without application to historical reality. In some cases new partial theories will be offered when it is not clear that any existing theory can do the job.

All the way through the book the student will be confronted with examples of reasoning drawn from the historical or theoretical literature. Until we have a better basis for understanding, these conclusions constitute the evidence of the discipline of international relations. Certain international situations are analogous to formal bargaining situations in game theory; therefore they may be treated in game theoretic form. Other situations present analogies to the market competition of firms or to two individuals striving to maximize their utility positions in the division of two goods. Where these occur, economic reasoning may be used. In the case of deterrence, it is possible to devise a mathematical deterrent model which shows what variables one should change in order to make peace more likely. Where the formal theories of balance in small groups apply to international circumstances, they will be used. In many cases the incentive structure of international politics approximates that of a game of strategy and can be treated accordingly.

This is by no means always the case. Some decisions made by national leaders are based more completely on an attention to domestic constituents and to the domestic decision-making network than they are to international factors. In this case, states are not players and the game, if it occurs at all, is likely to be found in the domestic decision-making process. The results are likely to produce unpredictable actions at the international level which cannot be understood in formal terms. Particularly at this juncture, we have to learn from history what others have done in similar circumstances. History is the record of miscalculation and misapprehension. It may be that studying international situations of the past can alert us to conditions in which irrationalities might apply in the present or future. We may thereby learn more about how to avoid them. National leaders sometimes become angry and appear not to calculate the consequences of their actions. War is most likely under these circumstances. How can they be eliminated in the future? Or is this a hopeless task? History is a crucial guide to understanding on this score.

Beyond this, history helps to tell us whether theory is correct. It gives examples of balance of power, of different forms of polarity, of arms races. It portrays the influence of domestic factors. Perhaps even more important, it offers the record against which new theories may be generated and compared.

The theories offered throughout the book take the following form:

x (war) is a function or partial function of y (explanatory variable)

Hence, if y increases, one can expect x to change in a predicted direction. In each chapter we seek to find variables or factors which if suitably changed, would reduce the chances or prospect of major war. These questions are at the core of the international relations field. Most of the scholarly literature of the past twenty years has dealt with the question of how conflict can be mitigated or eliminated and how cooperation can be increased in international relations.

Before turning centrally to these questions, we shall first set the stage by looking at the development of the modern state system and at the record of international history of the past two centuries. Then we shall examine international *systems, objectives,* and *techniques* as determinants of peace and war. What kind of international systems are most conducive to peace, which to war? What national objectives can be pursued without causing conflict, which are likely to lead to hostility or violence? What techniques can nations use which will avoid the extremes of conflict and which will not produce aggressive behavior or the part of other states? If these questions can even be partially answered, we may have a better basis for policy-making efforts towards peace than has existed before. Mankind has not achieved peace, and even limited wars have become more destructive. If the discipline of international relations can contribute to the establishment and maintenance of peace among nations, the justification for studying it seems clear.

NOTES

1 See Raphael Littauer and Norman Uphoff (eds.), *The Air War in Indochina* (Boston: Beacon Press, 1972).

2 See among others: Kenneth N. Boulding, *Conflict and Defense* (New York: Harper and Row, 1962); Anatol Rapoport, *Fights, Games and Debates* (Ann Arbor: University of Michigan Press, 1960); L. F. Richardson, *Arms and Insecurity* (Chicago: Quadrangle Books, 1960); K. W. Deutsch et al., *Political Community and the North Atlantic Area* (Princeton: Princeton University Press, 1957); Kenneth N. Waltz, *Man, the State, and War* (New York: Columbia University Press, 1959); John Herz, *International Politics in the Atomic Age* (New York: Columbia University Press, 1959); Stanley Hoffman (ed.), *Contemporary Theory in International Relations* (Englewood Cliffs, N. J.: Prentice-Hall, 1960); Richard Rosecrance, *Action and Reaction in World Politics* (Boston: Little, Brown, 1963); Raymond Aron, *Peace and War* (New York: Doubleday, 1966); Quincy Wright, *A Study of War* (Chicago: University of Chicago Press, 1942); Bruce Russett,

Community and Contention (Cambridge, Mass.: MIT Press, 1963); Ernst B. Haas, *Beyond the Nation State* (Stanford: Stanford University Press, 1964); Ernst B. Haas, *The Uniting of Europe* (Stanford: Stanford University Press, 1968); Charles McClelland, *Theory and the International System* (New York: Macmillan, 1966); F. H. Hinsley, *Power and the Pursuit of Peace* (Cambridge: Cambridge University Press, 1963). To single out these works is merely to underscore typical foci. Other equally representative studies could be cited which center on the same problems.

3 See L.F. Richardson, "Generalized Foreign Policy," *British Journal of Psychology Monographs Supplements* 1939; and Quincy Wright, *A Study of War* (Chicago: University of Chicago Press, 1942).

4 See R. Rosecrance, *Action and Reaction in World Politics* (Boston: Little, Brown, 1963).

5 See R. Rummel, "Dimensions of Conflict Behavior within and between Nations," *General Systems Yearbook,* 1963; and R. Tanter, "Dimensions of Conflict Behavior within and between Nations, 1958-60," *Journal of Conflict Resolution,* 1966.

6 See Karl Deutsch and David Singer, "Multipolar Power Systems and International Stability," *World Politics,* April 1964.

7 See Michael Haas, "International Subsystems: Stability and Polarity," *American Political Science Review,* March 1970.

8 See R. McNamara, *The Essence of Security* (New York: Harper & Row, 1968).

9 See S.M. Lipset, *Political Man* (Garden City: Doubleday, 1960).

10 See F.H. Hinsley, *Power and the Pursuit of Peace* (Cambridge, England: Cambridge University Press, 1963).

11 See A.F.K. Organski, *World Politics* (New York: Knopf, 1968).

12 See K. Deutsch, *Nationalism and Social Communication* (New York: Wiley, 1953).

13 See K. Deutsch et al., *Political Community and the North Atlantic Area* (Princeton: Princeton University Press, 1968).

14 See K. Deutsch and D. Singer, "Multipolar Power Systems and International Stability," *World Politics,* April 1964.

15 See Singer and Small, "Alliance Aggregation and the Onset of War," in Singer (ed.), *Quantitative International Politics* (New York: Free Press, 1968).

16 See A.L. Burns, "From Balance to Deterrence," *World Politics,* July 1957.

17 See J.W. Burton, *International Relations* (Cambridge: Cambridge University Press, 1965).

18 See I.L. Claude, *Power and International Relations* (New York: Random House, 1962).

19 See K. Waltz, *Man, the State and War* (New York: Columbia University Press, 1959).

20 See F.H. Denton, "Some Regularities in International Conflict, 1820-1949," *Background,* 1966.

CHAPTER TWO

Essentials of
International Relations

THE EVOLUTION OF INTERNATIONAL RELATIONS

International relations is the study of the relations of nations. But nations did not always exist. Strictly speaking one cannot apply the term *international relations* to the period of the Greek city-states, because the Greek *polis* did not include all Greeks; it had no hinterland beyond the city. Furthermore, while a citizen of the Greek city-state was a vigorous participant in all its affairs, there were many who were not citizens and hence were deprived of the rights of political action and participation.

At the end of the medieval period and the beginning of the Renaissance, the Italian city-states emerged as concrete and cohesive political entities. They were, however, neither usually representative, nor could they speak for all Italy. The Italian nationality was not coterminous with the tiny states of Florence, Venice, or Milan.

It was not until the Peace of Westphalia in 1648, perhaps not until the eighteenth century, that it became possible to talk of *international relations,* a term invented by the English philosopher Jeremy Bentham. During the eighteenth century princes gradually increased their hold on national territory to the extent that in some cases, at least, nation-states emerged, i.e., states which embraced or nearly embraced the entire national group of which their population was composed. France came to include all or nearly all Frenchmen. England embraced all Englishmen, and the United Kingdom included

Scotland, Wales, and Ireland as well. Germany was not yet united into a single national state. Italy remained divided. States, however, were coming closer and closer to becoming nations.

The development of the nation-state was also connected with another important change in historic political life. Until some point in the seventeenth century political life was not fully secular. States were not autonomous independent units because of the allegiance they owed to external religious authority. The kings of Europe were supposed to be the loyal servants of the church, and to yield personal and national interests before the authority of the medieval papacy. The Reformation of the sixteenth century offered a decisive challenge to papal authority.

NATIONS AND NATIONALISM

With the development of the nation-state came the phenomenon of nationalism. Nationalism is fundamentally the creation of "we-feeling" among members of a nation to the point where national loyalties take precedence over most other obligations. Germans wish to advance the interest of Germany, Frenchmen of France, Americans of America, even at the expense of other countries or universal moral norms. Nationalism expresses itself in sentiments like: "my country, right or wrong." When carried to its ultimate conclusion, nationalism would have the citizens of the nation-state substitute an overriding loyalty to the nation for loyalty to family, friends, the church, or international moral principles.

In some ways it is surprising that nationalism should have been such a potent force and that it remains largely undiminished today. During the nineteenth century the major forces in world politics (technology, economics, and ideology) were international in character. The force of industrialism was worldwide; it did not wish to be confined in the parochial structures of the nation-state. Ideological principles were directed to reforming society throughout Europe, first in a liberal, then later in a socialist direction. In reaction the old eighteenth century aristocratic cliques wished to reinstate elite rule of societies, to restrict popular participation, and to prevent both working classes and middle classes from acquiring their full share of influence in government. None of these doctrines was national or sectarian.

By the outbreak of World War I in 1914, however, nationalism had triumphed over all three factors: the world economy was shattered with the impact of war; one national-industrial combine was pitted against another in manufacturing the munitions of war. The ideological forces of reform, whether they were liberal or radical, fell before the greater power of nationalism. When the crunch came citizens of all social classes and representatives of each economic stratum put their loyalty to their nation-state ahead of universal economic or political forces.

In part this was because the development of popular influence upon government had proceeded to the point where peoples identified almost willy-nilly with their state. After the political and economic reforms of the French Revolution, citizens tended to see the nation-state as the creative element within society protecting and later extending previous social gains. Eventually perhaps some came to view the nation as an embodiment of their own political desires and aspirations.

The development of nationalism was strengthened by feelings of power-lessness in the face of other impersonal social forces. The average man could not control or even affect the conduct of worldwide business enterprise; he could not influence the development of ideological movements in other states; he could not regulate the pace of technological innovation. But the nation-state, whether in practice or in theory, was supposed to be his instrument to take actions which publics mandated and to eschew those policies which publics disliked. Thus, in the period of popular influence upon government, the national state has become the public's device for striving to control impersonal social forces. It is not surprising in this context that the citizen returned undue loyalty in exchange.

The force of nationalism today is perhaps the greatest barrier to international peace. As long as nations will not moderate their claims against each other, as long as each public believes its own state is the most desirable on earth, when conflicts emerge, governments will not be tempted to compromise. Spurred on by a nationalist citizenry, war may be preferred to national humiliation. As we shall see later, relations among states were much more harmonious in the eighteenth century before nationalism had come to dictate international morality.

THE GOALS OF NATION-STATES

Since the rise of nationalism the political leaders of nation-states have been largely free to chart their courses, and to select their goals without outside limitations. They have usually chosen to advance their own interests as against those of other states. In the nineteenth century particularly, it came to be recognized that governments were responsible to the governed; they could be dismissed if they wasted the national patrimony and did not serve the interests of the people. If important sections of the public were demanding territorial aggrandizement or economic expansion, leaders had to heed their cries. If foreign states were aggressively expanding, they had to be resisted. The goals of nation-states would vary: at one point in time they might include national expansion—the acquisition of empire; at another, national consolidation and self-preservation.

The goals of nations have sometimes reflected ideological views: conservative, liberal, socialist or communist. They have often, however, been concerned solely with maximizing the interest of one nation against others, to advance its power. Sometimes the two ambitions have been conjoined, as in the policy of the conservative coalition leagued against Napoleon. The European monarchs wished to protect and even advance their conservative positions against the French revolutionary emperor. At the same time, they wished to prevent French dominance on the continent. In other cases, nations have not always been able to combine ideological and realistic concerns. American President John Adams would probably have liked to help the French against conservative European forces in 1798; instead he stayed out of European quarrels because American power was not sufficient to sustain such participation. In 1935, the British would have liked to enforce sanctions against the aggressor, Italy, after the latter attacked Ethiopia. They dared not do so, however, because they were hoping to get Italian support against the German dictator, Adolf Hitler. Through all this, national leaders and people have been aware that the standard for choosing foreign policy goals was that they should improve the national position in a field of competing nation-states.

THE TOOLS OF NATION-STATES

The means of improving or sustaining a national position are multiform. States will use diplomatic techniques to persuade other states of their point of view. If these are not successful, they may resort to economic pressure, seeking to use economic resources in such a way as to bring cooperation. For a period of time when the United States foreign aid budget was very large, the threat to cut off aid to another country offered the United States a very considerable leverage in the affairs of recipient countries. During the period of mercantilism, which lasted until the end of the eighteenth century, states strove to develop favorable balances of trade, sending exports abroad and restricting imports. This was designed to lead to an accumulation of debts by other countries which could only be paid in gold. The country which acquired the most gold would be seen to have the greatest resources for financing wars and external expansion.

In recent years these techniques have been supplemented by the use of revolutionary propaganda. Even the French revolutionaries used to appeal to foreign peoples over the heads of their governments. In the Middle East, as one example, the Egyptian regime under Nasser was able to exert such an influence upon political developments in Jordan, Syria, and other countries through the appeals of Cairo Radio that it often made life very difficult for the regimes in power. Revolutionary appeals together with some degree of on the spot subversion certainly contributed to the fall of regimes in Syria, Iraq, Lebanon, Yemen, and Libya.

Today, in fact, nations are "permeable"[1] to outside ideological influences to a greater degree than they have been at any time since the eighteenth century. Governments cannot completely monopolize the media of communications; messages from the outside world manage to get through. Since governments must to some degree reflect the aspirations and wishes of their citizens, as those public tides of sentiment change (and as they are manipulated), governments must take account of them. It is striking today to find that many political programs and sentiments in one country have counterparts in others. The influence of the American radical student movement upon European countries has been profound. Maoism and Castroism have had a dynamic effect upon the publics of the third world. The Americanization of the consumer in many other countries, both developed and less developed, has led to new demands for government services and new access to capitalist markets. For better or worse, consumer tastes and cultural life-styles of nations are in process of being reshaped.

Entirely aside from these nascent shifts of sentiment, governments have paid servants in other countries, suborned to do their bidding. Diplomatic officers regularly "place" articles favorable to their own country in the newspapers of their choice. Labor unions, student organizations, and intellectual groups may receive explicit or covert support from foreign sources.

Propaganda, subversion, and accessibility to outside influence, however, are not the only tools that a nation may use in its foreign policy besides more traditional diplomatic persuasion. In the final analysis, if a nation cannot get what it wants, it may be tempted to fight for it. War has always been the *ultima ratio* among nations. War or the use of military pressure by one power in turn places great emphasis upon other nations to support a military policy. Through the ages one of the most usable military concepts has been that of *deterrence.* One nation would presumably not attack another, if he could not defeat his adversary, or if the costs of winning would be greater than the gains. But how was one to guarantee deterrence? First, there had to be some circumstances under which a nation would fight; otherwise national threats or ultimatums would be empty gestures. Even given that willingness, a nation had to have the means to carry out its threats—to be able to defend against an adversary, or to hurt him beyond endurance. In the latter part of the nineteenth century particularly, nations came to recognize that military preparedness was the sine qua non of survival. If they were not ready to give battle when attacked, or to back up their threats, they could not deter hostile action.

But how was a state to obtain the wherewithal to support its military stance? For these purposes a range of resources was necessary: an adequate national and per capita income; a trained and sufficiently large population; resolute domestic political support; perhaps a favorable geographic position or situation; sufficient access to modern technological development to be able to fashion weapons to cope with those an enemy might use; perhaps allies to protect oneself if national resources were inadequate. Finally, some access was needed to the raw material and mineral resources that sustain modern armament and modern war. States that have suffered critically in regard to these categories of strength have not heretofore remained as independent actors very long in international relations. They have either been eliminated, become nonparticipant neutrals, or have become dependent upon the protection of larger powers.

Today, along with the traditional military and resource categories, one of the most important strengths which a nation can develop is domestic cohesion and resolve. If the national populace strongly and even well-nigh unanimously supports its government in its foreign actions, it will have much greater influence and power internationally. Even powers greater in resource and material terms may not be able to sway it. As examples of the striking effect of unswerving domestic resolve, note the great influence of North Vietnam and Israel in current international politics. Even superpowers have not been able to dictate, or greatly influence, their courses of action. As publics are mobilized to political participation and activity in the third world, it will be increasingly difficult for great powers to exert influence in their internal politics. In one sense, therefore, a contemporary paradox presents itself: societies are now permeable to outside influence in a way they have not been since the eighteenth century, but they are also becoming more obdurate to influence wielded by specific external states. While there has been a devaluation of the governing power in many nations, external powers have not always been able to capitalize upon the internal weakness of their foes. If the domestic rulers of a society cannot govern it, foreigners have been able to do little better. The difficulty of external rulership, moreover, is likely to become accentuated with time.

INTERNATIONAL RESTRAINTS

If the nation-state remains paramount in current international politics, it is nonetheless true that nations are subjected to a number of external restraints, some formal, some informal. The most obvious check on national policy is the inadequacy of resources to carry out goals. Since the June war of 1967 Egypt has been eager to regain the territories occupied by Israel. But she did not launch an attack in 1971 despite President Sadat's designation of 1971 as the "year of decision." Presumably Egyptian military resources were inadequate to defeat Israel. States also generally seek to avoid actions which will result in major counteraction by other states. In 1962 the Soviets thought they could get away with establishing a missile base in Cuba. They are very unlikely to attempt such a feat again, however, because they know that American action would swiftly follow. Thus, in many circumstances, a state's power position may simply be deficient in comparison to its ambitions.

Alternatively, a state may be so bound up in a network of political and contractual obligations that separate national action does not emerge as a realistic alternative. The nations of the Common Market have had to make an important coordination of their commercial policy and have now commenced a great effort to coordinate monetary and fiscal policies as well. In these fields independent action against the common framework is virtually unthinkable. Even those states like France, which have sought to retain monetary autonomy in the context of developing coordination of trade and social policy, have found their leeway limited. In the world economy as a whole, the developed nations have such an intricate degree of interdependence that currency and reserve arrangements are now aligned multilaterally. The American import surcharge and suspension of gold payments of August 15, 1971 led to a revaluation of all major trading currencies and to new reserve arrangements as well. The change in the position of the United States dollar was so marked that it produced a fundamental revision of the monetary system established at Bretton Woods in 1944. In this process all nations, including the United States, had to make major adjustments in their economic objectives to accommodate the interests of others. If any of the major participants in these negotiations had refused to compromise, agreement might have been lost and the world economy shattered. Thus, nations may sometimes be forced to take account of external factors in their national policies.

International institutionalization is also having an effect on the network of cooperative restraints. Intergovernmental organizations have burgeoned and proliferated. Nations which seek to act in a functional area of activity like trade, finance, labor, economic development, health, agriculture, and so on find a large number of international agencies have preceded them. As they join in the work of these organizations, they are in turn hemmed in and enmeshed in institutional restraints.[2] Even in more political areas, institutionalization disciplines national policy. As new members of the United Nations the Chinese have found they have had to moderate some of their foreign policy stands in order to work with other states in UN forums. The strident expression of their policy has also been toned down. In more general terms, the development of international institutions, even non-supranational institutions, has proceeded to the point where national participants, though technically free to act against the international framework, find themselves entwined in a network of institutional cooperation. This in turn refines and helps to regulate the expression of their policy.

Finally, there are restrictions of international morality and international law which condition the behavior of states. In nations where domestic opinion has some impact on foreign policy, governments find that unpopular actions raise internal political problems. While the international and domestic outcry against American policies in Vietnam may not have brought Washington to terminate this sorry episode, it as least has had an important effect on other involvements. The international reaction has also probably influenced certain other governments against continuing commitments of this sort.

International law has had a small but positive effect upon relationships among states. The juridical equality of nations, largely legitimized by international recognition and membership in the United Nations has probably modestly restrained major states in their treatment of minor ones. It is not possible to be fully definite on the matter, but it seems plausible that if the Vietnamese episode had occurred in the nineteenth century (when Indo-Chinese states were not recognized members of the international community) the United States would probably have invaded North Vietnam. It would have used whatever force was necessary to assure a favorable outcome. Today, in addition to the threat of resistance by other great powers, there is recognition that great powers ought not be too brutal in their relations with smaller states. This does not mean, of course, that major states no longer use such methods, as for example in the Russian suppression of Hungary in 1956 and Czechoslovakia in 1968. But the international restraints on such actions are greater now than they were a century ago.

Further, positive international law rests on treaties which are honored most of the time. The degree of international institutionalization strengthens international law for it means that the web of contractual relationships and treaty engagements will be much more developed than would otherwise be the case. This does not always restrain conflict, however, for the structure of international treaties and obligations is sometimes conflicting and inconsistent. In 1887 German Chancellor Bismarck undertook military obligations to Russia that partially conflicted with previous obligations to Austria under the Triple Alliance. In Europe today the existence of two multilateral defense pacts does not help to prevent conflict in a crisis, because they are directed against each other.

In sum, international law represents a modest addition to the forces in world politics working for peace. It is sometimes disregarded, as, for example, when the Germans attacked Belgium in 1914, denouncing the treaty to respect Belgian neutrality as a "scrap of paper." Second, since international law deals by definition with those areas of international politics where legal interpretations can be made, it does not affect the political areas where law either does not exist, or has not been fully developed. Finally, international law is not like domestic law. In domestic societies government exists to enforce law. But there is no government in international relations to perform the same function. Strictly speaking, politics among nations if a form of anarchy.

DOMESTIC SOCIETY AND FOREIGN AFFAIRS

This leads to the most fundamental characteristic of international relations—the absence of a supreme arbiter or authority over nations. Relations are *inter*-national; they subsist among equal juridical entities. They are not subordinate, reflecting the predominance of a world government. It follows, therefore, that there is a basic difference between domestic society and foreign affairs. International politics is politics among equals. Domestic politics is politics under the aegis of the state. Excesses of conduct which would not be tolerated in domestic society are endemic to foreign affairs. There are no world police; no world courts have powers of enforcement. (The International Court of Justice does not have such powers.) Violators cannot be apprehended as occurs in domestic society. Even more important perhaps, since the participants in international relations are nation-states, individuals cannot be punished for their crimes unless nations have first been defeated in war. Thus the attempt to bring an offender to justice may sometimes cause more damage than the evils he has perpetrated. In 1914 France and Britain had become convinced that Germany needed to be stopped, by war if necessary. But the ravages of World War I brought more death and destruction than had been caused by previous German policy. While war is sometimes the only remedy for attempts at world domination, it is characteristic that the cures for aggressive action in international relations are far too gross, and in some cases they are worse than the disease.

Although there is a fundamental distinction in principle between domestic and international affairs, it is true that in recent years the gulf between them has narrowed. This is not particularly because of any great limitation of conflict in international relations, but rather because domestic affairs are becoming more conflictual. Political elites have lost authority and legitimacy because domestic publics have not always been able to support their acts. Government policies have been seen in many countries as increasingly coercive, and citizens have become alienated. There has been a devaluation of the internal governing power.

This trend, however, does not offer great comfort to those who wish to prevent war. The restraints on national action levied by international law and organization are slight and tenuous. They do not greatly limit conflict, and they certainly do not prevent purposeful aggression. While some limitations affect Western and developed powers, smaller states do not hesitate to go to war with one another. Nor are great powers capable of preventing lesser states from doing so. In the June war of 1967 certain great powers went to considerable lengths to prevent either party from attacking, yet failed. In the Indo-Pakistani conflict of 1971 great power influence did not dissuade either participant from an aggressive stance, nor did it prevent war. Certain types of major war have not been employed since 1945, but large-scale violence still occurs and millions are killed. The problem of war has by no means been solved.

In the next chapter we shall look at the evolution of international relations in slightly greater detail. How have we arrived at our present plight? By what stages have changes taken place in the patterns of international history? Are any features of that history common to our period? If so, how can we utilize historical knowledge to prevent future war?

NOTES

1 See John Herz, *International Politics in the Atomic Age* (New York: Columbia University Press, 1958).
2 E. B. Haas, *Tangle of Hopes* (Englewood Cliffs, N.J.: Prentice-Hall, 1969).

CHAPTER THREE

Patterns of
International History

HISTORY AND THE STUDY OF
INTERNATIONAL RELATIONS*

We become interested in international history because it offers perspective on present discontents and problems. Also, though historical processes are not repetitive, history is a laboratory in which our generalizations about international politics can be tested. While the entire set of historical circumstances varies greatly from one epoch to another, similar phenomena have existed in all historical periods since the onset of the modern state system in the sixteenth century. Alliances have been a means of gaining security for more than three centuries. Wars have occurred to shatter that security. Various patterns of alignment have existed in the international system, ranging from unipolar to multipolar. Ideological forces have existed as perturbant influences at least since the French Revolution. Nationalism and patriotism are not new. They were major factors in nineteenth century international politics.

International systems of the past have had to accommodate rapid technological change. While nuclear weapons are unique to our post-World War II era, the dangers of first strike capabilities with new weapons have existed previously. Today one talks about revolutionary domestic ferment and its impact on international relations. But this phenomenon has been well portrayed in past international politics. Even the extension of the inter-

*Note: Those who have a limited knowledge of modern European history may wish to consult the brief historical chronology which is offered at the end of this chapter.

national system to include new developing states is not a novel aspect of current world politics. The international system was greatly extended toward the end of the nineteenth century. New actors had to be adjusted to. The breakup of the Turkish, Austrian, and Russian empires at the end of the nineteenth and the beginning of the twentieth centuries has important similarities with the breakup of colonial empires in Africa, Asia, and the Middle East after World War II.

Thus, a survey of international history may show us how statesmen coped with problems not totally unlike those we face in the present era. Inevitably any such survey will contain subjective elements. History, at least as presently studied, lends itself to varying interpretations. Historical data does not constitute a fixed, integrated body of knowledge. What follows, therefore, inevitably remains partially impressionistic, though it does reflect some of the innovations in international research of recent years.

INTERNATIONAL RELATIONS IN THE EIGHTEENTH CENTURY

From any standpoint, the eighteenth century was a moderate age in international relations. While there was a considerable amount of warfare, it was not severe, nor did war prevent later cooperation among opponents. More than any subsequent age, the *ancien régime* which lasted until the French Revolution in 1789 was international in character. Important legal class divisions operated within a country, so that social cooperation across class lines was minimal. Before the French Revolution, moreover, there was little sense of national loyalty. Diplomacy, military force, and international relations—these were the domains of monarchs, princes, or aristocrats. The ordinary man, even the wealthy bourgeois, did not intrude into them. The state did not belong to the people. Rather, people were the subjects of the ruling princes of Europe. Europeans who could travel discovered that they had much in common with citizens of their own class in other countries. The European literati spoke a common language—French; they shared common philosophic convictions; they had similar criticisms to make of existing society in different countries. Their values were international. Intellectuals and members of literary salons did not glorify the national achievements of one state or one people; they tended rather to look at the achievements and possibilities of *man* in the generic sense. The values of patriotism and national loyalty were at a nadir.

This European cosmopolitanism facilitated limited diplomacy and militarism and maintained the international orientations of the age. States could not pursue extreme policies; they could not eliminate another member of the European system; they could not engage in unlimited war or total diplomacy. Statesmanship and soldiering had become international. Kings hired diplomats and chancellors from other states. Princes turned to other countries to find their generals and admirals. Even the common soldier was not necessarily a national of the state whose honor he defended. Soldiers were mercenaries who fought for pay. "The French Army before the Revolution was half-composed of men who were not French; and the army of Frederick William I was one-third foreign. Frederick the Great's army some years later was more than half-filled with foreign mercenaries, prisoners of war, and deserters from enemy armies."[1] Officers of one nationality regularly served foreign monarchs. Englishmen served as Russian admirals. Irishmen became Spanish generals and foreign ministers. Germans were found as leading statesmen, diplomats and commanders at the Russian, Danish, and English courts. George I of England was a Hanoverian by birth and upbringing, and Catherine the Great of Russia had previously been a German princess. The commingling of aristocrats, monarchs, and generals was matched by the internationalization of the common soldiery. One writer observed, "The common soldier was a sort of workman of the military corporation, who toured the world and stopped wherever the trade was good—that is, where war, falling upon some fat country, could nourish its artisan."[2]

Since soldiers were fighting for pay and not for their national fatherland, they were not willing to make great sacrifices or to undergo great exertions on behalf of their national employers. If the military artisan was not relatively well paid and nourished, he would desert. Eighteenth-century military campaigns, therefore, depended upon long baggage trains and an elaborate system of supply magazines to sustain the forces. Armies could not rely on foraging or enforced requisitioning from the populace, for to do so would disrupt civilian life. There were in consequence severe limits on military mobility. If armies were to be maintained intact, they had to be marched in formation with officers guarding against desertion. Forced marches, dispersed campaigns in the forest, and night marches provided irresistible temptation to the potential deserter and thus were studiously avoided.

Since armies were composed of paid hirelings, they could not be idly hazarded in chance engagements. Large-scale battles between armies were not to be tolerated. In any event battles could not be fought until marching columns had been arranged in battle formation; by this time an enemy might have decamped. Maneuver and position were more important than frontal assault. Generals were reluctant to give battle in any event, for fear of losing some part of their expensive force. Under these circumstances it might be better to cede a province than to lose an army. In any event, battles were seldom decisive. As one military historian observes " . . . the contrast between eighteenth-century and Napoleonic battles is especially clear. After Blenheim, Malplaquet, Fontenoy, or Rossbach, the war dragged on for years. After Marengo, Austerlitz, Jena, Wagram, or Leipzig, peace overtures began in a few months."[3] Given the archaic social structure of the old regime, states could not fight wars of annihilation. These were not possible until after the

French Revolution when citizen armies were fighting to protect their fatherland.

If diplomats, officers, and soldiers were unwilling to go to great lengths to dispose of an opponent, monarchs and princes were even less willing to do so. The kings of the eighteenth century were often related by blood. They spoke a common language and shared common ideals. In general terms, the higher the social group in eighteenth-century society, the greater the solidarity with counterparts in other countries. Thus, members of the nobility, clergy, and royalty were the least likely to express persistent enmities to their counterparts in other countries. After the French Revolution, however, this was no longer true. Because nationalism had begun to replace the internationalism of the eighteenth century, rulers began to have more in common with their subjects than they did with princes from other states. This change is shown diagrammatically in Figure 3-1. Before the French Revolution there were

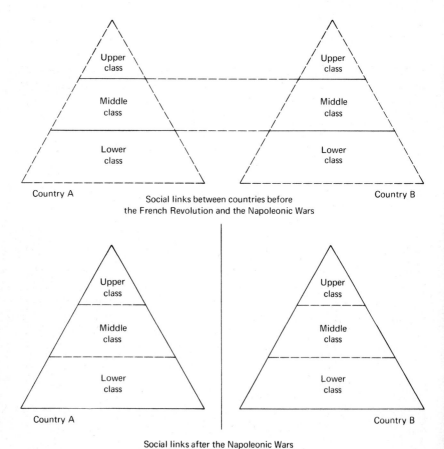

Figure 3-1

some international class alignments. National boundaries did not mean national loyalties. After the French Revolution the national bond became primary. Links at the international level were broken or weakened. Horizontal links between states in the *ancien régime* were replaced by vertical barriers between states after the period of Revolutionary and Napoleonic wars.

The means of controlling conflict in the eighteenth century was the balance of power. No perverse ideological issues existed to disrupt the free play of a balance mechanism. States combined with or opposed one another on grounds of power—what they might attain in territory or prestige. There was also a general commitment to equilibrium: no state should get too much; no state should receive too little. If one gained disproportionately, the others were to be compensated with tribute elsewhere. Since nationalism had not yet arisen territories could be shifted back and forth between sovereigns.

The balance of power system actually had little to do. Since states were not unified social mechanisms, no policy could be carried too far. Sovereigns did not possess the economic resources or the popular support necessary to wage a *guerre à outrance*. Conflicts were thus strictly limited; wars were indecisive; neither gains nor losses were irrevocable. Furthermore, while kings and princes had rivalries for prestige and position, they were linked formally and informally by blood and aristocratic ethos. They had both manners and decorum, and would not work to undermine each other. While the balance of power did not prevent conflict, it strictly limited its excesses. In many ways the eighteenth century was a halcyon age in international relations.

INTERNATIONAL RELATIONS IN THE FIRST HALF OF THE NINETEENTH CENTURY

The Development of Nationalism

Probably the most important change in modern international history occurred with the French Revolution. The Revolution of 1789 ended aristocratic rule in France and established equality before the law for all citizens. Ecclesiastical privileges were abolished. Nobles were no longer given legal priority. Middle-class professionals, townsmen, and even artisans were given basic political rights. Before the French Revolution Frenchmen had not had much influence upon French government. The policy of France had been the policy of the king—Louis XIV, Louis XV, or Louis XVI. Not surprisingly, people who lived in France did not identify themselves with *France* as a political entity. And in one sense there was no France—only the domains and realms of the French monarch. Frenchmen did not identify themselves with the actions of the king. After the Revolution, however, and after the development of popular influence upon government, the acts of the government became, indirectly at least, the acts of the citizens. If people could influence or determine government policy, they became identified with that policy. Thus, popular government led to nationalism.

More importantly, however, when a nation with crusading nationalist zeal entered the international arena, it immediately had an effect upon non-nationalist states. First, the French were interested in protecting their revolutionary reforms against attack from without. After the revolutionary wars with conservative states began in 1792, however, the French soon desired not only to protect their own revolution, but to extend it to other countries. Thus, they sought not only to defeat conservative princes in battle, but to depose them from their thrones. Ideology became a force in international politics. After 1792 regimes were fighting not only to protect their territory, but also to protect their internal system of government.

The End of Eighteenth Century Moderation

Inevitably, therefore, in the years that followed the French Revolution international politics took on an unlimited quality. No longer was there a European consensus, a philosophic cosmopolitanism, which united states. Rather the issues of liberalism and nationalism tended to divide them. There thus arose two international groupings: liberals and conservatives. Liberals were those who supported the freedoms won by the French Revolution. They wanted to end the privileges of nobility, establish equality before the law, bring popular participation in the selection of government, and they sought to remove the state from regulation of all aspects of economic activity. Conservatives were those who wanted to maintain elite aristocratic rule and keep liberal middle-class elements from gaining power. With the French Revolution, liberals were temporarily victorious in France. But in other countries conservatives held sway. If either group failed to compete successfully in the international arena, it would not be able to compete successfully in the domestic sphere. To protect one's internal regime, it was necessary to prevent attack internationally. At first France was the only power in the first category: the only liberal state bent on internal and external reform. After the Napoleonic Wars and internal political change, however, England joined the liberal forces. During the period 1830-1848 many of the outcomes of international politics in Europe were determined by the competition between the Liberal Two (France and England) and the Conservative Three (Russia, Prussia, and Austria).

A New Regulative Mechanism to Control Conflict

The enormously changed international system, and the extremes to which regimes would now go in defending their own position or attacking that of others led to a new attempt to regulate violence among states: The Concert of

Europe. The Concert was designed to ensure that no domestic or international transformations would take place without the consent of the five major European powers. At the end of the Napoleonic Wars in 1815, states recognized that reliance upon the eighteenth century balance of power mechanism would not be sufficient to produce peace. By the time it had mustered a predominant coalition to cope with the French, grievous damage had already been done to the external and internal social order of Europe. The advantage of the Concert was that it would be able to act at the first hint of domestic turmoil, before that turmoil spilled over into the international orbit. The theory of international relations adopted by the Concert was that domestic revolution was the cause of war. If internal revolution could be prevented, it could not lead to an attempt to revolutionize other European social orders by force.

During the period of the Concert's greatest effectiveness the five great powers governed the domestic and international lives of most of Europe. They intervened to put down revolutions in Spain and Naples. They did not permit ideological issues to stand in the way of an overriding concern to promote peace. The fury and destructiveness of the Napoleonic Wars had given rise to the conviction that war should not be allowed to occur again. Metternich of Austria and Castlereagh of England labored mightily to prevent a resurgence of war. But the Concert was not omnipotent. It could not stand in the way of domestic reform or revolution in all European countries. By 1822 England had refused to sanction Concert intervention in the domestic affairs of other nations even if intervention were necessary to prevent revolution. By the late 1820s Englishmen found themselves sympathizing with the Greek revolution against Turkey. When the Belgian revolution against rule by the Netherlands broke out in 1830, the French and the British stood together against intervention by the three conservative courts, and Belgium gained her independence.

The Development of Partial Bipolarity

As a result of the reform and revolutionary movements of the early 1830s Europe was changed into a partially bipolar international order. The liberals opposed the conservatives. Each wished to complete the social processes set afoot by the French Revolution: the liberals wanted to carry the revolution to its final conclusion in the conservative monarchies; the conservatives wished to complete the counterrevolution and reinstall legitimist monarchies. In the long run, however, neither was successful. Each protagonist was too strong to be eliminated by the other. Further, the bipolarity was never total. Issues of material interest in the Near East and elsewhere blurred the ideological cleavage. England sometimes acted with Russia to restrain France. France sometimes acted with Austria. The Anglo-French combination was partial and intermittent. It did not even endure until 1848.

Further, war was prevented by virtue of the consciousness on both sides that it could not be tolerated. The Napoleonic Wars were the most violent conflict since the Thirty Years' War. Conservative and liberal states had suffered almost equally. Liberals, moreover, came to the conclusion that domestic victories could be won in other countries without military action. The liberal seed, once planted, would germinate and grow by itself. The conservatives, while resolved against revolution, would not lightly start a war in order to prevent it. They realized that the social chaos caused by prolonged and catastrophic warfare would also be a major cause of revolution. The conservatives were afraid to take a strong line against domestic reform and against the mild revolutionary currents of the 1830s and early 1840s. Fear of major war on both sides, then, helped to limit conflict.

INTERNATIONAL RELATIONS IN THE SECOND HALF OF THE NINETEENTH CENTURY

The Revolutions of 1848

The relative stability of international politics which followed the Napoleonic Wars was broken with the revolutions of 1848. Political upheavals occurred in France, Austria, the German, and Italian states. At first it appeared as if the liberals and nationalists would win. The Austrian emperor was forced to concede reforms in his domains. The French king was overthrown and a republic established. In the German and Italian states, new and liberal constitutions were proclaimed. Whereas England and France had already attained national unity under a single government, the German states were broken into two large powers—Austria and Prussia, and many smaller principalities. The Italian states were also disunited. German and Italian nationalists saw the revolutions as a heaven-sent opportunity to consummate the unity of their nations. In both instances this meant removing Austrian influence. Austria blocked political unity in the Italian states; she also stood against German unification in central Europe. In 1848 liberals and nationalists appeared to win out. A Frankfort Parliament of all the Germanies was to devise a plan for German unity on liberal principles. In Italy there was a movement for national consolidation.

The Success of Counterrevolutions

In both instances, however, the success of unification efforts depended on liberals remaining at the helm of the major states. While rulers had yielded to the initial revolutionary tide they had not, except in France, lost their thrones. By the summer of 1848 they sought to reassert conservative control. And even in France, 1849 brought Louis Napoleon to power as French president supplanting a more liberal French republican regime. Conservatives were then in a position to restore order in their dissident provinces. Austria put down the revolutions in Italy with military force and regained her old territorial position. Russian troops intervened to depose the independent regime in Hungary and to restore Austrian control. In Germany, the most important state, Prussia, refused to go along with liberal plans for German unification. By 1849 the revolution had either been defeated or was on the defensive everywhere

Consequences of the 1848 Revolutions

This failure had profound international implications. In a sense the failure of the revolutions of 1848 temporarily discredited the influence of ideology in international politics. It had always been assumed that when a new revolutionary outburst occurred one side or the other would triumph. Either the revolution or the counterrevolution would be victorious. In a sense, if either had won, the result would have been better for the European system. Ideological harmony would have been restored, and the danger of ideological wars of the Napoleonic variety would have been eliminated. Yet neither won. As one historian remarks "The success of the revolution discredited conservative ideas; the failure of the revolution discredited liberal ideas."[4] Even in France, Louis Napoleon was a pale replica of his uncle, Napoleon I. Far from extending the revolution to other countries, he did not even pursue it resolutely at home. In Austria and Prussia conservative leaders were so threatened that they did not dare embark on a counterrevolutionary crusade to expunge liberalism everywhere. Having been so thoroughly challenged by the revolutionary tides of 1848, they felt it was essential to secure their own position. Rulers would use any means to do so, even if they violated previous ideological tenets, and even if they entailed war. Thus the age after 1848 has been described as an age of *realpolitik,* an age in which violent means were not disdained if they suited their user's purpose. Since England and Russia were untouched by revolution, they did not have to engage in extreme behavior to reinsure their domestic stability. But in Austria, Prussia, and France new gains had to be made to gain popular adherence for the shaky regimes in power.

In all three cases the means found were nationalism and national unification. In France, Louis Napoleon appealed to the glory of the nation, though he did little to threaten other states. His only concrete expeditions were the Crimean War against Russia, 1854 to 1856, which, unlike his great forebear's campaign, was a limited and episodic affair, and the short Franco-Austrian war of 1859, in which Louis Napoleon paved the way for a partial unification of Italy. Still, even though the French Emperor did not threaten the European peace as his uncle had done, it was still essential to make gains in foreign affairs to ensure popularity at home. For Austria and Prussia the situation was more desperate. If German unity were carried through under Austrian auspices, it would ensure the Austrian conservatives of their hold on power. If it were achieved under Prussian auspices, it would represent the same fillip to conservative causes in Prussia. There were two conceptions of German unity, in one (the Prussian), Austria would be excluded from Germany or only her German provinces would be permitted to join; in the other (the Austrian), the entire Austrian Empire including its southern provinces would be admitted, thus dominating the other German states. At first it appeared that the Austrian conception might be victorious. But in the Austro-Prussian War of 1866 Prussia triumphed, and all but the south German states were combined in the North German Confederation. Finally in the Franco-Prussian war of 1870 to 1871, the German Chancellor, Prince Otto von Bismarck, succeeded in adding the South German states as well, and the German Empire was born.

Realpolitik and War

During the period of *realpolitik* the European Concert could not prevent war. States were, in fact, often forced to wage war, if only to reinsure their domestic position. As we have seen, however, wars were no longer ideological. The most important struggle of the period 1848 to 1871 was that between Prussia and Austria, two conservative states. By the time of World War I the ideological issue had been completely submerged, and the war was fought between Triple Alliance and Triple Entente. The Triple Entente included England and France, the two most liberal states, and Russia, the most conservative empire. The Triple Alliance included two conservative states, Germany and Austria, and one, Italy, of more liberal complexion. The disappearance of the ideological question is one of the most interesting outcomes of modern international history. It had not been foreseen. At mid-nineteenth century all informed observers had expected an eventual conflict of the rallied forces of conservatism and liberalism, settling the issue once and for all.

That this did not occur was a tribute both to the weakness and to the strength of the two camps. They were weak in that they could no longer think in terms of engaging in a purely ideological struggle against the other side. Each liberal and conservative state thought solely in terms of protecting itself domestically. They were strong in that each ideological strand was well entrenched and fortified against assault from without. The conservatives had partly learned the lessons of the French Revolutionary era: they understood that a regime had in a measure to pursue popular causes if it was to remain in power. They therefore conceded universal manhood suffrage and benefited from the enfranchisement of the conservative peasantry. More important, they sought new legitimacy and support through sponsorship of nationalism.

The Triumph of Nationalism

It is not surprising that the conservatives learned this lesson. Nationalism intrinsically was not a social doctrine that would appeal to liberals alone. In an age of romanticism, traditional elements in society, even the working classes, could find succor and solidarity in a policy of forwarding the national unification of their country. In the latter part of the nineteenth century they could identify themselves with the national and imperial expansion of their fatherland. The conservatives were aware of this, and they were ready to use nationalism to distract attention from the lack of social and political reform. The conservatives could not give ground in terms of conceding political power; they could not displace themselves. But they could offer placebos and palliatives to tranquilize the electorate.

As the social issue developed, moreover, the conservatives were not the only political group to use nationalism to deflect social discontent. The liberals themselves, in power in France and England, found their doctrines gradually being outpaced by events. Economic freedom, parliamentary rule, laissez-faire (freedom from government economic regulations), and free trade had far less application to the Europe of the fourth quarter of the nineteenth century than they did in the second quarter of that century. By 1875 industrial conditions, depressions, and unrestrained economic competition showed the need for greater government control of industry. They also showed that the working man, unassisted by government, could not cope with either the legal-contractual or the economic results of unfettered laissez-faire. He needed direct economic and legal support. Thus, the proponents of a sectarian liberalism were increasingly out of harmony with social and economic trends. A powerful political working man's movement arose to shift the center of political power to the left and to change the economic and social policy of liberal regimes. Even in liberal states, therefore, governments desirous of avoiding concessions used nationalist expansion as a means of focusing attention elsewhere. Imperialism was in part a device to discharge social discontent at home.

Imperialism and War

To acknowledge this, however, was ultimately to acknowledge war as a means of coping with domestic problems. Universal imperialism is not a prescription for peace. Sooner or later competing imperialists collide. This was not true in the 1880s when chips of real estate in Africa and the Far East were just beginning to be carved out. By the 1890s extra-European territory was well-nigh divided up, and that decade was characterized by conflicts in Africa, the Near East, and the Far East. But the worst situation was to follow: after extra-European territory had been divided, the imperialists would turn their expansionist energies back into Europe itself with lethal consequences for general peace. World War I emerged out of competition for the spoils of the Ottoman Empire on the fringes of Europe.

The Enfeeblement of the Concert

If the Concert of Europe had been able to constrain international behavior, this result might not have occurred. But after 1848 the Concert no longer exerted much control on international outcomes. It met to help settle the remnant issues after the Crimean War in 1856. But the wars of 1864, 1866, and 1870 were neither prevented by the Concert nor were their results affected by Concert deliberation. It was not until the Congress of Berlin in 1878 that the Concert made a disposition of general issues which might have led to a wider conflict, one involving Russia, Austria, and England. After 1878 the Concert failed to function as a major instrument of great power rule over the rest of Europe.

The Tolerability of War

The reason for this decline in power was partly that fears of war which had been constant during the first half of the nineteenth century had greatly declined by the second half. As a result of the five wars between 1848 and 1871 the statesmen of Europe knew that war did not necessarily lead to social chaos and to revolution. Thus, their deductions were opposite to those which had been drawn in 1815 after the Napoleonic Wars. Indeed, after 1871 precisely the opposite conviction began to develop. Wars would be decided rapidly. The decisive battles in the Austro-Prussian War of 1866 and the Franco-Prussian War of 1870 had all been fought within six weeks. The victor had won cleanly but not destructively. His opponent had not been humiliated. As we have seen, wars were partly viewed as a preventative of revolution. By emphasizing social solidarity on national grounds, they contributed to unity. Thus, wars were no longer a disadvantage, and some historians even tended to glorify them. Statesmen did not have to try very hard to prevent them.

Political and Military Consequences of War

At the same time, while warfare did not necessarily transform a state's material position, it did influence prestige. In this respect Germany was in the ascendant after the Franco-Prussian War; French vaunted military prestige had sunk to a new low. The French, moreover, wanted to get back Alsace-Lorraine. This meant, ultimately, that they had to be prepared for war with Germany. It also meant that the consequences of war, for a defeated power, could be serious, though not disastrous. Indeed, in one sense, the military and political results of warfare had been interchanged. In the early nineteenth century, the military consequences of warfare—the killing, the destruction, the social chaos—were the major source of worry to political leaders. The political transformations of Europe which followed at the Congress of Vienna in 1815, on the other hand, were tolerable. In an age in which nationalist sentiments had still not developed to a high point, territories could be transferred and boundaries redrawn without great political disadvantage. By 1871 this was no longer true: the military consequences of the Franco-Prussian and Austro-Prussian Wars were far from serious. What was troubling was the political consequences. The seizure of Alsace-Lorraine from France was historically too late. It depended on an inchoate, not a fully developed nationalism. Thus, the provinces that could so easily be reshuffled in 1815 could no longer be alienated by 1871. The political results of war came to have greater significance than their military results.

Changes in Military Technology and Strategy

For all these reasons nations had to be prepared to wage war when it threatened. Military technology had changed since 1815. The telegraph, the railway, the breech-loading rifle, and the rifled artillery piece—these had transformed warfare. Plans for war had to be formed long in advance. Armies had to mobilize their reservists, who would then be provisioned and rapidly shuttled to the front by railway. Thus, concentration and rapid movement now made possible stunning offensive operations. An army which could mass and invade first could disrupt the opponent's mobilization and railway time-tables, thus winning a relatively easy victory. The breech-loading rifle and the new artillery piece added to the effectiveness of both offensive and defensive operations. Their accuracy and rate of fire, however, had a devastating effect. It seemed one side would quickly defeat the other. The side would win which had better prepared positions from which to deploy the new weapons. In any event, victory or defeat would come rapidly. The side which mobilized first had a great offensive advantage.

Alliances and the Concert of Europe

These new military techniques preempted diplomacy. The Concert of Europe had presumed that time would be available: time to compose a counter-coalition to any disruptive power; time to take the field. Yet the Concert was now evermore behind events. By 1856 it ceased to control events in advance and came merely to deal with the consequences of war, to construct a political settlement. Thus, it could no longer prevent war, but only decide whether the war would be profitable and to whom. Nations came, therefore, to try and find alternative means of preventing war, or if it could not be prevented, of winning it. Alliances usurped the role of the Concert on both counts. If war were to be prevented or deterred, alliances would perform the critical function. An alliance combination, particularly if it implied advance military planning, would deter an adversary's attack. If the attack nevertheless took place, the alliance would make victory much more certain. Allies would offer military aid on a short time-scale. Respective military obligations would already be spelled out. Alliance partners could concert their military means fast enough to cope with the greater rapidity of modern technological warfare. Thus, states ceased trying to find security through the ponderous operations of the multilateral Concert of Europe and relied instead on allies, pledged and ready in advance.

However, as soon as alliances began to usurp the security role previously played by a conference of great powers, the Concert's role was further circumscribed. The Congress of Berlin in 1878 was the last instance of general Concert determination of basic political and military issues. The Congress did revise the terms of the peace treaty ending the Russo-Turkish war of 1877, and it did restrain Russian belligerence in the Balkans. Further, it did so in a manner in which all European states generally concurred. But there was an enormous difference between the Congress of Berlin and the Algeciras Conference in 1906. By the latter date, alliance arrangements had become the focal point of European concern and attention. The Algeciras arrangements on Morocco were not legitimized for all participants: they reflected a temporary predominance of an Anglo-French as against an Austro-German combination. But as soon as the conference was over, the dissentients began to seek ways of undoing its results. The Concert by the end of the nineteenth century therefore no longer stood above partisan national interest: it became identical with the wishes of the strongest alliance combination at the time. Thus, international outcomes were no longer accepted by all the major participants. International relations, once de jure, became de facto.

Military Technology and Warfare

The final development which paved the way for World War I was the growing attractiveness of preemptive war. War, as we have seen, was no longer thought disastrous; it could be waged. Even more important, as a political crisis impended, it became crucial not to let an adversary seize the military initiative. If he did so, the success of his initial offensive operations might determine the outcome of the war. Thus, the diplomats had only so much time before the militarists demanded control of national policy. If they could settle a crisis quickly, so much the better. But if the crisis dragged on, or even got worse, at some point the military would want to have its way. The Schlieffen Plan—the German plan for a two-front war against France and Russia—depended upon a German offensive against France, wheeling through Belgium, and turning the French left flank. Victory over France had to be obtained in short order before the weight of the enormous Russian mobilization could be felt in the East. After a quick defeat of France the German armies could turn their undivided attention to the Eastern front. If the French could not be quickly routed, however, there was no certainty of favorable results against Russia. Thus the German timetable depended inordinately on the beginning of Russian preparations. When the Russians began to mobilize, the fate of France was already sealed: the Germans had to attack. The international system no longer prevented war; it made it more likely.

INTERNATIONAL RELATIONS FROM WORLD WAR I TO WORLD WAR II

Lessons of World War I

International relations between the wars was determined by the attempt to apply the lessons of World War I. After the war many concluded that it had been a tragic accident which different international institutions might have prevented. Sir Alfred Zimmern, presenting the view of the British Foreign Office, argued:

> And was not the war itself due, at least in large measure, to the absence of a system of regular Conference under the Concert of Europe? Did not the catastrophe become inevitable from the time that the European powers formed themselves into two sharply divided groups, the Triple Alliance and the Triple Entente, each with its own system or, at least, habit of consultation? And was not this division, which hardened so rapidly into opposition, due to the absence of any obligation to come to sit regularly at a common table, under conditions permitting of frank and friendly discussion? Could not arrangements be devised which would make it morally impossible for a state, or a group of states, to remain apart and drift into an attitude of suspicion and bitterness.[5]

If a conference had been held on the eve of war, discussion would have illuminated the likely outcome, and reasonable men would have stopped short. This view, which was so influential in the creation of the League of Nations, stemmed from the fact that after the Algeciras Conference there were no general European meetings dealing with crucial political questions until after the war. If a conference had been held in July 1914 a better understanding, even a meeting of minds, might have occurred. But as we have seen, a conference would not have neutralized the effect of alliances and the alliance system. Two blocs were poised against each other. Even the Algeciras meeting had not produced durable agreement; it merely offered grounds for further dispute and contention. What more could a conference in 1914 have done? It was nonetheless true that during the nineteenth century the habit of consultation among Great Powers had gradually weakened and finally broken.

A conference after years of unilateral and separate action might have done little. A conference which reflected and extended existing patterns of consultation on the other hand might well have produced peace. If the Concert of Europe had not broken down well before 1914 it might have functioned in 1914. It was therefore possible to believe that a habit of consultation could be re-created, and the vehicle, of course, was the Council of the League of Nations. Disputes could be dealt with immediately, before they became decisive for the general peace. The League of Nations would institutionalize a regular international conference system.

The British not only saw the League Council as a remedy for defects in nineteenth-century diplomatic practice, they also sought, in their own policy, to prevent the revival of exclusive alliance combinations. There should be no more Triple Alliances or Triple Ententes. The best way of ensuring this was to avoid commitment in Britain's own relations. Thus, in the 1920s and 1930s, the British studiously avoided any commitment or understanding with the French that might re-stage the eve of World War I. As a result the French had to go it alone against Hitler's Germany. Without major supporters the French conceded point after point to Hitler in the period 1935-1938. For a considerable time the British conceived their policy to be that of balancer between Germany and France; they thought of France as the most powerful continental state. Even as late as the spring of 1938 the British told the French that they would not go to war even if Hitler seized the Sudetenland areas of Czechoslovakia. At the Munich Conference in September they formally ceded these areas to Hitler.

The Philosophy of Appeasement

British Prime Minister Neville Chamberlain, more than his predecessor, operated on an explicit philosophy of appeasement, by which he meant healing and binding up the wounds of the late war and remedying the inequities of the Versailles Treaty. Germany had been discriminated against in that Treaty: she had been forced to give up her colonies; to assume the total responsibility and guilt for the war; to remain disarmed; and to demilitarize the Rhineland. She had also lost German areas to Poland in the East, and Austria, though now separated from her non-German territories, was forbidden to unite with the other German states in the German Empire. To many it appeared that the discriminations against Germany were also inconsistent with the nationalist principle: that the members of one nation in ethnic and linguistic terms should be allowed to live together in the framework of a single nation-state. When Germany remilitarized the Rhineland in 1936, when she completed the union with Austria in 1938, and when she asked for cession of the German-speaking Sudeten areas of Czechoslovakia later that year, she was only requesting vindication of the principle of nationality and national self-determination. Hence the British, for one, would not resist her. The Versailles Treaty was particularly inconsistent on the point for it tried to implement the principle of nationality in Eastern and Southern Europe, but to implement it in Central Europe would leave Germany too powerful and in a position to wage war again. Thus the British desire to ease relations among states and work for cooperation was accentuated by the belief that Germany had suffered under a punitive and discriminatory peace settlement. Appeasement was justified not only in terms of lessening concrete grievances, and thereby making for a less strained international atmosphere, it was required on international principles of national self-determination. Indeed, it was not until Hitler completed the occupation of Czechoslovakia in March of 1939 (and thereby violated principles of national self-determination) that Chamberlain gave up his quest for peace through appeasement. Until then the British believed that World War II could be prevented by means which would have prevented World War I.

New Ideological Conflicts

It would surely have taken a much more powerful international organization to prevent World War II than would have been required to prevent World War I. Alternatively, it would have taken a much more thoroughgoing policy of appeasement, one which would have given Germany a free hand on the continent, to have avoided war. The first was not possible in the circumstances of the time. The second, even the British would not have agreed to. One of the reasons for the greater difficulty in producing peace in 1939 than in 1914 was that a new ideological conflict had come to the fore in Europe and the world. As we have seen, whatever the issues of World War I, they were not ideological. The social and international struggle between liberals and conservatives had been given up or compromised at some point in the latter half of the nineteenth century. There was no ideological reason for World War I, though there was a security reason. In addition, regimes were increasingly out of harmony with their populations in social, economic, and political terms. War or aggressive expansion overseas was one means of discharging social discontent at home. In the end even the Marxist German Social Democratic Party voted for the war in 1914.

After the war one might have anticipated that those tendencies which had been interrupted by conservative tactics of nationalism in the nineteenth century would be resumed in the twentieth. The old conservative empires collapsed: the Russian, the Austrian, and the Turkish. Woodrow Wilson refused to make peace with the Kaiser: he insisted on the establishment of a more liberal and democratic regime in Germany. Why, therefore, would not liberalism finally emerge triumphant? Why would not the war ultimately be a force for ideological unity on liberal principles?

Disjunctions of Liberalism and Nationalism

The answer was complex, and it had to do with the tension between liberalism and nationalism in reformist theory. The old nineteenth-century liberals, like Mazzini, had always assumed that the two would everywhere move in tandem. The victory of true nationalism would promote liberal governments. The victory of liberalism would mean national unification. Indeed, nineteenth-century reformers could not think of nationalism being satisfactorily carried out under conservative auspices. In this view, they were wrong. Liberalism was essentially a middle-class doctrine. Nationalism could appeal to elements of all classes. It was therefore possible to use nationalism for conservative purposes. At the end of World War I there was still the question of the relative emphasis to be accorded to each. Liberal governments had been installed in Europe, but would they survive? The reason they did not survive, particularly in Germany, had to do with the results and impact of the war. The war had been equivalent in its internal impact to that of a social revolution. The war-caused inflation, the printing of money to finance the war, had pauperized those classes which lived on fixed incomes. The salary-earner, the white-collar class, the *petit rentier*—these were grievously affected. The savings of many of the lower middle classes were wiped out. On the other hand, the entrepreneur, the businessman, the war profiteer—those who could adjust their incomes to the inflation, who could charge higher and higher prices as the inflation progressed—benefited from the war. Indeed, in a real sense, they profited at the expense of the rest of their countrymen.

Class Divisions

Thus, when the prospects of liberal middle-class government loomed, its foundations were already partly discredited. The middle class was divided against itself, the lower middle class rejecting the leadership of the upper middle class. Further, what the upper middle class had done, in profiting during the war, had been to act against the interests of the rest of the nation. They had become an internationalist force, reaping gains while their nation suffered. At the end of the war, then, to gratify nationalism was to chastize and punish the entrepreneurial class. To gratify liberalism was to give them even greater political influence.

Unappeased Nationalism

When the choice was eventually posed, the masses of Germany and of Italy chose nationalism. They chose nationalism not only for economic reasons, but also because nationalism was unappeased. Germany had lost the war, and Italy had failed to gain from it. The notion was circulated that traitors had been guilty of a "stab in the back." In truth, the German people were not aware of the reality of German defeat: there was no collapse on the Western front; there was no invasion of Germany; there was no occupation. It appeared that their leaders had surrendered without reason. Thus, the lesson of World War I for the Germans was not that nationalism was discredited; it was that it had almost been victorious, and they waited for the next play of the game. It might still be vindicated.

In France and England, on the other hand, precisely opposite notions were entertained. The British and the French had won, but at catastrophic cost. Having won, they were not tempted to repeat the venture; having grievously suffered, they could believe that war was not worth the cost. The Germans suffered, but strangely, they did not suffer enough, or they suffered too much. They did not suffer enough because they were not disabused of nationalist war as a solution to international and internal problems. They suffered too much in that they could not forget the war and felt ever afterward that their honor had to be redeemed. It is not surprising in this context that Hitler and his National Socialist Party could achieve power in 1933. Hitler provided the vehicle for restoring German prosperity, hurt by war and later depression, and of reviving German nationalist fortunes. Thus liberalism was undercut at the very time when the old conservative enemies seemed to have been swept away. It failed because it was not nationalist enough, and national honor still had to triumph. There was no universal conviction that war was no longer tolerable.

At the international level two different lessons were inculcated. The British and French believed that war could not be allowed to occur again; it was far too disastrous. At least at a certain point Germans came to believe that it might be desirably repeated. Thus it was almost foredestined that Britain would appease and appease, and that Hitler would demand and demand. But since Hitler was not opposed to war, there was no concession which would be sufficient. Britain would have had to give Germany a free hand on the continent for war to be averted, and even then there would still have been war between Germany and France, and between Germany and Russia. National Socialist totalitarian ideology now took on great significance. The French and the British did not really understand the new ideologues in Germany and Italy, and they were not capable of dealing with them. In the broadest sense, therefore, the conditions of World War I led directly to World War II. War broke out in September 1939.

INTERNATIONAL RELATIONS AFTER
THE SECOND WORLD WAR

A New Ideological Conflict

The ideological conflict between liberal democracy and fascism in the interwar and wartime period was succeeded at its close by a conflict between communism and liberal democracy. Though many at the time believed that this conflict would be as vital and irrevocable as the conflict between democracy and fascism, there was never the same impetus to it. Hitler conceived of National Socialism as inseparable from a violent transformation of European relations. The Soviet Union, on the other hand, was not willing to sacrifice vital Russian national interests to the violent pursuit of an international ideology. Caution has been the trademark of Soviet practice and behavior. War was not seen by Soviet leaders as the only nor as even a desirable way of advancing Soviet or Communist interests. Further, and perhaps most important, Hitler was a revisionist in the sense that he was fundamentally dissatisfied with the pattern of international outcomes and wished to change them, through force if need be. *Mein Kampf*, Hitler's prison autobiography, offered a concrete program of German expansion in Central and Eastern Europe. It called for a repudiation of the Versailles settlement and a resumption of German liberties.

The international doctrines of Lenin and Stalin, however, were neither as programmatic nor as specific. They consisted of ideological notions which were subject to exegesis and reinterpretation. They did not pledge Russia to take specific actions at specific times to bring about the fall of capitalism in the rest of the world. The theory of communism could be reshaped and revised to come to grips with current realities. More than this, the Soviets in 1947 had thirty years of socialist construction behind them. They would not lightly hazard these major gains. Hitler, contrastingly, began to plan for war from his very moment in power. His *raison d'être* in foreign affairs was to make a break with the discredited policy of fulfillment pursued by his predecessors. Nazi dissatisfaction with the German position in Europe in 1939 was far greater than Soviet dissatisfaction with the Russian position in 1947. Russia would be the more conservative.

The Western response to Soviet policy after the war was also very different from the response of Britain and France to German policy in the 1930. In one sense it was a desirable response, in another it was erroneous. It was desirable in that the Western alliance provided a useful counterweight to Soviet power in Europe and other areas. As the Napoleonic episode proved, a revolutionary power may not abide by limits unless these are buttressed by outside strength. Stalin was not an expansionist in quite the same way as Hitler or Napoleon but he was quite prepared to take advantage of weaknesses in the Western position whether they were in Berlin, Czechoslovakia, or Korea. It would have been absurd for the Soviets to have limited their penetration of Eastern Europe. They needed a buffer to insulate themselves against Western and German influence. Further, none of the Western nations were disposed seriously to interfere with this region of Soviet concern. Where the Western coalition organized itself, however, the Soviets were much more cautious. Whether they did or did not harbor visions of taking over the rest of Europe, they were certainly never tempted to test frontally Western strength in that area. Thus, the organization of a Western coalition of nations coped with the disorganization of the post-World War II world in a manner that did not present irresistible opportunities for Communist expansion. In this sense the Western nations avoided the mistakes that Britain and France had made in the interwar period.

Lessons of World War II

In another sense, however, the precedents of American and Western action in the early years after the war were likely to lead to mistakes later on. Essentially, as we have seen, what the West did was to invoke policies which, if applied in 1935, might have prevented World War II. Little account was taken of the ways in which the postwar world was different from that of the 1930s. There were two errors to be avoided. The first was to opt for policies which allowed an opponent an unrestricted field of expansion or encroachment. The second was to follow policies which, because of concern for the first task, actually increased the risks of war and confrontation. Today there is a fine line to be drawn between the one task and the other. On the one hand, if commitments are not made, there is no ex ante deterrence of opponent action; he is given full freedom of action. On the other hand, commitments themselves, if they are challenged by opponent powers, raise the risk of war. In some cases, moreover, as in the Middle East case, the commitments one gives to client states may actually get one into larger conflicts partly against one's will. Further, commitments may be challenged even when there is no diabolical or purposive intent on the part of an opponent. Revolutions may occur; coups may take place. Smaller allies of a major antagonist may take initiatives without permission. One's own allies may take actions that one cannot dissociate from. In a period in which conventional and unconventional tactics can rapidly change the balance of force in an area, big powers are likely to be faced with the temptation to intervene and with the threat of opponent intervention in a range of contexts.

A Transformed International System

The international system, of course, has changed drastically since 1945. A bipolar confrontation has been modified, first by the introduction of smaller, non-aligned states. It has been transformed, secondly, by a change in the relations between the bipolar powers themselves. Both the United States and the Soviet Union are now aware of the dangers of overcommitment, of the paramount need for crisis management so that commitments do not get out of hand. Both recognize that a major war would be most deleterious to their own positions, while it might even advantage lesser states. Both are coming to see that a diffusion of power and cohesion to the nations of the Southern Hemisphere would not be in their bipolar interest. In various ways, there are hegemonial features to the emerging international system—with two largely status quo powers, the United States and the Soviet Union trying to safeguard their positions against inroads from developing and revisionist states. At the same time, it has not been in the interest of either superpower merely to stabilize relations or to prevent war at the extremities of the system. Each state has sought to advance its own position to the disadvantage of the other. The United States wants a less cohesive Eastern Europe, one more amenable to Western and American influence. It wants to prevent successive Communist gains in Southeast Asia. America wants to keep Soviet military bases out of the Caribbean. The Soviets are striving to increase their influence in the Arab world and to acquire a larger foothold in the Mediterranean and in the Indian Ocean. Neither power accepts as fixed the preexisting sphere of influence of the other. In this jockeying for position it is possible that moves will be made which will provoke a crisis, as they did in 1970 on the Jordanian-Syrian frontier.

It would of course be optimistic if one could say that either or both powers would renounce national expansionist ambitions whenever they seemed likely to disrupt the overarching stability. As we have seen in the past, however, what to one power is a disruption of international peace is to another a vital move for national security. It is not at all clear that self-limitation can be relied on. Nor is it transparent that if one power alone restricts itself the results will be beneficial. In the 1930s one group of states abstained from belligerent activity while a second did not do so. The results were portrayed in World War II. Neither total abstention nor total isolation is likely to be a vehicle of peace unless all powers abstain equally.

The Overuse of Commitment Strategies

Given these limitations on how far any nation can "opt out" of world politics, it is nonetheless true that some states have been too highly participant. The United States has made a fetish of viewing post-World War II international politics as if they merely replayed the issues of the Munich Conference of September 1938. The American prescription for peace has been commitment and deterrence: draw a line, and then threaten to go to war if that line is crossed by an opponent. Since, as we have seen, some reasons for challenge to a commitment are not those that can be laid at the doorstep of a major adversary, if one automatically responds to challenge, the commitment itself has become a factor for war. Further, all deleterious actions by an opponent or his allies cannot be rationally deterred. No matter how serious one makes the sanctions upon aggressive behavior, that behavior cannot entirely be ruled out. Some actions may be the result of accident, miscalculation, or unauthorized behavior. Some may be strictly irrational. To respond in the preprogrammed way to such aggression then may merely be to do infinite harm to both sides.

Wholesale reliance upon commitment strategies, moreover, tends to leave the contours of one's own interests to be defined by enemy action. One responds where the enemy challenges, regardless of the intrinsic importance of the area involved. There would be no disadvantage in such a strategy if it were clear that deterrence and commitment would be one hundred percent effective. There would then be few costs associated with the strategy. At the present time, however, the United States has commitments to more than forty other nations on an overt basis, and to several more informally. Since these understandings were made in the late 1950s or early 1960s, the cumulative probability that at least one of them would be challenged has grown year by year. With such large numbers of commitments the cumulative probability of a major United States involvement is now fairly high. It is therefore not at all surprising that the United States has been heavily involved in Vietnam; it is rather surprising that United States involvements in Vietnam have not been accompanied by major force investments and military conflicts in other places. It behooves the United States, therefore, to calculate much more precisely than it has done before whether its commitments add to the greater likelihood of major war or whether they serve to deter that war. Some network of commitments is probably unavoidable, but they should be those which are strictly in the United States' interest, and they should not be numerous.

Beyond Nationalism?

There is a further quandary about contemporary world politics which must be considered. The force of nationalism has considerably diminished as a factor in great power policy since the early years of this century. We have already noticed that the introduction of nationalism with the French Revolution at the end of the eighteenth century transformed international relations. National states would go farther in their relations with one another than the old dynastic states. Popular support, popular sacrifice for military victory, the nationalist demand that opponents be humiliated, that unconditional surrender be the minimum basis for peace—all these have made warfare more terrible and long-lasting. The first checks to the intensity of nationalist feeling were not administered until World War I. After that war Britain and France at least began to ponder the desirability of a doctrine which made compromise more difficult and war more likely. Englishmen began to debate whether they would fight "for king and country." But the problem as we have seen was that Germany, under National Socialism, had succumbed to radical or integral nationalism at the same time that Britain and France were questioning their own nationalist credentials.

After World War II a congeries of newly nationalist states were created with the breakdown of the old French, British, and Dutch empires. It is not at all clear that Soviets are less nationalist today then they were immediately after the war, but they are coming to recognize their position at or near the top of an international status quo. They are not willing to jeopardize that position in high-risk international ventures.

Elsewhere, in Europe and the United States, a potentially beneficial phenomenon has been the development of an antinationalist protest movement. In part this sentiment has crystallized as antiwar, but actually it has represented a much more fundamental critique of existing institutions. In effect it reflects alienation from the entire corpus of institutions and policy-outputs at the decision-making center. It is therefore not at all surprising that it is also antinational. Not entirely unlike the French philosophes in the waning days of the *ancien régime* the radical critics of existing Western society place patriotism at the bottom of the list of virtues. Unlike the Enlightenment thinkers, however, the radical critics of today do not possess a well-developed and consistent alternative philosophy and political theory on which a new society might be based. More importantly, there is the danger of portents similar to those of the Napoleonic era in which some nations were indeed antinational and others ultranationalist. If the radical protest movement is to be successful as an antinationalist force, it must be universally successful. All states together must lose their nationalist credentials. Nor must these be supplanted, as they were after the revolution in France, by an expansionist nationalism on the part of the revolutionary regime. The worst of both worlds would be obtained if the radicals were successful only among Western nations. The peace of balance of power may possibly be acquired by balancing nationalism against nationalism. The peace of *détente* and repose is acquired if there is no nationalism at all. But utter conflict eventually results if one-half of the world is nationalist and the other not.

Beyond Militarism?

If the future of modern nationalism is opaque, so is the question of the dominance of military factors. Since 1945 military weaponry has been developed to supreme effectiveness, at least in nuclear technology. Confrontations such as the Cuban missile crisis in 1962 have revolved around nuclear superiority and inferiority. The spread of nuclear weapons to other states— first to England, France, and China and probably soon to Israel, India, and Japan—have been cited as indications that military capabilities will continue to predominate in international politics. The nuclear bipolarity of the past will be transformed into a nuclear multipolarity of the future. Commitment, threat, and deterrence will be king in this era as they have been in our own.

There is at least a chance, however, that military variables will be less important in the future. In the past ten years there has been a development of new currencies of power in world politics; military factors now have to share pride of place with economic factors. Japan and Germany have risen to prominence on their economic, not military strengths (though clearly the former capability is capable of being transformed into the latter). In discussions among developed nations rates of economic growth, price stability, size of reserves have been as important in recent years as military technology and hardware. While France and China have become nuclear powers, it would be difficult to assert that both have gained more ground in international politics over the past ten years than Germany and Japan.

Further, the rise of economic factors has paralleled and reflected a growing interpenetration between the economies of developed states. Far more than is true in the military area, in economics it has become less and less sensible to talk about the American economy or the Japanese economy in national or strictly geographic terms. The role of Japanese products and Japanese capital in the American market makes the United States in some sense an extension of the Japanese sphere of economic activity. United States economic growth cannot meaningfully be separated from the growth of United States multinational corporations in Europe and elsewhere. Europe is in this sense an adjunct of the United States. Europeans are increasingly investing in United States securities and markets. Japan will be opened up more and more to outside economic influence. In security or military terms there is clearly a major interdependence of Western interests. In the economic field such an interdependence may be even more marked: developed economies must progress together or the entire edifice of economic expansion may collapse. Periods of crisis emphasize military relationships, but economic factors are crucial in peace.

It is possible, therefore, to speculate about the future of world politics in terms which transcend purely military variables. Strategic polarities may be less relevant in the future than the web of economic interrelationships which increasingly are uniting developed polities. If this is true, the likely tensions of the future (assuming economics to be a dominating factor) may very well be tensions between the developed and less developed worlds, where interpenetration and mutual interdependence has gone much less far than it has among developed societies. But these are possibilities whose true relevance one can only conjecture at the moment.

This chapter has sketched some of the lineaments of international history of the last two centuries that we must take into account if we are to design a world order which promotes peace. History is an essential part of our investigation, for history is a laboratory in which the peace-keeping techniques that men devise are tried out. If devices did not work previously, they may not apply today. If, on the other hand, certain methods did reduce violence at the international level in conditions analogous to those of today, they may be worth trying once more. The analysis which follows takes international history as its essential point of departure.

Chronology of Modern European History

1789-1799

The French Revolutionary era. The king is overthrown; aristocrats and clerics are deposed from positions of influence. Equality before the law is established. Citizens are given a share in their government. Frenchmen rally to support their state against Austrian conservative invasion designed to put the king back on his throne and to reinstate rule by royalty and aristocracy.

1799-1815

The Napoleonic era. Napoleon (I) attains power in France. He desires not only to protect the liberal, social, and economic reforms that have been won by the Revolution but also to extend them to other countries. This results in a prolonged period of war with the leagued conservative coalitions of Europe. France defeats Prussia and Austria. Her invasion of Russia in 1812 leads to disaster, culminating in a rout of French forces. After withdrawal from Russia Napoleon's forces are defeated by coalition armies at Leipzig in 1813. In 1814 Napoleon is forced to abdicate to the Isle of Elba. He returns to France in 1815, however, raises an army, but is again defeated by the other European powers at Waterloo. Henceforth Napoleon is banished to St. Helena and the French Bourbon monarchy is restored with Louis XVIII on the throne.

1814-1815

The Congress of Vienna meets to make a political and territorial disposition of European issues. Legitimate monarchs are returned to power throughout Europe. France loses territory to bordering states.

1814-1815

The Concert of Europe, including England, Russia, Prussia, and Austria is formed to prevent a renewal of French aggression. The Concert also agrees to intervene in countries which are menaced by revolution to prevent liberals from seizing power. After the restoration of monarchy in France, France is admitted to the Concert. In the period from 1818 to 1822, the Concert authorizes interventions in Spain and Naples to put down revolutions against the conservative order.

When the Greek revolution breaks out against Turkey, however, the powers cannot agree how it should be handled. Eventually England decides to leave the Concert. Liberal sentiments are bubbling to the surface in England, and she no longer agrees to do conservative bidding.

1830   The revolutions of 1830 lead to the installation of a moderate liberal regime in France, headed by the Orleanist king, Louis Philippe, and to Belgian independence from Holland. For a considerable period between 1830 and 1848 the Liberal Two (France and England) work together against the Conservative Three (Russia, Prussia, and Austria).

1848   Liberal revolutions break out in France, Prussia, Austria, Hungary, and the Italian states. Louis Philippe is deposed. Eventually, however, the French republican regime gives way to the Second Empire presided over by Louis Napoleon, the nephew of the great Napoleon, who assumes the title of Napoleon III. In Prussia, Austria, Hungary, and in the Italian and German states, however, liberal revolutions are put down. With Russian help, Austrian and Prussian conservatives are returned to power. Since conservative regimes have been so drastically challenged by the revolutions of 1848, however, they must find a new means of gaining popular support and acquiescence to resist the liberal onslaught. It is clear that whichever conservative regime gets the credit for bringing about the unification of Germany will gain a new lease on life. Hence, from 1852 on, Prussian and Austrian conservatives compete to gain German national unity.

1854-1856   The Crimean War between England and France on the one hand, and Russia on the other. The Crimean War is one of the last wars in the nineteenth century which has an ideological flavor, with liberal states against a conservative power. Formally the war is about the Russian-asserted right to protect Orthodox Christians against the Turks; informally it has much to do with French and English attempts to punish the leading conservative power in Europe. After much bloodshed, the Russians are defeated.

1859-1861

The Franco-Austrian War of 1859 is another ideological conflict, designed to paralyze the Austrian grip on the Italian states. France wins, and the House of Piedmont (Sardinia) leads a successful effort to unify the Italian peninsula.

1864-1866

Austria and Prussia disagree over the division of the spoils of their joint conquest of Denmark.

1866

Prussia defeats Austria in the Austro-Prussian War. The Austrian defeat enables Prussia to set up the North German Confederation in 1867. Now all except the South German states are united under Prussian leadership. Austria is excluded.

1870-1871

France quarrels with Prussia concerning compensation for French neutrality during the Austro-Prussian War. This leads to the Franco-Prussian War. Prussia defeats France. As a result the South German states join Prussia in the German Confederation. The united German Empire is proclaimed in 1871. Austria is left out. Germany takes Alsace-Lorraine from France.

1877

The Russo-Turkish War. Turkey had been weakened by a series of revolts in her European provinces in Bosnia. Russia capitalizes on her weakness to attack, ostensibly as the protector of her European and Christian peoples. Turkey is defeated but only after putting up stubborn resistance at Plevna. As a result of Russian victories, England and Austria become increasingly alarmed, fearing that Turkish independence might be extinguished. When the Treaty of San Stefano is signed, setting up large areas of erstwhile Turkish territories that would become virtual protectorates of Russia, the powers decide to intervene.

1878

At the Congress of Berlin in 1878 Russian gains in the Turkish war are substantially pared down. Austria gains as much as Russia. The Russian-sponsored "Bulgaria" is cut in half. Russia emerges angry and vindictive from the Congress, feeling shabbily treated by her sister powers. She is particularly incensed at Germany's role, feeling that she deserved the support of German Chancellor Bismarck.

1879   Austro-German Alliance. The Dual Alliance was the first long-term alliance in peacetime in European history. It was directed initially against Russia.

1882   The Triple Alliance. The Dual Alliance is expanded to include Italy, which has concerns about disputes with France and potential disputes with Austria (which are hereby allayed).

1880-1912   The decade of the eighties witnesses the outbreak of European imperialism. Beginning with the efforts of Belgians in the Congo, the entire African continent is partitioned between France, Britain, Germany, and Portugal. In the Far East France, Britain, Japan, and Russia get large concessions or sections of erstwhile Chinese territory.

1887   The Reinsurance Treaty between Germany and Russia. While Russia has been excluded from the Triple Alliance, it is always Bismarck's policy to keep on relatively good terms with both Austria and Russia. This is to prevent them from coming to blows over their rivalry in the Balkans. It is also to make sure that France will not find an ally to gain revenge for the outcome of the Franco-Prussian War.

1890   After the fall of Bismarck, his successors decide not to renew the Reinsurance Treaty with Russia, preferring instead a connection with England. That connection never materializes, however, and Russia is left free to find alternative allies. She turns to France.

1894   The Franco-Russian Alliance overturns the bases of German policy. Now there are two alliance combinations in Europe: the Triple Alliance and the Franco-Russian Alliance. For a time, Bismarck's successors do not worry overmuch, however, for they believe that England could never come to terms with Russia and France. Thus they confidently rebuff English alliance overtures during 1899 to 1901.

1904   The conclusion of the Anglo-French Entente. England and France agree to settle colonial disputes. Essentially France stops challenging the British position in Egypt in return for British support in Morocco. The Entente undercuts the basic presumptions of German policy. Germany seeks to either undo the new arrangement or else to get Russia on her side.

1905   The German Schlieffen Plan involves preparation for a two-front war against both Russia and France. France is to be defeated first in a wheeling movement through Belgium designed to turn the French left flank and then encircle Paris. After the defeat of France, Germany is to throw its whole weight against Russia.

1906   Algeciras Conference. Germany seeks to prevent France from establishing a foothold in Morocco, but France is supported by England as well as Russia and wins a temporary victory. Germany is bent on humiliating France and preventing a French protectorate in Morocco.

1907   Anglo-Russian Entente. This completes the building of the Triple Entente—England, France, and Russia.

1908   The Bosnian crisis occurs between Austria and Russia. Austria and Russia had secretly agreed to further mutual encroachments upon Turkey. Russia was to get concessions in Constantinople in return for Austrian annexation of Bosnia. Austria does not wait for joint action, however, and annexes Bosnia unilaterally. Austria is strongly supported by Germany while France does not strongly support Russia.

1912-1913   The Balkan Wars occur in which Turkey is weakened once again and a strong, independent Serbia emerges as a threat to the security of the Slavic portions of the Austrian Empire.

1914   Assassination of Austrian Archduke Franz Ferdinand in Bosnia is attributed to Serbian complicity. Austria resolves to punish Serbia at all costs. First she obtains a "blank check" from Germany to act. Then she issues an ultimatum which Serbia does not fully accept. Russia, however, will not stand by and see Serbia destroyed, and issues partial mobilization in response to the Austrian mobilization against Serbia. Germany is bound to mobilize fully to protect Austria even if Russia does not mobilize against Berlin. Russia however cancels partial mobilization and mobilizes against both Austria and Germany. France then goes to war to support Russia. After German troops violate Belgian neutrality on the way to attack France, England declares war on Germany. The Schlieffen Plan is improperly executed and German troops are stopped on the Marne. After years of carnage, marked by Russian collapse in 1917, and America's entry into the war in the same year, the British, French, and Americans are victorious over Germany and Austria.

1917   Bolshevik Revolution in Russia. Following the March revolution in which liberal constitutionalists take power from the Tsar, the Bolshevik Revolution occurs in November. During the summer, the provisional regime was unable to meet the demand of the peasants for an end to the war and acquisition of the land. Workers were rioting for food. The Bolsheviks seize power on the slogan: "Peace, bread, land!" Although only a tiny minority of the Russian electorate, they manage to hang on to power by ending the war and signing the humiliating Brest-Litovsk treaty with Germany. At first the Russians try to follow the Marxist-Leninist program of worker and peasant control; later they realize that central management control is essential to their own position and to efficient production. After a period of experimentation with state-sanctioned private enterprise in both agriculture and industry, 1921 to 1927, they launch a major industrialization and collectivization of agriculture in 1928. All vestiges of private property and enterprise are eliminated.

1919

The Versailles Settlement. The Versailles Treaty was more punitive toward Germany than the Vienna settlement had been in respect to France a hundred years previously. Germany lost Alsace and Lorraine to France, a strip of territory to Poland, and territory to Belgium, Denmark, and Lithuania. Her colonial empire was stripped away. She was forced to accept all guilt and responsibility for the war, and to pay an indefinitely large reparations bill. The Rhineland was demilitarized, and strict limits were placed on German military forces. Any union with Austria, forming a greater Germany, was proscribed.

The Versailles settlement also provided for the creation of the League of Nations, designed to serve as a permanent concert of the great powers and lesser states, to protect the peace. The heart of League obligations occurred in Articles X and XVI in which members were obligated to respect and preserve against external aggression each other's territorial integrity and political independence; and which also provided for the application of sanctions against states in violation of the League Covenant. In addition, the League called for submission of disputes to arbitration or to the League Council and for a moratorium on action while these procedures were in process. This was designed to permit the development of strong public pressure—the hue and cry of international opinion—against potential or actual aggressors.

The Versailles settlement and the end of the war also witnessed the establishment of a series of independent states in Eastern Europe, successors to the Russian and Austrian empires: Poland, Latvia, Lithuania, Estonia, Czechoslovakia, Yugoslavia, and an enlarged Rumania. It should be noted that while the objective of President Woodrow Wilson is "national self-determination," the frontiers that actually emerge do not conform with this premise. Czechoslovakia and Poland have large German populations in their western and frontier areas.

An integral part of the Versailles settlement from the French point of view is a treaty of guarantee with America and Britain, designed to protect France against a renewal of German expansion. This Treaty is nullified, however, when the U. S. Senate refuses to ratify both the League Covenant and the Treaty of Guarantee.

1919 also sees the creation of the German Weimar Republic, an apparently liberal successor regime to imperial Germany

1922	Benito Mussolini, leader of the Fascist Party, gains power in Italy.
1923	French Occupation of the Ruhr. When the Germans default on reparations payments, the French occupy the Ruhr valley. The Germans support their passive resistance to the French by printing money. This results in a drastic inflation which, combined with the previous wartime inflation, helps to wipe out the savings of the German lower middle class.
1929-1930	Onset of the Great Depression, causing great unemployment in most industrial countries.
1931	Japan occupies Manchuria.
1933	Attainment of power by Adolf Hitler and the National Socialists in Germany. Hitler purges dissidents, and has the German legislature vote for an enabling act which essentially vests all power in the Chancellor. Hitler wins when the economic crisis and the sense of nationalist grievance combine to reject bougeois liberal or socialist parties, and also the conservative parties of the old empire. His program is fundamentally that of remaking the map of Europe, and regaining for Germany the territories and prestige lost at Versailles. His program of expansion is basically directed toward Eastern Europe and Russia, but he must eliminate France and Britain to succeed in such goals.
1934	Hitler begins rearmament.
1935	Italy begins her attack on Ethiopia. France

and Britain in the League agree on "harm-less" sanctions against Italy.

1936   Germany marches troops into the demilita-rized Rhineland.

1938   Germany forces a union (Anschluss) with Austria and later demands the cession of the Sudeten (German) areas of Czechoslovakia. This is conceded in the Munich Pact (Britain, France, Germany, and Italy).

1939   Hitler takes the rest of Czechoslovakia and provokes a crisis over Poland. Britain and France agree to stand against any infringe-ment of Polish sovereignty. The Russians agree to give Germany a free hand in most of Eastern Europe in the Nazi-Soviet pact. Shortly afterward, Hitler makes war on Poland and World War II is declared.

1941   The United States cuts off supplies of raw materials for Japan (oil and iron). Later, Japan attacks Pearl Harbor, and Germany declares war on the United States. Germany makes war on Russia.

1945   Germany and Japan are defeated. The Soviet Union establishes an area of predominance in Eastern Europe. The United States and its allies are predominant in Western Europe. Disagreements between the two groups lead to the cold war. The United Nations organi-zation, with the Security Council capable of taking enforcement action against an aggres-sor (assuming unity of the Big Five: China, France, Britain, the United States, and the Soviet Union) is created. Given disagree-ments, however, such action is never taken. The detonation of the first nuclear weapon.

1948-1949   Berlin blockade.

1950-1953   Korean war.

1952   The successful testing of the hydrogen bomb.

1954-present   Major United States involvement in the Vietnam war.

1957   The successful testing of the first intercon-tinental ballistic missile and the first earth satellite.

1958-1959	Berlin crisis, with threatened closing of Western access routes.
1961	United States sponsored invasion of Cuba at the Bay of Pigs fails. Construction of the Berlin Wall.
1962	Cuban Missile Crisis.
1963	The Nuclear Test Ban Treaty.
1968	The Nuclear Non-Proliferation Treaty.
1969	Man's first landing on the moon.
1971	The admission of the People's Republic of China to the United Nations.

NOTES

1 R. Rosecrance, *Action and Reaction in World Politics* (Boston Little, Brown, 1963), p. 20.
2 E. Lavisse, quoted in R. B. Mowat, *The Age of Reason* (Boston: Houghton-Mifflin, 1934), p. 55.
3 R. R. Palmer, "Frederick the Great, Guibert, Bulow: From Dynastic to National War" in E. M. Earle (ed.), *Makers of Modern Strategy* (Princeton: Princeton University Press, 1953), p. 52.
4 A.J.P. Taylor, *The Course of German History* (London: H. Hamilton, 1954), p. 68.
5 A.E. Zimmern, *The League of Nations and the Rule of Law, 1918-1935* (New York: Russell and Russell, 1969, pp. 190-1.

CHAPTER FOUR

Determinants of Peace and War:
Systems, Objectives,
and Techniques

This book is about possible strategies for coping with the problem of maintaining peace. What causes large-scale international instability of the sort that existed during the Napoleonic Wars, World War I, and World War II?[1] What factors tend to promote a stable order in which there is no recourse to violence on a massive scale? In particular, can we elaborate a theory that can actually be applied in the context of current world politics, or are real solutions utopian? If we were to conclude, for example, that only a world government would foster a peaceful world environment, we might have to admit the remedy was impossible to put into practice. But even if our solutions are applicable, can we be sure that we have come up with the right approach? As we have seen, past international theorists have tended to devise remedies which would have prevented the previous war, but which have little or no relevance to the next one. Can any truly international theory be put into effect in a period in which the nations of the world are turning inward toward a new concentration on domestic problems? This is significant in light of the fact that the British and French publics in the 1930s did not respond to Hitler partly because of their domestic preoccupations. Are we bound to repeat such errors?

SYSTEMS, OBJECTIVES, AND TECHNIQUES

There are many possible ways of seeking answers to these questions, and many conceptual formulations which might be employed in approaching

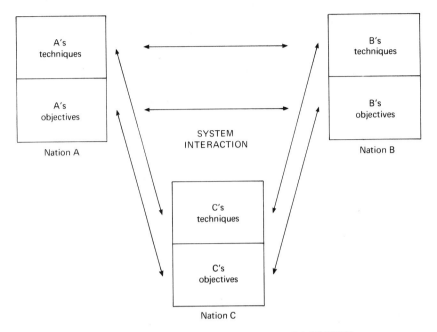

Figure 4-1 SYSTEMS, OBJECTIVES, AND TECHNIQUES

them. Theorists may divide the subject matter of international relations in any manner they please, provided that the division yields fruitful insights or theories. This book examines three key means by which conflict may be generated or controlled, three key determinants of peace and war. These areas are: systems, objectives, and techniques. The way in which they might be described spatially is shown in Figure 4-1.

International *systems* refer to the interaction among states. They are therefore external to the perspective of any given state. A nation can of course decide what it wishes to do in world politics (choose objectives); it can select means to achieve its ends (specify techniques); but it cannot control the reactions of other members of the system. It may try to anticipate the reactions of others and to be prepared for them. If it is very successful, it may even cope with many of these reactions. But in some measure it must also adjust to them. Napoleon thought he could dominate Europe and revolutionize European society as well. But the responses of states like Russia and England ultimately upset his calculations. Systems, then, refer to relationships among states. If there are no relationships—positive or negative, friendly or unfriendly—a nation does not have to take account of the attitude or policy of other states. In such an instance there is no international system.

In some cases the responses of other powers may be institutionalized and expressed through an international organization. In a very few instances the response of an international organization, as formulated by its permanent officials, may differ from the sum total of national responses. Such an instance occurs when an international organization has power of its own and some independent decision-making latitude. In most circumstances, however, the system displays national reactions of individual states apart from and independent of international organization. Even during the heyday of international organizational effectiveness—in the early years of the Concert of Europe—nations did not refer all of their disputes to the Concert, nor were all reactions expressed in Concert forums. Today, most important national initiatives and responses take place outside the framework of the United Nations. Even attempts at peacemaking have largely bypassed the UN in recent years. Increasingly, the UN has been used as a propaganda forum in which policies formulated elsewhere are explained and rationalized before world opinion.

Once there are system responses (by individual states) to the policy of a nation, it becomes clear whether the initiating policy will be successful. As a result of the pressures and responses of other states, a nation may have to change its policy or to alter its techniques. In 1946 the Soviet Union occupied Azerbaijan, a northern part of Iran, hoping to make it part of the U.S.S.R. The United States demanded Soviet withdrawal, and members of the UN Security Council also protested. Eventually the Russians withdrew. Occasionally a nation will find its policy reinforced as other national actors lend support to carry its policies further. Whether the system will facilitate or restrain the policies of a nation-state is affected by the form or structure of the system, by the type of controls levied by the system, by the way in which the members of the system interact. If system responses are rapid, united, and powerful, a state may not be able to make aggressive or expansionist moves on the stage of world politics.

Secondly, outcomes in international relations are affected by the *objectives* which states seek. Objectives are not external to the perspective of a given state. They are formulated within that state's perspective. While they may take into account probable systemic interactions and responses, objectives are fundamentally the expression of the internal political life of a state. They are a manifestation of its hopes and desires in the international realm. Inevitably, the internal process of deciding upon objectives cannot comprehend all the external influences that may affect success and failure. If it could do so, all states would be successful in the objectives that they chose, for they would only select goals that could be effectively achieved. Objectives also only partially apply to the entire international scene. States do not pay attention to all that is going on around them. Nations may wish for isolation; they may seek to concentrate upon domestic tasks; they may become involved in major international questions only episodically. Very rarely do states have goals which apply to all other nations and regions of the world.

Only then do their objectives become coextensive with the entire international system.

Just as international systems affect international stability by restricting or reinforcing state behavior, so stability is also partly dependent upon the type of objectives which states choose. If states have unlimited ambitions, they are bound to have conflict with one another. Where nation-states advance contending ideologies a certain amount of conflict is inevitable. As one state succeeds in promoting its ideology, another fails. On the other hand, if states seek goals like economic development or an increase in world trade, these objectives can be realized without creating antagonism with other nations. If goals do not conflict, there are no rational grounds for war. This, of course, does not mean that there can be no war where goals do not conflict. States, acting irrationally, may believe they conflict when they actually do not.

Thirdly, stability and instability will be influenced by the *techniques* which states use to achieve their goals. The choice of techniques, like the selection of objectives, emerges from the internal decisions of nations. Techniques, however, are practical; objectives are expressions of national desires. Objectives are what states want; techniques are what they do to get them. Almost inevitably, objectives and ambitions exceed what states can realistically achieve. In practice, therefore, most nations will only try to realize certain of their most fundamental objectives. Techniques are not usually designed to accomplish the entire corps of objectives. They are fundamental, however, for they are actually what states do.

The direct impact of techniques on the chances of peace cannot be overemphasized. Some techniques produce war; indeed, they are themselves the waging of war. Some help maintain peace. Military and economic threats may not result in war, but they involve a risk of war. They may be necessary, however, if an aggressive nation will not limit its behavior short of threats from its neighbors. In 1937 to 1938 the British did not object to what they understood to be Hitler's goals: that of regaining German territory lost in the Treaty of Versailles. They were willing to see adjustments in both Czechoslovak and Polish borders to implement such changes. But they were not prepared to see Hitler take these areas by force or by the threat of force. Ultimately, it was Germany's employment of military threat that led Britain and France to cease acquiescing to Hitler's demands. If military measures are likely to produce such hostile responses, however, diplomatic techniques and international negotiation are much less dangerous to the peace. Attempts to improve another state's economic position may be positively beneficial and may directly contribute to a relaxation of international tension. In one sense, techniques offer the last clear chance of peace. For even if the system does not constrain aggressive action, even if objectives seem bound to produce conflict, war does not occur until a resort to violent means actually takes place. As long as nations are prepared to carry on their disputes by means other than the use of force, war can be avoided.[2]

Systems

International systems help to determine the outcomes of world politics in four different ways. First, the interaction of state policies in the international realm may be such as to *regulate* bellicose national behavior. Every historical international system has clearly shown that persistent violent or aggressive behavior ultimately calls forth opposition to try to halt that behavior. This attempt to regulate the system, to prevent the extremes of hostile action, is not always successful. Sometimes, instead of restraining the aggressor, the attempt to regulate his behavior precipitates war. On the eve of World War I, for example, the Triple Entente was trying to regulate the expansionist behavior of Austria, a member of the Triple Alliance. But the attempt to restrain Austria, particularly on the part of Russia, did not succeed. It led only to greater German support and finally to a larger war. Regulative forces must be adequate to contend with disruption; if they are deficient in the strategies which they can use, the attempt at regulation is likely to precipitate war or even to make it worse. If the Triple Entente had not tried to prevent Austria from acting against Serbia, there might have been an aggressive war in the Balkans but it would not have engulfed the rest of Europe. On the other hand, when the Concert of Europe was at its height after 1815, all potentially disruptive powers were brought to heel. Russia was prevented from intervention in Greece. France was chastized and later returned to the family of nations. When the Concert began to become identified with alliance systems in the later part of the nineteenth century, German Chancellor Bismarck maintained the peace by organizing a predominant alliance combination. No power could act against the central coalition. Bismarck balanced off his alliance partners as well so that there was no temptation to challenge the existing international arrangement.

Until the Napoleonic Wars a balance of power system maintained the equilibrium in Europe. Wars did take place, but they were of limited scope and intensity and they nowhere threatened the existence of a great power. In the eighteenth century military ventures were means of producing marginal adjustments in the distribution of territory, prestige, and influence. After 1815 a Concert of Europe, consisting of irregular meetings of the major European powers, maintained peace for a considerable period. It was most effective in its first ten years of operation. Thereafter it became less important as agreement among states dissolved and the fear of war began to wane.

After World War I a regular peace-keeping mechanism was institutionalized through the League of Nations. With the League, and later the United Nations, it was hoped that the world would not have to rely solely on the national decisions of major powers to keep the peace. It was felt that a council of great powers could produce basic agreement which in turn could be used to enforce peace in the rest of the international system. In neither case, however, did international organization fulfill its purpose. The League and the UN have occasionally been able to regulate the disputes of small powers when the great states were in agreement. But neither the League nor the UN has been able to produce great-power agreement on all questions of major importance. Neither League nor UN, facing disagreement among great powers, has been able to regulate their conduct. Today great-power conduct is regulated only by the behavior of other great powers. This does not mean, however, that regulation is not performed in the contemporary international system. Nations hesitate to adopt extremely aggressive policies for fear of the responses of other nations.

Secondly, the international system helps to preserve stability and peace by affording an adequate *environmental supply* of the goods and resources which states demand. Even if regulation is unsuccessful, environmental supply may ensure against war. Conflict in international relations ensues when states cannot simultaneously obtain their objectives. Suppose for the moment that the major objective of states is the acquisition of territory. If there were plenty of territory to go around, territorial expansion would not lead to conflict. There would not be war, in short, if the environmental supply of the desired resource (in this instance, territory) is abundant enough to provide for all concerned. Suppose, on the other hand, that states aim not at territorial acquisition, but at the propagation of their ideology, ultimately seeking to spread it to the entire world. If states have different and conflicting ideologies, there is no way in which they can achieve their goals simultaneously. Victory for one is defeat for another. The environment cannot gratify all at the same time. If states aim at security, whether they will be able to attain it cooperatively will depend on the conditions of military technology and warfare. In some technological environments there may be an enormous premium upon striking an offensive blow, hitting an opponent before he can strike back. If security depends upon being able to strike first, then all cannot be secure. The environmental supply of security is deficient. Conversely, if modest defensive preparations are sufficient to bring security, many states can find security without going to war. Security for one is consistent with security for others.

International systems reduce or mitigate conflict either by regulating national behavior, or providing a sufficient environmental supply of the goods which states seek. If regulation is effective there is no conflict, for states are directly prevented from engaging in actions which would be detrimental to others or to international stability. If environmental supply is adequate there is no war, for states can get what they want without recourse to violence.

How successful international systems can be in applying either of these remedies for conflict, however, depends upon two other factors: system *structure* and system *interaction.* System structure, the third means by which international systems may effect peace or war, refers to the way in which national units are aligned or distributed. If the structure is bipolar, for example, it will be very difficult for an external balancer or an international organization to regulate the behavior of either major camp. At the same time, if the two blocs are evenly matched, each may deter the other from aggressive action. Regulation through a predominant coalition or through international or regional organization is likely to be more effective if there are five or more states or blocs. Either the coalition can restrain an aggressive member, or an international organization can develop a consensus against a miscreant state which may prevent further hostile expansion. Regulation will also be affected by the degree of homogeneity in the system. If all powers have the same ideology and political form their conflicts will be less strident and violent than if they represent different ideologies or political types.

Finally, the success of the system in maintaining peace will be influenced by system *interaction*. A loosely interacting system in which the interests of one state have little relationship to the interests of another may offer considerable scope for environmental satisfaction of national objectives. If the pursuit of an objective by one state does not adversely affect the goals of another, there is little reason for them to come to blows. On the other hand, a loosely interacting system will have greater difficulty in regulating the behavior of its members. If states do not fully participate in general international politics, they may not understand the importance of preventing an aggressive state from expanding militarily. They may not see that unfettered expansion would eventually pose a threat even to their own interests. In these circumstances it will be difficult to form a regulative coalition to prevent action by the aggressive state.

Objectives

If international systems fail to prevent aggressive behavior—if the restraints on state policy at the international level are inadequate—whether war occurs will tend to depend on the objectives which states seek. If national objectives call for a radical change in international politics and in relationships to other countries, conflict will likely result. If objectives are more modest, but depend for their achievement on frustrating the goals of others, there will still be grounds for war. On the other hand, if the goals of one state do not interfere with those of another, or if they can be achieved in tandem, the pursuit of national objectives is likely to reinforce peace.

What states ultimately seek depends in turn upon the way in which objectives are formulated. They may be largely *internally* or *externally* determined. If they are internally determined and do not take into account the probable policies of other powers, they are likely to be very disruptive. Indeed, those states whose objectives are formulated without significant attention to the external system can scarcely be desirous of avoiding war. A nation wants what it wants, regardless of what other states think. If we are to maintain peace, we cannot allow states to think only of the internal and not of the external constituencies. Internal determination, moreover, may lead a state to oscillate between the extremes of isolation and intervention. While it may then try to remold the system, it is likely to relapse into an isolationist lassitude and cease to participate in general international relationships.

Externally determined objectives are likely to be more tractable. If states pay primary attention to what is going on around them in the outside world, they will tend to formulate their goals in terms of what is possible. They will be less intent on overturning or radically transforming the international system. Goals will be chosen on the basis of the state's position in a field of competing nation-states. Objectives will be formulated with a keen appreciation for their international impact. Weaknesses in the regulative structure of international relations will be exploited; states will seek to advance their position where they can, but without overthrowing the system.

The effect which objectives have upon international stability will also depend on the way in which they are combined and integrated. In previous periods, and to a limited extent today, national objectives have had a diffuse character. Goals were not necessarily related to one another in strict hierarchical form. No final priorities had been established; statesmen were not themselves quite sure how to rank goals of territory, prestige, glory, security, or ideological gain. As time passed, however, objectives tended to become fused into a particular hierarchy, with national interests of security and power taking precedence. This inevitably posed problems for the control of conflict: fused objectives were much harder to alter and adjust at the behest of international imperatives than diffuse objectives. The more clear-cut priorities are, the more difficult it is to change them by negotiation.

The particular objectives which states will stress tends to depend upon the pattern of historical development. The kind of demands which a state makes upon the system is partly determined by the nature of its participation in international relations. A state that is completely secure, that has a long international history of independent existence will be likely to aim at derivative objectives. It will tend to seek marginal adjustments in the outcomes of the international system, redistributing prestige, territory, or influence in its favor. Its concerns will be basically material, involving a better access to the rewards of the system. States which are less secure and have only recently come to participate in international relations on a continuing basis may consider that their status is not sufficiently high. They may believe that they can validate and reinsure their position only by rapid political or even military gains at the international level. Such gains, however, may in turn be regarded as challenges to the existing order by other nations. States that have just undergone the throes of domestic revolution may be tempted to try to export their revolutionary ideology to other states. Having just survived a test of national existence, a revolutionary regime may wish to make converts externally, if only to solidify the revolution at home. Such regimes will pursue ideological objectives. The need for the pursuit of ideology tends to arise when a nation's right to an independent existence has been challenged.

Still more fundamental than ideological objectives is the quest for security. While all nations retain security as a major goal, it does not become fully operative as a proximate objective until it is felt to be challenged. As long as it is not threatened, a state can pursue other less important aims. When threats to a regime or nation multiply, however, the question of security becomes predominant. In some cases ideological and security objectives may be sought simultaneously, particularly where the external threat is also a threat to extinguish a particular political regime or constitution. When challenges to the very existence of the state emerge, ideological gain tends to give way to the protection of minimal national security. After the Russian Revolution the new Bolshevik regime did not move into a phase of ideological offensive, striving to carry the revolution to the rest of Europe and Asia. The challenge to Soviet security was so great that the new regime had all it could do to protect itself against foreign intervention and attack. Western capitalist states intervened in Russia, challenging the ideology of the Russian Communist regime, but Lenin could not afford to lash out against his tormentors. If he had done so, Western armies might have resumed an advance on Moscow and put an end to Bolshevik rule. Security, therefore, dictated caution.

Sometimes, of course, national leaders may become convinced that there is a threat to their security when the threat exists only in their minds. If this is true, national responses will be similar to those where real security interests are involved. On the eve of World War I, Austria-Hungary undoubtedly overdid the threat which Slavic Serbia presented to her southern frontiers. In Vietnam, a succession of United States decision makers have exaggerated out of all proportion the danger which even the most blatant Communist take-over would cause to American interests. In deciding to attack the United States in World War II the Japanese thought that their fundamental security interests were imperiled. Their security required an attack on the United States, however, only if they insisted on maintaining their empire in East Asia, which in turn brought them into conflict with America. If they had been willing to withdraw from their conquests they would not have faced the necessity of war with the United States.

The quest for these three different objectives has an immediate impact on the stability of the system. Where security is not in jeopardy, the desire for material objectives permits a generally relaxed international atmosphere. However, under conditions of security and seeming peace, nations may be led to expect or to demand too much. They may miscalculate the responses of potential opponents. Believing themselves fundamentally safe, they may become overconfident and seek larger shares of international resources.

When security is threatened, a nation tends to concentrate only on its more central goals. Its demands on the system will be more limited, but they will also be pursued with great tenacity and resolution. Under certain conditions of military technology they may even be easier to satisfy than material objectives. But nations will always be near the brink of war, if only because they believe themselves in danger of attack. In such circumstances, some may be tempted to attack others, if only to forestall attack upon themselves at a later time.

On balance, peace is most likely to be obtained under two opposite conditions: in one, states feel quite secure and therefore do not have to engage in desperate measures to achieve security; in the other, their security position is in such great jeopardy that even warfare will not retrieve it. The most worrisome situation is an intermediate position—where security is in question but appears obtainable by force. In these circumstances nations may launch major offensives on the world scene to regain security.

Techniques

The final determinant of peace and war is that of *techniques*. While states employ various means to advance their policies in international relations, three general methods stand out above the rest. A state can seek to advance its position through diplomacy and negotiation, through military preparedness, and through economic transformation. Reliance upon these techniques has not been uniform throughout history. Two hundred years ago diplomatic negotiation had a rather more important place in the armory of national techniques than it does today. War and military force were seldom decisive. Objectives were strictly limited. Since military measures did not decide contests, diplomacy had great importance. With the development of more effective military tactics in the Revolutionary and Napoleonic wars, and with the development of nationalism, however, diplomacy gradually receded into the background. Diplomatic techniques were now less important than military ones. Nor could diplomacy bring about a reordering of the objectives of nations. By the end of the nineteenth century nationalism had made it impossible to tamper with sacred national goals. Diplomacy was circumscribed: greater emphasis was placed on purely military strategies, on the acute international crisis, and on the fait accompli.

It is not necessary to point out that diplomatic negotiation and economic strategies are less likely to lead to war than military techniques. Even in an era in which military techniques are paramount, however, it does not follow that they must inexorably produce war. For the past twenty-five years the spectre of cataclysmic consequences seems to have successfully prevented the extreme form of violence, the use of nuclear weapons. Balancing in the international arena has taken place partly through changes in the arms budget of various powers. Doctrines of nuclear deterrence have been developed to prevent an expansionist power from simply seizing what it wants. Under some circumstances, military techniques enjoin caution on a potential aggressor and thus foster peace. But the ever present threat of the use of weapons of mass destruction does not lead one to believe that war is best avoided by an arms race, by threat, and by military ultimatum. The threat of use of such weapons introduces an uncertain element in international politics.

CONCLUSION

Systems, objectives, and techniques together determine international outcomes: peace or war. They are also interdependent and influence one another. A particular form of international system may require or predispose states to work for particular objectives. If a system is bipolar, a state's room for maneuver is limited, and the objectives it can pursue already partly defined. The pursuit of certain objectives in turn affects the form of the system. If a state wants to extend its ideology to other nations and there are two major ideological theories contending for influence, the system may become bipolar. If, on the other hand, a state seeks economic growth and minimal physical security against attack, a much less structured international system may emerge. In this case, the attainment of one nation's objectives need not prevent others from gaining similar objectives: there may be no vital conflict within the system.

Objectives and techniques are also interrelated. States pursuing unlimited objectives will go to great lengths to achieve them. The techniques they employ will include the undermining or destruction of other regimes. In this way objectives help to determine the techniques that are used. At the same time the adoption of particularly aggressive or violent techniques will call forth an extreme reaction on the other side. This in turn will affect the objectives the parties are seeking to gain. The initially moderate objectives of World War I became more extreme as battles turned into a frightful carnage. At the end of the war nothing short of an absolute humiliation of the defeated power was acceptable to the victors.

In the same way systems and techniques affect one another. If the system prescribes a relationship of players in which all advance their positions simultaneously, recourse to violent or destructive techniques will be ruled out. Resort to such techniques will, however, clearly alter the relationship of states in the system. If each is violently attacking the other, not all can gain.

The net result is a complex interrelationship of factors. Systems, objectives, and techniques influence each other. It is impossible to say finally in which direct causation proceeds or which are independent and which dependent variables. Systemic constraints take the most general form, but they can be reshaped as states adopt different objectives and techniques.

Objectives and techniques emerge from a domestic context, but they are vitally conditioned by the nature of the international system and the restraints that exist within it. The three factors together determine the outcomes of international relations, and they specify whether those outcomes will be stable and peaceful or unstable and productive of war.

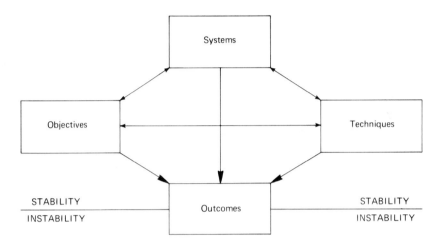

Figure 4-2 OUTCOMES AND STABILITY

NOTES

1 It should be noted that in this analysis *stability* and *peace* are normally linked. There is a slight difference between them, however, and on two counts: (1) If the fundamental structure and state-units of the international system are maintained intact over time, the system would be described as stable. Minor wars, however, might occur without disrupting that stability. Major wars in which populations and resources are totally involved, however, would not be consistent with stability because both structure and state-units change as a result of such wars. Stability is therefore sometimes consistent with minor war. (2) Peace is sometimes consistent with instability in that it may be better secured by a change in the units or structure of the system. A system change may sometimes produce peace, because it adjusts system structures in ways that make war less likely. In general terms, however, large-scale system change is likely to produce an international uncertainty and insecurity which is conducive to warfare. Despite these differences, in the remainder of the text the terms will be used virtually synonymously.

2 Kenneth Waltz, *Man, the State, and War* (New York: Columbia University Press, 1959). He views the international system as the permissive cause of war, in that if states do not restrain themselves, it is the international system which permits them to go to war. This is of course correct, but it is the states themselves which take the action which makes war.

2

Systems

Systems are the first of the three international determinants of stability and instability which we will consider. *Systems* refer to relationships among states, to the way in which the objectives and techniques of states interact. Systems can produce peace, irrespective of other factors, if they either provide a sufficient ability to *regulate* the behavior of disruptive powers, or if they offer a sufficient *environmental* supply of international goods so that states can all be satisfied without coming into conflict. Whether either regulation or environmental supply can be adequate to this task is in turn dependent upon system *structure* and system *interaction*. The next four chapters deal in turn with each of these concepts.

CHAPTER FIVE

Regulative Forces

As we have seen, the international system stands outside the control of any single state (unless the system is unipolar). When a nation acts, the other members of the system will respond. The response will determine whether the state will succeed or fail, whether it will be able to proceed with its policies, or will have to change them. Some actions will cause conflict if they are allowed to continue unchecked. At this point other members of the system or international organization may intervene to *regulate* the behavior of the disruptive party.

Regulation may be of many types. A balance of power system may cause opposing alliances or alignments to be formed, impinging upon the security of the potential expansionist power. A bipolar system might lead a second camp to take action to offset the gains of the first. A concert of European powers or another type of international organization might bring the potential disruptor before the bar of world opinion to mobilize international support against its action. If the contest is between two superpowers, even a slightly increased danger of war might cause an offending party to reconsider its position and adopt more limited policies.

International regulation, however, is not universally successful. Sometimes the attempt to regulate national behavior does not produce accommodation or a reduction of aggressive action. Occasionally the powers seeking to regulate the system are weak relative to the magnitude of disruption. In the Napoleonic Wars the various conservative coalitions were not strong enough to face down the French emperor or to prevent French aggression. In July 1914 the Triple Entente was not strong enough to prevent Austrian action against Serbia. The attempt at regulation merely broadened the war by involving more parties: Russia, Germany, France, and England. In 1939 the peaceful nations were unable to prevent Hitler from going to war. Despite their appeasement of the German Chancellor they could not induce him to limit his ambitions, nor could they deter him from acting by mounting a common front against him. If regulative forces had been stronger, if they had had a wider variety of moves to play, major war might have been avoided.

The response of the international system to national disruption is similar to that of mechanical systems like refrigerators or hot water heaters to disturbance from the outside. In a refrigerator the thermostat (regulator) will start the cooling mechanism when interior temperatures begin to rise above a certain predetermined point. In a hot water heater the gas will be turned on when temperatures within the boiler have fallen below a set limit. In each case disruption from outside (in one instance, perhaps the opening of the refrigerator door; in the other the turning on of the hot water tap) will be countered by regulative action from the cooling or heating system. The regulative activity will be designed to return outcomes (in these two cases, temperatures) to acceptable (stable) ranges. But the regulative mechanism will not always be able to produce desired outcomes, just as international regulation does not always produce peace. A hot water heater will probably not be able to cope with a tenant who turns on all the hot water taps full blast. Sooner or later the heater will not be able to heat water as rapidly as it is used. A refrigerator's cooling mechanism will not be able to cope with a careless housewife who leaves the door open. In both instances temperatures inside will eventually change in ways that defeat the purpose of the system.

The success of regulation in mechanical or international systems depends on the number and variety of disruptive strategies with which it must cope. No system can cope with all forms of disturbance, but it must be able to counter the most likely ones. It follows that regulative forces must have a variety of regulative strategies to play if they are to counter a variety of disruptive inputs. The more strategies which a regulator can employ in response to disturbance, the more likely regulation is to be successful. Let us imagine a regulator which can play three strategies (A, B, and C) and a disturbance or input which can play five strategies (1, 2, 3, 4, and 5). Let us also assume that k is the desired or stable outcome. Figure 5-1 gives the series of outcomes in response to the strategies played by both regulator and disturbance. One can see by inspection that the regulator successfully copes with all possible strategies of the disturbance, producing k no matter which strategy the disturbance employs. If the disturbance (D) offers strategy 1, the regulator (R) will counter with Strategy C; if D chooses strategy 2, R will play strategy A; if D selects 3, R will use C, and so on. For each strategy chosen by the input D, the regulator can guarantee the outcome of k. On the

Disturbance strategies	Regulator strategies: A	B	C
1	*h*	*j*	*k*
2	*k*	*m*	*n*
3	*o*	*p*	*k*
4	*k*	*q*	*r*
5	*m*	*k*	*p*

(Cells: Outcomes)

Figure 5-1 OUTCOMES OF REGULATOR-DISTURBANCE INTERACTION

other hand, if the desired outcome is not *k,* but *m* or *p,* the regulator cannot always produce it. The regulator can obtain *p* only if the disturbance plays strategies 3 or 5. The regulator can gain *m,* only if the disturbance offers strategies 2 or 5.

As can easily be seen, the effectiveness of the regulator in producing *k* is dependent on the regulator's ability to control more than one strategy of the disturbance with a single strategy of the regulator. The regulator's strategy A produces *k* when D chooses either strategy 2 or strategy 4. The regulator's strategy C produces *k* when D chooses either strategy 1 or strategy 3. If this were not so, the regulator could control disturbance strategies only by adding new regulator strategies. Therefore, to control five strategies of input or disturbance, one would need at least five strategies of regulation. Successful regulation depends, then, upon a wide variety of regulative strategies. *Only variety in regulative strategies can force down variety in the outcomes, can hold outcomes within stable limits. Only variety can destroy variety.* (This is Ashby's Law of Requisite Variety.)[1]

This insight explains why international regulation is so difficult, and in particular explains why regulation by international organizations has been so relatively unsuccessful. Nation-states have a wide variety of international techniques (strategies) at their disposal. They can use military force, economic pressure, diplomatic persuasion, propaganda, and even subversion. What is more, individual nations can easily decide what to do, and they can continue a course of action on the basis of national decisions for an indefinite period. International organizations have no military forces of their own; they depend upon contributions from their members. They cannot use economic pressure unless that pressure is applied by member states. Their diplomacy depends upon the positions of major states. But most important, since the decisions of international organizations are essentially collective decisions of individual nations, they may change from one time period to the next. Even if a strong regulative stand is taken at one point, it may be modified and later watered down as individual states shift their positions. This is precisely what happened when the League of Nations resolved on economic sanctions against Italy in response to her invasion of Ethiopia in 1935 to 1936. Since Italy was grossly in violation of her covenants under the League, other powers agreed to deprive her of trade and raw materials. Britain and France, however, were unwilling to embargo crucially needed oil because they wanted Italian support against Hitler. Thus the League imposition of sanctions failed. International organizations function best as regulators when there is a strong international consensus supporting their work. When that consensus weakens, they have few instruments to use to ensure regulation.

FORMAL AND INFORMAL REGULATION

There is consequently an important difference between formal and informal regulation. Formal regulation refers to regulation by an international agency or organization. Informal regulation means regulation by nations or blocs. Informal regulation does not depend upon legally defined powers or specific institutional arrangements. An informal regulative mechanism like a balance of power system can function without an explicit definition of its powers or boundaries. In a bipolar context two blocs may check and limit one another without advance agreement concerning the scope and limits of regulative action.

This means that formal and informal regulative procedures have different strengths and weaknesses. An informal regulative system is likely to have a greater variety of strategies at its command than a formal system. Since the range of moves allotted to a formal regulative instrument will have to be legally conferred by nation-states when the institution is devised, they will be likely to be clearly defined and strictly limited. The institution will find it difficult to exceed its granted powers. If it does exceed them, it will be brought up short by one of the great powers. When a crisis impends, the regulative institution may not have a sufficient armory of strategies to counter a disruptive national actor.

It also follows that a formal regulative agency, specifically endowed with powers by nation-states at a given point in time, is unlikely to pose an independent threat to the stability of the system. If anything, its powers are likely to erode with time, as nations are tempted more and more to separate national action and as the originating international consensus dissipates. A formal system, in short, may not regulate adequately, but it does not impede regulation. An informal system, on the other hand, may turn its more varied set of strategies to purposes of disruption as well as regulation. A balance of power system does not merely hold powers in equilibrium. It also reflects the aggrandizing desires of its participants who wish to improve their access to territory, prestige, and influence. At the outset of World War I, the Triple Entente tried to regulate the behavior of the Triple Alliance. It failed and World War I was the result. But alliance combinations do not merely seek to hold each other in check. They do not have the primary objective of maintaining peace, even though that may be an important secondary objective. Their primary goal is to frustrate the desires of an opposing camp and to improve their own position. In the case of World War I the objectives of each group went beyond regulation of the actions of the other side; they included victory over that side. Before World War I, as we have seen, warfare was a perfectly acceptable means of achieving one's goals.

Today the Soviet Union and the United States regulate each other's international conduct, but it is not clear on either side that the objective sought is simply and primarily preservation of the general peace of the world. Achievement of national or bloc objectives comes first; the avoidance of crisis or war second. Since this is true, one can never be sure that in a major world crisis or confrontation the parties will universally agree that avoidance of violent conflict is preferable to attempts to gain a local success. Antagonists may misperceive each other's intentions. Informal regulation, then, offers more strategies than formal regulation, but its goal cannot always be confined to the maintenance of a stable and peaceful international order.

In theory, an ideal solution to this dilemma would be to create a formal regulative mechanism with much greater power, perhaps a world government. It would clearly be in the interest of the world governmental organization to prevent conflict among constituent parts, to rule out war among member states. It would therefore be as concerned to safeguard stability and peace as either the League of Nations or the United Nations, and it would have many more strategies to employ. In practice, however, and under contemporary conditions, it is less clear that world government would be the solution to the problem of international conflict. Indeed, since World War II there have been many more violent civil wars and instances of domestic violence than inter-national conflicts. Some international wars, moreover, such as those in Korea and Vietnam, have grown out of previous civil conflicts. Only if a world government were capable of regulating conflicts within domestic society would it be likely to prevent recourse to large scale violence. If it could not prevent such conflicts or limit the weapons which would be used in fighting them, a world government would merely transfer the locus of violence from a previously international to a national plane. It might not reduce the incidence of violence overall.

ECONOMIC AND POLITICAL REGULATION

In addition to differences between formal and informal regulation, there appear to be contrasts between economic and political regulation. *Political* regulation refers to regulation of vital national and security matters. *Economic* regulation refers to the regulation of external financial policy by international agencies. In the case of political regulation, many nations refuse to allow outside nations or organizations a role in the determination of their vital national interests. Political regulation, therefore, is difficult at best. Economic regulation is perhaps more easily accomplished both because it affects a less vital sphere of interest and because, with the increasing integration of the world economic system, individual nations can wield less influence than they can in political foreign policy and defense.

Owing to developments since World War II, economic sovereignty no longer means what it did thirty or forty years ago.[2] Unlike the situation in the twenties and thirties, states now recognize that they cannot simply violate established rules of economic conduct. Rather, they must persuade other nations and international organizations that an exception to the rules is justified. Today nations do not normally devalue their currencies, for example, without considering the interests of others. If they did so, the affected nations might respond in kind, leaving the initiator even worse off than before. Strictly national approaches to economic security and solvency, therefore, are at a discount. More and more a solution to international financial difficulties is being found either in the provision of new kinds of financial resources or in agreed changes in currency values. As a result multilateral institutions like the International Monetary Fund, the Organization for Economic Cooperation and Development, and the United Nations Conference on Trade and Development are coming to play a greater role. It is far more true today than it was a generation ago that nations are turning to international economic organizations to find a solution to their financial problems. With the creation of Special Drawing Rights (SDRs) under the IMF, the future growth of world reserves will be partly determined by an international organization.

Because of the new saliency and importance of these economic agencies, even the United States has been forced to adjust and modify its economic policies in response to pressures of international organization.[3] As a result the ability of the international system to regulate the economic policies of member states is greater than its ability to govern their political and military policies. The international organizations which exist in this field are stronger than their political and military counterparts. One might even conjecture that if the international system appears to be confronting the breakdown of political units into smaller decision-making entities in the military and diplomatic realms, in economic and functional areas there has been a movement toward integration. Economic agencies like the IMF, OECD, and the

European Economic Community seem likely to gain greater power over their membership while political agencies like NATO, SEATO, and even the UN lose effectiveness. If so, the international ability to cope with a financial miscreant will be greater than the power to handle a political or military disturber. Economic regulation will be more efficacious than political or military regulation.

REGULATION VERSUS RESTRAINT

In the international system there has been a continued interplay of regulation and restraint. In the European *ancien régime* of the eighteenth century, the balance of power system was not the only means of maintaining stable and, to a degree, peaceful outcomes. There was an important measure of national self-restraint in the formulation of policy. Aggressive behavior was limited not only because of the possible formation of an opposing coalition, but because state objectives were modest. Since states themselves did not seek to transform the system or to eliminate a central member, a balance of power system did not have much to regulate.

After the French Revolution had altered national objectives and shown that new tactics of militarism and the *levée en masse* could produce dynamic victories and redraw the map of Europe, however, nations were less willing to restrain themselves. Liberal states could hope to undermine conservative empires. The monarchs of Russia, Austria, and Prussia developed new military machines that were supposed to be capable of administering decisive defeats to liberal nations. Ideological differences also led states to espouse far greater ambitions. At least until World War II, moreover, it seemed that revolutionary and expansionist objectives could in fact be attained. Until the First World War it appeared that the arts of military technology made possible a quick, decisive, and relatively painless victory over an opponent. And even after World War I had underscored the triumph of the defense—the trench fortification, the machine gun, and artillery—some nations continued to believe that major victories could be won through persuasion and propaganda. Hitler could aim at unlimited objectives not only because he had developed a new military strategy of blitzkrieg, but also because he could paralyze the national wills of his opponents by playing upon their fervent desires for peace. As long as his cause could be effectively rationalized and legitimized, others could not take a stand against him. Thus at least until World War II it seemed that nations might be able to pursue imperial ambitions without great disadvantage to themselves.

Since World War II, however, and particularly since the advent of the thermonuclear bomb, major nations have had an interest in diminishing, or at least strictly limiting, the claims they make on the world environment. If the superpowers become involved in an armed conflict, nuclear escalation can easily follow. As a result, for perhaps the first time since the eighteenth century, major powers have tended to follow rather limited objectives, fearing the possibility of a nuclear holocaust. Indeed, in certain respects, the objectives of the superpowers have been less ambitious than those of certain lesser states. There is an important difference between the two eras, however: in the *ancien régime* of two hundred years ago, states and principalities pursued limited aims because their desires were limited. They were not forced to restrain themselves. Today, the major powers apparently do not limit themselves because they would not like to achieve more. They restrict themselves because of the potential consequences of striving to realize unlimited aims. Today powers are coerced into restraint. Today formal regulation in the military realm is quite ineffective. What prevents major war is informal regulation by blocs and a judicious self-restraint on the part of great powers.

REGULATIVE INSTRUMENTS

The Balance of Power System

The balance of power system in the eighteenth century by no means prevented war. What it did was prevent the excesses of war, and make sure that no state emerged from a conflict without salvaging a modicum of prestige, territory, or diplomatic position. Alignments in the old regime were fluid: there were no perverse ideological issues which tended to divide states or to insure particular combinations. At mid-century alliances reversed: what had been a traditional rivalry between France and Austria became the famous Kaunitz coalition in which France, Austria, and Russia opposed a beleaguered Prussia, assisted only by England. Frederick the Great of Prussia managed to fend off attacks in Europe while England assumed the initiative in the New World, permitting a modest triumph in the peace negotiations. In the operations of the balance of power system, states which lost did not lose too much; states which gained were not permitted to gain disproportionately. Even losers were compensated.

As a result, states neither sought large accretions in power, nor were they able to win them. Opposing alignments developed when it appeared that a state might succeed in a limited power grab. Agreement upon an ideology of eighteenth-century conservatism, moreover, meant that the princes of Europe were all seeking to advance the same social objectives. The ruling classes of the period formed a kind of international fraternity. They all got on better with people from their own class in a different country than they did with people from a different class in their own country. There were thus limits on the objectives which princes set; there were methods which they would not employ. Further, on the fringes of Europe and in the American hemisphere, there was ample scope for territorial expansion. It was not necessary to seek large territorial gains in central Europe.

Wars occurred, but they were strictly limited wars. No prince was ready to make major sacrifices politically, socially, and economically in order to dominate other rulers. The balance of power worked because no monarch was ready or eager to challenge it. Compared to more recent international systems, the *ancien régime* was a moderate age in diplomacy.

The Concert of Europe

The formation of the Concert of Europe after the Napoleonic Wars transformed modes of international regulation. The balance of power system operated informally; it did not require periodic meetings of the major states to decide the fate of Europe. Since there was prior ideological agreement upon aristocratic rule and monarchical solidarity, conferences did not have to be called to ensure cooperation. Since national policies were on the whole moderate ones, they did not have to be scrutinized and approved by an international institution. After the Napoleonic Wars, however, restraint on the part of either liberal revolutionaries or conservative aristocrats could no longer be guaranteed. Statesmen could no longer rely on the automatic operations of a balance of power mechanism and presume that all nations would be equally concerned to preserve moderate behavior. A formal conference of great powers would be necessary to make sure that states cleaved to their obligations. Since there were now ideological disagreements, a forum was needed in which argument and conciliation might facilitate consensus. Not only this, but after the rigors of the Napoleonic period, it became imperative to develop a formal resolve against war. In the eighteenth century this had not been necessary, for wars had not been devastating or serious.

For the first half of the nineteenth century, the Concert of Europe operated to reduce conflict. After 1825 it ceased to control national policies, but it did settle disputes and facilitate compromise. It also provided an international imprimatur for important changes in the international scene such as occurred in Belgium and the Near East. In addition it limited the conflict between liberal and conservative states. After mid-century, however, the Concert failed to prevent war, and had to content itself with disposition of the spoils of war. From 1854 to 1871 there were five wars of international significance, but only after the first was the Concert to have much of an influence in creating conditions of peace. By 1871 a habit of separate and unilateral action had developed that the Concert was unable to control.

From 1871 to 1890 the Concert functioned only once as a multilateral instrument when it convened as the Congress of Berlin in 1878. Otherwise the Concert was increasingly replaced by alliances and alignments of European states. Gradually Prince Otto von Bismarck of Germany drew a series of alliance combinations around him that by 1887 linked all great powers save France into a central coalition governed from Berlin. No state was capable of acting against this powerful grouping, and peace was maintained by military might. As long as this combination continued, no countercoalition could be formed. After Bismarck was replaced in 1890, however, the new German rulers dropped the alliance with Russia. This led in 1894 to a Franco-Russian alliance. The Anglo-German links were gradually loosened, and by 1904 an Anglo-French entente was consummated. Russia completed an understanding with England in 1907, and the Triple Entente was formed as a rival to the Triple Alliance. No longer, therefore, could alliance combinations restrain disruptive action. In 1914 the Triple Alliance was not deterred from action by the possible involvement of the Triple Entente. The Triple Entente was not prevented from acting to restrain Germany and Austria for fear of the Triple Alliance. The bipolar alliance framework did not prevent war; it made it more likely.

The League of Nations

As the Concert of Europe had been formed in response to the Napoleonic Wars, the League of Nations was the response to World War I. Two major ideas were embedded in the Covenant. The first was that of a standing international conference of great powers, embodied in the League Council. Since many reasoned that if a conference had been called on the eve of World War I, the conflict might have been avoided, the League Council was to afford such an opportunity in future crises. Secondly, some theorists related war to the absence of open or liberal democratic political structures among nations of the world system. After polities had been democratized at the end of the war, their publics could be relied upon to issue a hue and cry against aggressors. A three-month waiting period before parties to a dispute could resort to force would permit the mobilization of world and national opinion, hopefully bringing an aggressor to heel. The founders of the League placed great stress upon public opinion as a pressure on governments and believed that one of the reasons for conflict at the end of the nineteenth century had been the absence of liberal or democratic political systems in many countries.[4]

The League, like the Concert of Europe before it, had no enforcement power. Once a nation was in violation of its covenants under the League, all members were supposed to subject it to sanctions. But what some members considered to be punishable, others did not. And when sanctions were actually applied, as they were to Italy in 1936, Britain and France, anxious to draw Mussolini to their side against Hitler, watered them down until they had no effect. The League Council also failed. The notion that a standing international conference of great powers would keep the peace by eliminating causes for misunderstanding, was rendered vain and ineffective by the presence of nations like Germany, Japan, and Italy, which sought territorial expansion and were quite ready to use military means to achieve their ends. The League had no power to prevent aggression.

Nor did public sentiment prove itself a reliable force against expansionism. The German and Italian publics were apparently pleased at the gains their leaders laid at their feet. Public opinion in France and Britain was against taking a warlike stance against either Hitler or Mussolini. United States public opinion was certainly not willing to countenance war against Japan despite the Manchurian incident and the Japanese attack on China in 1937. Neither theory proved adequate to keep the peace.

The United Nations

Under the United Nations Charter the UN could take enforcement action against an aggressor if the Permanent Members of the Security Council agreed. Unlike the League Council, the Security Council could decide whether aggression had occurred. It could then decide what action to take, including resort to enforcement measures. Permanent members were supposed to make forces available for implementing UN enforcement actions under the Military Staff Committee.

Of course the members of the Security Council did not usually agree. The cold war between Communist and Western nations frustrated the Council's work. Its record in settling disputes or repelling aggression is not a satisfactory one.

The failure of the Security Council to carry out peace and security functions placed greater emphasis upon the General Assembly and on the office of Secretary General. Neither agency, however, was capable of regulating the international system. The Secretary General could in practice enter a dispute only if invited, and he has been reluctant to diminish his political capital by involving his office too centrally in the more difficult and intransigent conflicts. Nor has the General Assembly been a more effective arbiter of the peace. At one period in the late 1950s it appeared that the Assembly might undertake a mediating or balancing role between the two power blocs. By the early 1960s, however, it became clear that the Assembly would not develop a third pole in world politics. Increasingly the General Assembly has taken the somewhat irresponsible role of gadfly, critic, and obstructionist of policies on which the major powers were agreed. In sum, the institutions of the United Nations do not regulate international conflict. (This does not mean that they do not assist in the settlement of disputes.)[5]

Contemporary International Regulation

The contemporary international system is not regulated by international organizations but by the interaction of powers and blocs. For a considerable period of time after World War II there were two bloc leaders competing for influence in a field of lesser states. A balance of cooperation and competition emerged that inhibited either major state from adopting an extremely aggressive stance. The competition between the United States and Russia enhanced the role of lesser powers. They obtained leverage on the great powers and made economic and political gains as a result. Neither the United States nor the Soviet Union, however, wished to press its competitive designs to the point where lesser states might have become arbiters or balancers between the Big Two. For the period from 1963-1968 the Soviets and Americans recognized some common interests in preventing too great a growth of strength or cohesion on the part of other nations. Russia and America agreed on a treaty to prohibit the proliferation of nuclear weapons to other states. They stopped competitive donations of economic aid. Sensing that they were at the top of the political hierarchy in world politics, both powers saw common interests in resisting overt or implicit challenges to their high estate. Yet there was no tendency to transform the power alliances, with the United States and the Soviet Union joining forces to oppose the rest of the world. Deep-seated rivalries between the two major powers in the Middle East, South Asia, and elsewhere have prevented any such outcome. Among lesser powers, including both Europe and the developing countries, there are so many differences of economic and political form that a consolidation against the two superstates has been impossible.

The emergence of China as a diplomatic and military factor in world politics, however, has changed the previous system of balance and opposition. It appears that China has decided that the Soviets represent a greater long-term threat to their interests than does the United States. Accordingly a modest *détente* is in progress, holding the possibility that the Chinese and Americans will work together for limited purposes in certain areas of the world. South Asia would appear to be a prime candidate though it is possible that cooperation could be extended to Southeast Asia after the Vietnam imbroglio is over.

Even more important than the current Sino-American *détente,* however, is the longer term prospect of tripolarity in the international system. China provides a much more effective regulator of the conduct of either the Soviet Union or the United States than lesser nations have done in the recent past. By inclining this way or that, China can make it difficult for either superpower to carry on very adventurous policies. Just as a Sino-American combination deters Russian action, so a Sino-Russian link would make the United States position very difficult. For the time being at least, the emergence of China probably rules out any lasting accommodation of the United States and the U.S.S.R. over the heads of the field powers.

In the future the tripolar tendency of the moment will give way to a quadripolar or quintipolar arrangement with Japan and Western Europe as new pivots of the system. This may well contribute some features of traditional European power balancing in the 1970s and 1980s. While balancing systems have sometimes avoided war, they have by no means universally done so. In the future, it is not clear that the variety of regulative strategies will be great enough to ensure that disruption will not succeed. In the emerging quintipolar world, great powers have many more resources at their command than do international organizations; but in multipolar balancing systems regulative coalitions are not always formed. Informal regulation has often failed. Other means must clearly be found to limit conflict in the system.

NOTES

1 See W. R. Ashby, *Introduction to Cybernetics* (New York: Wiley, 1956), pp. 206-207.

2 See Raymond Vernon, "Economic Sovereignty at Bay," *Foreign Affairs*, vol. 47, no. 1, pp. 110-122, October 1968.

3 See Ernst B. Haas, *Tangle of Hopes: American Commitments and World Order* (Englewood Cliffs, N.J.: Prentice-Hall, 1969), p. 134.

4 See A. E. Zimmern, *The League of Nations and the Rule of Law, 1918-1935* (New York: Russell and Russell, 1969), pp. 265 ff.

5 See Ernst B. Haas, *Collective Security and the Future International System*, The University of Denver. The Social Science Foundation and Graduate School of International Studies Monograph Series in World Affairs, vol. 5, no. 1 (Denver, Colorado, 1968).

CHAPTER SIX

Environmental Supply

As we have seen, regulation refers to the ways in which the international system controls disruption. If nation-states engage in policies which are likely to produce conflict, regulative mechanisms may seek to counter them. A nation faced with opposition from a coalition or action by an international organization will be tempted to moderate its policies, reducing the disruptive impact. Essentially then, regulation of the international system succeeds when states are prevented from doing some of the things they may otherwise wish to do, when they are forced to trim their objectives and limit their policies. Regulation of the system would not be necessary if there were no conflict of objectives. If states could get what they want without impinging upon the interests or objectives of others, there would be no war, even in the absence of regulation. Thus, if there is an abundant environmental supply of what states need, seek, or demand, conflict can be avoided. In the best of all possible international worlds, the environmental supply of resources would increase proportionally to an increase in national demands upon the system. In such a beneficent situation there would be a constantly expanding pie of environmental resources. If, for example, D (demands) and R (resources) were related to each other in the following numerical way (where k is any constant):

$$D = k \times R$$

then any increase in demand would automatically result in an increase in the supply of environmental resources to meet those demands. Demands would be virtually self-fulfilling. There would also be a kind of international harmony of national interests, for the realization of one nation's objectives would not depend upon frustrating the objectives of others.

On the other hand, if there is a constant pie of environmental supplies of resources, all states may not find their demands gratified. International stability will then depend upon effective regulation: nations will have to limit their objectives if conflict is to be avoided. Suppose the resource pie in world politics looked like Figure 6-1. Any increase in the size of A's slice of the pie

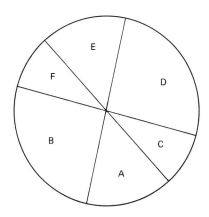

Figure 6-1 HYPOTHETICAL RESOURCE PIE

must come at the expense of the slice of another national actor, B or C. To put the relationship another way, the sum of the national slices equals a constant (k):

$$A + B + C + D + E + F = k$$

Under these circumstances, an improvement in the position of one country can only take place at the expense of one or more others. All nations cannot improve their resource positions simultaneously, because the sum of total resources in the system is a constant. The constant-sum game is also the most general form of the zero-sum game:

$$A + B = O$$

In the zero-sum game, not only is it true that if A goes up, B must go down, it also follows that A and B cannot both have positive or favorable positions. If $A = 3$, $B = -3$, and so on. Thus if a zero-sum game existed among states, even a status quo situation could not be stable, since one party would always have an incentive to improve his position. In the constant-sum game, conflict is inevitable only when one power strives to advance his position. If all remain at their *status quo ante* positions, it is conceivable that all may be satisfied to some degree, for the sum of resources in the system is positive.

ENVIRONMENTAL SUPPLY OF TERRITORIAL RESOURCES

For long periods of history, international stability tended to depend more on the environmental availability of resources than upon the existence of really powerful regulative instruments. In the eighteenth century, for example, a great deal of colonizable territory was available for preemption on the fringes of Europe, in Asia and the New World. One of the reasons for the relative moderation of conflict in the *ancien régime,* then, was not simply the success of the balance of power system in regulation, but rather that states could acquire territory to compensate themselves for gains made by other powers. Colonizable territory was still not used up. Indeed, the very principle of compensation which was claimed to be integral to the operation of the balance of power system depended upon the existence of international resources from which states could compensate themselves.[1] Perhaps the best examples of this principle occurred in the three partitions of Poland (1772, 1793, and 1795) which, except for a brief interlude, eliminated Poland from the map of Europe until after World War I. But it was also reflected in the struggles of the Seven Years' War which, outside of Europe, had to do with territorial divisions in the New World and South Asia.[2] Of course the principle of compensation could never have operated if territory had not been available for appropriation. An international system of this kind may take the form:

$$A + B + C + D + E + F + T \text{ (territory)} = k$$

As long as advances in the position of powers A through F take place only at the expense of T, there is no inevitable conflict among the powers themselves. Only after the supply of unappropriated territory is reduced to zero, do further attempts to expand result in direct conflict between states.

In the nineteenth century a similar mechanism reduced collisions between states during the heyday of European imperialism. Actually, it was not until the 1880s that Europe began a major quest for colonies in the overseas world. In that decade, Africa, the Near East, and Asia were targets for colonization or colonial concessions by France, Britain, and Germany. In the 1890s the situation worsened, and that decade was marked by limited colonial conflicts as European nations began to exhaust available territory in the overseas areas. France and Britain confronted one another in the Sudan and in Indochina. Russia and Britain had conflicts in the Far East as well as in areas surrounding the Black Sea. By the first decade of the twentieth century, the situation had become very serious indeed. Extra-European territory had already been divided up, and any further attempts to expand one's empire could only take place at the expense of some other European power. In the years before World War I the colonizing urge was turned back toward Europe itself, and the conflicts which led to war took place in the most dangerous areas of all, right on the fringes of Europe—in the Balkans and in North Africa. Further attempts to expand in these centrally important areas could only produce enormous hostility, and the attempts to do so had much to do with the origins of World War I. To seek territory when it has already been divided up, is to encroach upon the interest of some other central power.

In the post-World War II world there has also been a question of the availability of territorial resources. The decolonization of much of the world occurred with great rapidity after 1945. The Dutch, the French, the Belgians, and the British either gave their empires independence willingly or were forced to do so. Only the Portuguese still cling to large territories in Africa. Since the successor states have been recognized, joined the United Nations, and become members of the international community, there is no possibility of regarding them as subjects for future colonization by either European or non-European powers. If at one point in time the existence of such territory provided a kind of outlet or safety valve for conflict among the major states, that outlet no longer exists.

One of the problems of the post-World War II era, however, was that, for a time at least, neither the United States nor the Soviet Union was willing to restrict its demands for new ideological and alliance converts. Both wished to extend their big power alliances to the less developed countries of Africa, Asia, and the Middle East. These desires, however, were not fulfilled. The less developed countries refused to be drawn into either alliance system. Many subscribed to policies of formal nonalignment. Since both superpowers tended to regard developments overseas as crucial to the outcome of the cold war, however, this did not deter either the United States or Russia from seeking new adherents and converts in extra-European realms.

But there was a difference between the policies of the two major powers and those of the European imperialists in the nineteenth century. The imperialists of yesteryear wanted new territory, new chunks of real estate. The United States and the Soviet Union wanted ideological converts; they believed for some time that the competition between them would be decided by the expansion of their ideologies to new states. Owing to the resistance of the developing countries, however, the supply of potential converts was never exhausted. This meant that the extra-European realms continued to offer a safety valve for central conflicts, leading the major powers to seek a resolution of their rivalry in a struggle for new adherents overseas. Since the supply of potential allies remained about the same, however, the pursuit of "ideological territory" did not result in the conflict which emerged at the end of the nineteenth century. As long as the two superpowers believed that their competition would be resolved by the commitment of new states to one side or the other, and as long as that commitment did not take place, an overarching stability could be maintained.

By 1962 to 1963, however, both the Soviets and the Americans had begun to realize that the neutralist states could not be won over. More importantly, they began to think of the uncommitted nations as secondary factors in world politics. In the variety of world crises from 1958 to 1962, the nonaligned states had played practically no role. The United States and the U.S.S.R. began to neglect them. There were therefore fewer attempts to try to convert the rest of the world. There was less stress on dividing up the remaining T. While this was desirable in terms of the supply of environmental resources, it also meant that there was no longer a territorial safety valve for central world conflicts. From 1963 to 1967 the United States and the U.S.S.R. looked on themselves as the fundamental determinants of the system. All other powers were of secondary importance.

By 1971, however, the situation had changed once again. China and Japan had emerged as independent factors in world politics. Western Europe was taking a more self-reliant course. No longer were the two superpowers the sole determinants of international relations. At the same time, there was a rekindling of interest in extra-European developing nations. The preoccupation of both great powers with events in the Middle East raises questions about prior orientations. The Soviets, at least, seem convinced that the tradition of nonalignment in the Middle East and South Asia will not prevent considerable gains, politically and strategically. With the revival of interest in the policy of the uncommitted countries, it is possible that new inroads upon T will ultimately be made.

ENVIRONMENTAL SUPPLY OF IDEOLOGICAL RESOURCES

Territory is not the only desired good that states seek. In the past 150 years states have also sought ideological objectives. Ideologies do not necessarily conflict. One state may wish to set up democratic governments all over the world. Another may want to make sure that the citizens of all states have basic economic security. Since democratic regimes are concerned about the welfare of their citizens, there is likely to be a high degree of overlap between such ideological views as shown in Figure 6-2. State B (which prefers security to democracy) may be willing to accept an undemocratic regime which provides for the basic economic needs of its people. It would approve of the internal regimes of many of the Communist countries. State A (which prefers democracy to security) would not approve of Communist polities, but would accept Irish or even Indian democratic systems, even though basic economic welfare has not been attained for all citizens in those two countries. A and B would agree in approving most of the developed countries: Western Europe and Japan, Australia and New Zealand where both democracy and economic security have been achieved.

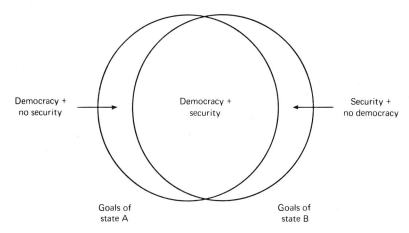

Figure 6-2 THE INTERRELATION OF THE IDEOLOGICAL GOALS OF TWO
STATES

Ideological goals, however, may sometimes clash. If state A wants a
Communist form of internal polity and state B wants a liberal democratic
form of domestic society, there may be no overlap of ideological goals shown
by Figure 6-3. Under these circumstances the attainment of the goals of state
A will completely frustrate the ambitions of state B, and vice versa. In these
conditions only if A and/or B are willing to postpone the attainment of their
goals will compromise be possible. When ideologies are not overlapping, there
is no way in which there can be a sufficient environmental supply of

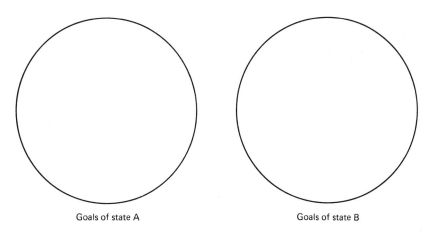

Figure 6-3 DISPARATE IDEOLOGICAL GOALS OF TWO STATES

resources. If one state gains its goal of converting other states to its exclusivist ideology, then its ideological opponent has failed. If one wins, the other loses.

In the eighteenth century ideology was not a divisive factor. States subscribed at least informally to a common ideology of conservatism which supported the social and political institutions of the old regime. Thus if one state succeeded in reinforcing conservatism in one particular political area, this was not a defeat for others. It was rather a victory since states were agreed on ideological objectives.

When the French Revolution occurred, however, this could no longer be true. Thereafter France and its ideological allies were bent on extending the revolutionary principles of liberalism to the social and political structures of other states: they wished to extend the revolution. There was no degree of overlap between revolutionary and conservative ideologies. The various coalitions opposing France wanted to prevent revolutionary infection and to reinstate a conservative regime in France, which they finally succeeded in doing in 1815. After a brief period of legitimate conservative regimes which followed the Napoleonic Wars, however, the ideological issue reemerged. By 1830 France had reaffirmed its liberal principles and England was fast acquiring them. At least until 1870 there was an implicit conflict between states on ideological grounds. France and England were seeking to advance liberal principles; Russia, Prussia, and Austria were trying to maintain aristocratic rule.

Ideological conflicts broke out again after World War I, and they were especially acute after the Second World War. One of the reasons why the cold war could not be contained by the international system was that there was no way in which the ideological goals of both camps could be realized. If the Communists achieved their objectives, the goals of the Western countries would be frustrated and vice versa. Unless the behavior of states could be regulated, the system would not be able to contain them.

While ideological differences prevent the environment from helping states to realize their objectives without conflict, it does not follow that ideological antagonisms must necessarily go on forever. The differences between liberalism and conservatism waned after 1870; the divergences between Communist and Western views of the world have been reduced since 1945. After 1870 both conservatives and liberals had reinforced their own social positions. The liberals were not likely to win an overwhelming triumph through revolution, and the conservatives were not likely to recoup their position through counterrevolution. Both groups were now more satisfied with the gains they had won; both recognized the difficulty, even the impossibility of eliminating the other camp. Thus compromise was possible. It is interesting to note that ideology had little if anything to do with the issues which led to World War I.

Somewhat the same process may have been repeated after 1945. The need to compete ideologically was most imperative when neither camp was secure in its position. Soviet apprehension of the United States and United States concern about Russia were greatest at the end of the war. As both parties have established firm spheres of interest and involvement and have reinforced those positions, the waging of ideological war has seemed less necessary, and if waged, less successful. Realistically, neither camp can expect complete victory over its opponent. In addition, there is a question if new adherents actually add to the strength of core powers. Newly communized states may demand large resources from the Soviet Union, but they may nonetheless follow independent policies. Cuba, China, Albania, and Yugoslavia received large amounts of aid from the Soviet Union, but nonetheless pursued policies which the Russians could not always approve. Western allies have demanded more in support from the United States than they have returned or are likely to return in cohesion or solidarity. The superpowers today may well question whether an increase in allies is wholly desirable. Thus the impetus toward ideological conversion of other nations is much less than it once was.

At the present time ideological differences are much less likely to lead to war between major powers than they are to cause conflict among lesser states. As states emerge from colonial status and seek to develop a new basis of legitimacy internally, they may be tempted to try to solidify their hold on domestic sentiment through gains in foreign affairs. Repute, prestige, and influence at the international level may help to stabilize a regime at home. Ideological appeals may more likely be proclaimed in new states that have recently emerged from conflict with a European ruler. To gain the strength to win independence, they have had to emphasize nationalist and ideological solidarity. Once the imperialist has departed, however, there is no enemy to rally the people against and less reason for domestic cohesion. An ideological policy in foreign affairs, therefore, may help reinforce domestic solidarity, but it can also create competing ideological demands and make it difficult for the system to satisfy all national actors. President Sukarno's Indonesia and Dr. Kwame Nkrumah's Ghana adopted policies of ideological expansionism that brought them into conflict with other states. In the former case Indonesia's "confrontation" of Malaysia led to an attempt to undermine the Malaysian province of Sarawak and to a guerrilla war with Britain along the Indonesian frontier. These policies were not terminated until Sukarno and Nkrumah fell from power.

ENVIRONMENTAL SUPPLY OF ECONOMIC GOODS

If the environmental supply of resources is always deficient when there is an ideological conflict, the pursuit of economic and financial gain does not lead to similar antagonism. From a long run perspective, a rising level of international trade depends upon domestic economic stability and progress in major trading nations. If a large importing nation suffers a reverse and must cut down on its imports, other nations will be affected. They will then sell less abroad and may similarly have to restrict their imports. The net result may be an international economic system in which trade has been reduced, thereby impoverishing the consumers of many countries. Conversely, one can imagine a situation in which domestic economic stability, leading to an increase in the exports of a nation, would also lead to an increase in imports. As a result of the favorable balance of trade, greater incomes from the export industry would ultimately mean more expenditure on consumption of imports as well as domestic products. The export industries of other countries would also benefit.

The process of economic growth, moreover, requires a setting in which governments are not pursuing deflationary goals. Economic growth and a modest level of inflation for one country, will be beneficial for the international trading prospects of others, creating a demand for the exports of other countries. If one country follows an inflationary policy and another a deflationary policy, however, the inflating country will suffer in international trade. This country should seek to persuade his deflationary colleague to pursue a policy of domestic expansion and progress. Oddly enough then, nations tend, with some inequities, to go up and down the international economic scale together. Pursuit by some of economic growth allows others to seek similar objectives. If, instead, deflation and economic contraction are a government's objectives, these will affect international trade and perhaps

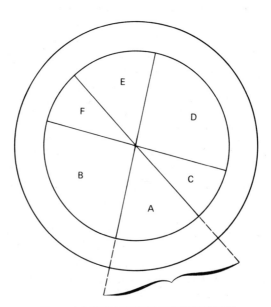

Figure 6-4 EXPANDING RESOURCE PIE

force other nations to pursue contractionist policies. In this sense, the economic realm is perhaps the only arena in which one can conceive of achieving the objectives of states through a constantly expanding pie of international resources. If we have the situation shown in Figure 6-4 then it is not necessary for nation A to expand its share of the international resource pie by encroaching on the slices of B or C. As a result of a larger and more abundant international economy and a higher level of international trade, nation A benefits from the increase in the size of the pie. He is led to encroach upon B or C only if he is not satisfied with a higher absolute share, but wants as well a higher relative portion of the pie. It is therefore easier to provide gratification of the goals which states seek in the economic realm than it is in the territorial or ideological realms. This means that the game of international trade is at least in part a variable-sum game. Instead of

$$A + B + C + D + E + F = k \text{ (a constant)}$$

we have

$$A + B + C + D + E + F = x \text{ (a variable)}$$

With increases in the sum of resources in the system, each state can be better off.

ENVIRONMENTAL SUPPLY OF SECURITY

The problem of security is unlike that of territory or economic welfare. Under some technological and political conditions states can achieve a minimum of security without infringing on the security of others. When the technological environment changes, however, it may no longer be possible for all states to be secure. Security for one may mean insecurity for another.

The original notion of a great power was that of a state so strong that even the rest of the members of the system could not defeat it. In the eighteenth century there were certainly great powers in this sense. During the Seven Years' War, Prussia, the weakest of the great powers, was attacked by France, Austria, and Russia; she received only limited financial help from England. Yet Prussia under Frederick the Great was not defeated. Nor were her adversaries. Provinces changed hands. Colonial real estate was exchanged. But there was no threat to the basic security or survival of any state.

With the Napoleonic Wars, however, security and survival itself were questioned. Prussia's defeat in 1805 was so decisive that it was not certain she would recover. Napoleon's armies occupied the capitals of other powers; the French revolutionized other nations' social systems, installing liberal reforms. The armies of France, utilizing the *levée en masse* (which was an approximation to mass mobilization), were citizen armies. They were willing to sacrifice more and to endure more hardships because, unlike the mercenaries of the eighteenth century, they were fighting for their *patrie,* their fatherland.

Thus the military potency of the revolutionary armies was far greater than that of traditional armies. Modes of politics and warfare made possible occupation and overthrow of other political systems. The problems of security and survival took on a new urgency.

In the third quarter of the nineteenth century the problem was compounded. The Austro-Prussian and Franco-Prussian Wars of 1866 and 1870 showed that decisive battles might be fought only weeks after the beginning of war. Technology had given primacy to the offensive—a state which could concentrate its troops through use of the railway network, which could move them rapidly from place to place, which could back them with modern artillery, which could throw masses of conscripts into the battle—this state would be likely to win. The new technology and the new militarism meant that nations could no longer rely on a stubborn and resolute defense. Security depended on how the war began and on who took the offensive. States therefore had to be ready to make war at all times. If a nation was unable to take the offensive, it might lose. This situation also meant that a state must be ready to mobilize on very short notice, and since the first to mobilize would be the first to take the offensive, mobilization meant war. When one power mobilized, his opponent could not afford to wait to see whether he would really make war: he had to make preparations on his own. Thus when the Russians ordered general mobilization on July 30, 1914, the die was already cast for World War I.

Because it was thought that wars would be decided quickly, nineteenth-century nations could not wait for the ponderous operations of an international conference mechanism to find supporters. They had to have allies pledged in advance with whom advance military planning could be concerted. One had to know how many troops an ally could engage, on what time schedule and against whom. Since military planning and preparation took time, alliances had to last for three to five years. Once negotiated, they would normally be renewed. If a power left an alliance, he might open himself up to diplomatic isolation or perhaps to attack by other states. In the late nineteenth century there were no reversals of alliance of the sort which occurred in the eighteenth century.

The difficulty in gaining security underscored the point that all powers could not be simultaneously secure. If one power or group of powers was secure, it was because they had reliable plans to assume the offensive. If other powers could not take the offensive and maintain it, they would be defeated. The problem was that the achievement of security depended upon successful preemption of another power's initiative. Inevitably there was a reciprocal fear of surprise attack. As war impended, each nation feared that the other would get in the first blow. When a crisis occurred, neither side could afford to delay action. Security—real security against attack—could not be obtained by all powers at the same time.

In 1972 it appears that security is much less dependent upon an ability to strike first. Under contemporary and emergent technological conditions, both superpowers have and will continue to have ample capacity to destroy an opponent in retaliation. Since this is true, major states can at least assume a defensive stance. To this degree the environmental supply of security is greater today than it was at the end of the nineteenth century. Fledgling nuclear states, however, may develop nuclear capacities which are vulnerable to attack. As nuclear weapons and capacities continue to spread, this will present a major threat to the stability of the international system.

ENVIRONMENTAL SUPPLY:
THE INTERACTION OF INTERESTS

In the previous sections of this chapter we have discussed a variety of situations in which the resources of the system (environmental supply) were either sufficient or insufficient to permit states to obtain their objectives without conflict. But clearly the supply of resources which states seek varies from case to case. One cannot say that international politics can be described wholly in terms of the constant-sum game. Nor can international relations be regarded purely as a variable-sum game. When nations bargain and negotiate, they find they have some interests in common and some which are opposed; in some cases resources are abundant enough for both to satisfy themselves; in some, if one gains, the other loses. The United States and the Soviet Union have a strong common interest in the avoidance of thermonuclear war, but this does not mean that they follow identical policies in the Middle East. They agree that nuclear weapons should not spread (though in fact they are spreading), but do not see eye to eye on Vietnam. In some cases they can improve their positions by joint action; in others, if one benefits, the other suffers.

If we assume that states A and B each wish to maximize individual payoffs, the payoff structure in world politics today is akin to the area of a circle.[3] In the diagram shown in Figure 6-5, A's payoffs are measured on the y axis and B's payoffs on the x axis. It follows that points north and east of the origin will benefit both parties. Instead of starting at the origin, however, let us begin at the center (K) of a payoff circle. All points on or within the payoff circle are physically attainable and A and B must decide which point they wish to attain. Note that point K is positive: that is both A and B receive substantial payoffs at point K. If A and B are already at point K, however, they will not want to retreat toward the origin, because any such movement would cause a decline in payoffs for both parties. Thus, neither A nor B will want to move to points within the quadrant *DKE* (certainly not to point *F*) because both would suffer. (As one moves southward from K to E, A suffers;

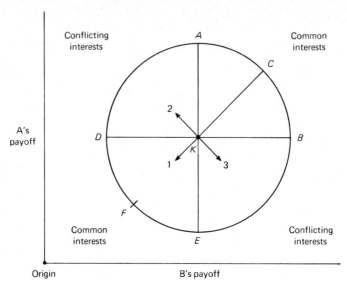

Figure 6-5 A AND B'S RELATIONSHIP OF INTEREST: CASE 1

as one moves westward from *K* to *D*, B suffers. At *F* and at any point between *D* and *E*, both suffer.) Thus there are common interests between A and B in avoiding any movement in this quadrant down toward the origin. Any movement in the direction of arrow 1 would hurt both. If we look at the other quadrants, however, the situation changes. In the quadrant *DKA*, A can benefit at B's expense. B suffers most acutely as A moves from *K* to *D*. A gains greatly while B gains nothing as A moves from *K* to *A*. Any movement in the direction of arrow 2 helps A and harms B. The opposite situation is revealed in quadrant *EKB*. Here B benefits at A's expense. Any movement in the direction of arrow 3 helps B and hurts A. Both A and B can agree, however, on a solution within the quadrant *AKB*, for in this region both improve their payoff positions. Point *C* in quadrant *AKB* would be the optimal position of greatest *mutual* benefit. The movement from point *K* to point *C* would be one of complete agreement between A and B for at each step along the line *KC* both increase their payoffs. Once *C* has been reached, however, any further movement within the quadrant will not gain agreement. A may wish to move from point *C* to point *A* (his maximum payoff in the payoff circle), but this could happen only at B's expense. B will want to move from point *C* to point *B* (his maximum payoff in the payoff circle), but this could occur only at the expense of A. A real conflict of interest, therefore, occurs beyond *C*.

This graphic illustration mirrors situations in the real world. When two nations start negotiating, they usually can find some points of mutual interest (equivalent to moving from point *K* to point *C*). But as each party seeks to improve its own position beyond a certain point of mutual benefit, the other will be likely to suffer (movements either from *C* to *B* or *C* to *A*.) During World War II America and Russia reached important agreements on military cooperation and achieved some coordination of military plans against Germany. But when they sought to move beyond purely military realms to the political future of Europe, they could not agree. (They could move from *K* to *C*, but disagreed on moves from that point on.) In some cases, of course, the room for improvement in the payoffs of two countries may be small. In case 2 (Figure 6-6) there is little that A and B can do to improve their joint positions. In case 3 (Figure 6-7) there is nothing they can do. They begin at a situation of complete conflict of interest.

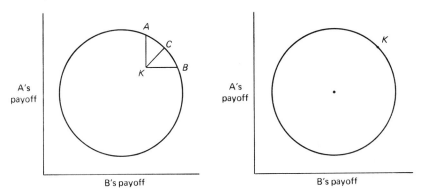

Figure 6-6 A AND B'S RELATIONSHIP OF INTEREST: CASE 2

Figure 6-7 A AND B'S RELATIONSHIP OF INTEREST: CASE 3

These graphic cases have to do with situations in which two powers can improve their positions simultaneously up to some point; beyond that, conflict emerges. It follows that they will cooperate initially; only later will one seek to disadvantage the other. In some circumstances, however, even though each will gain from cooperation, a power may gain more from not cooperating, if the other cooperates. Most teenagers are familiar with the game of "chicken." "Chicken" is normally played by two drivers who approach each other head-on along the center line of a highway. The first driver to veer to the side is "chicken," and the other "wins" the "game." It is perfectly clear that it is much better for both players to veer to the side, than for both to continue along the center line. Cooperation provides a much greater mutual benefit than a failure to cooperate (to say the least!). Yet if one veers to the side and the other continues straight ahead, the latter claims an even greater payoff. The payoff structure of such a game might be as shown in Figure 6-8. Clearly the best outcome for A is attained at $A_2 B_1$; and

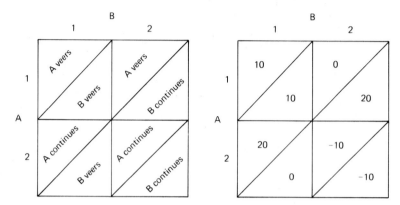

Figure 6-8 PAYOFF STRUCTURE FOR THE GAME OF "CHICKEN"

the best for B at $A_1 B_2$. But $A_1 B_1$ is far better for both than $A_2 B_2$. If both cooperate they achieve $A_2 B_2$. But if one cooperates and the other does not, they produce either $A_1 B_2$ or $A_2 B_1$. The practical rule in "chicken" is that if you are convinced that the other driver will not veer, you must do so. Thus teenagers have been known to sit in the back seat, tie the wheel, or even throw the wheel out of the car to convince their opponent that they will not deviate from the center line. To have any effect, of course, these measures must be observed by the antagonists. If he could drive, a blind and deaf opponent would be expected to "win" every time at "chicken." There are some international relations scholars who do not believe that "chicken" is ever exemplified in actual international situations. Nonetheless there are occasions when it appears that one power has set itself on a collision course with another unless the other "veers." President John Kennedy in the Cuban crisis was playing a form of this game, because he was clearly ready to use military force against the Cuban missile installations and the supporting Russian forces, if the missiles had not been withdrawn. Premier Khrushchev, recognizing this, did indeed "veer" and remove the missiles. Secretary of State Dean Rusk said: "We were eyeball to eyeball, and the other fellow blinked."

Much more common than the game of "chicken" in international politics, however, is a situation called the "Prisoner's Dilemma." Professor Tucker of

Princeton University named this game after a hypothetical case in which two prisoners were told individually that they could reduce their sentences if they informed on each other. On the other hand, if neither confessed, their sentences would not be reduced. If both confessed, they would both suffer long imprisonments. The utility matrix they confronted (Figure 6-9) was not unlike situations in international relations. It would appear that the best

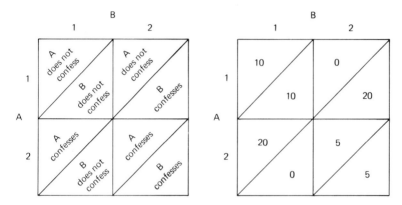

Figure 6-9 PAYOFF STRUCTURE FOR PRISONER'S DILEMMA

course of action for both is $A_1 B_1$, the cooperative solution in which neither informs on the other. On the other hand, A reasons: "If B cooperates (refuses to confess) and I confess, I will get an outcome of twenty which is better than the cooperative solution of ten." B reasons the same way and also chooses to confess. The final result is then $A_2 B_2$, a worse solution for both. It is easy to verify that no other solution is possible for rational players. $A_1 B_2$ is not a viable solution, for A will not consent to a zero payoff when he can improve his situation by playing A_2. For symmetrical reasons, B will not accept $A_2 B_1$. Yet the two cannot come to agreement on $A_1 B_1$, for as soon as it appears that cooperation is the better alternative, one player can improve on that solution by not cooperating. The structure of this game is more realistic than that of "chicken" for the penalties on noncooperation are not nearly as severe. Thus parties in such a game will strive less hard to avoid a noncooperative solution.

While game theory matrices never strictly apply to international situations, two nations often find themselves with similar incentives. They may have much to gain from cooperation, but it does not follow that both will play a cooperative strategy. In an arms race, for example, if both could reduce their military budgets, they would be equally secure with less expenditure. One power, however, fully recognizing the cooperative incentives, may still conclude that if his opponent halts arms preparations while he prolongs his own, he may be even better off. Both may therefore continue rearming at the old rate, and the cooperative payoffs are lost. The dilemma for international relations is precisely this: whatever the mutual benefits of cooperation, one power can often improve on the cooperative payoff by not cooperating. This is exactly what Hitler did in his bargaining with England and France over Czechoslovakia in 1938.

When Prisoner's Dilemma incentives exist, the only way to ensure the cooperative payoff is to provide physically or legally binding arrangements to prevent the choice of unilateral noncooperation. In the example shown in Figure 6-9 the reward for noncooperation is ten units $(20 - 10 = 10)$. If a penalty could be affixed to any noncooperative action of more than ten units, A_1 and B_1 would be preferred to A_2 or B_2. If, for instance, the payoffs were as shown in Figure 6-10. Then neither player would opt for his second

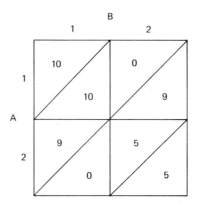

Figure 6-10 PAYOFF STRUCTURE OF THE PRISONER'S DILEMMA MODIFIED BY
BINDING AGREEMENTS

strategy. (If B played strategy 2, he would either get nine or five; if A played strategy 2, he would either get nine or five. But by playing strategy 1, both players can assure payoffs of ten.) These outcomes, however, depend upon legal or enforceable agreements between the two parties. In their absence (and they are often absent in international relations), Prisoner's Dilemma results may obtain.

What the Prisoner's Dilemma fundamentally shows is that the environmental supply of resources cannot produce harmony on its own. There will always be incentives to noncooperation and conflict, no matter what the abundance of international resources. Regulation by external powers or organizations is necessary to keep states on the straight and narrow path of cooperation.

CONCLUSION

In this chapter we have looked at a number of different relationships of state interests. Relationships may be of zero- or constant-sum in which case an improvement in the position of one party will take place only at the expense of at least one other state. If the resources of the system are not fixed, or if they are not already divided up, however, two parties may both increase their share of resources. If states seek additional territory and there is abundant territory to go around, expansion does not necessarily breed conflict. If the resource demanded is ideological gratification, whether conflict ensues or not is a function of the degree of conflict between ideologies. Some ideologies are complementary, or at least overlapping. Non-overlapping ideologies, however, raise problems. The pursuit of such ideologies is likely to produce conflict for the two states who cannot both get their way simultaneously. If one wins, the other loses. If security is the resource aimed at, conditions of military technology help to determine whether security can be achieved by all. If states can only be secure if they are able to get in a first strike on their opponent when war impends, then all cannot be secure simultaneously. Security for one is insecurity for others. Economics is the most benign constituent in the environmental supply of resources. States can improve their economic positions simultaneously, if they are in a position to benefit from increasing international trade. An expanding pie of economic resources can make a large number of states better off, and therefore render it unnecessary for them to try to encroach upon each other's share.

It should be noted, however, that an increasing abundance of the resources which states demand (an increasing environmental supply) only satisfies nations without engendering conflict if their desires are *absolute* and not *relative*. If each nation wants a particular stock of security, for example, and overall security can be enlarged, all can be satisfied. But if each nation wants more security than others, then conflict is inevitable. One of the reasons why war has not been constant is because many nations have used absolute criteria in seeking the resources of the international system.

Even where environmental supply offers an abundance of international resources, however, conflict is not always avoided. In games of "chicken" and the "Prisoner's Dilemma" the incentive structure is such that greater payoffs emerge from noncooperation when the opponent is cooperating. These games do not assume that players are seeking benefits on a relative basis; rather each seeks merely his own highest absolute payoff regardless of the payoff the other receives. But both games do assume that one player's payoff is a function of the strategy adopted by the other player. In international relations it is often true that if two states cooperate they can improve their mutual payoffs. But if one cooperates and the other does not, the second may even secure a greater benefit. As long as noncooperators are not uniformly sanctioned in the amount of the extra benefit, such strategies will be chosen. This places great emphasis upon the regulative capacity of the system, for regulation holds out the hope of penalizing such behavior.

NOTES

1 See Edward Vose Gulick, *Europe's Classical Balance of Power System* (Ithaca, N.Y.: Cornell University Press, 1955).
2 See Walter Dorn, *Competition for Empire: 1740-1763* (New York: Harper, 1940).
3 I am indebted to John Harsanyi for much of the analysis which follows. See his "Game Theory and the Analysis of International Politics" in J. Rosenau (ed.), *International Politics and Foreign Policy,* 2d ed. (New York: Free Press, 1969).

CHAPTER SEVEN

System Structure

If the international system is to prevent military conflict among states, it must do so either by preventing nations from engaging in highly disruptive activity or by providing resources so that states can get what they want without engaging in violent conflict. If the first tactic works, the system is effectively regulated. If the second tactic works, there is an adequate environmental supply of desired resources. Whether either tactic can be employed, however, is dependent on two other factors: *system structure* and *system interaction*. One kind of system structure will call for a different mode of regulation from another. One type of system interaction will affect environmental supply differently from another. Until we have looked at the form and interaction of the system, then, we will not know how and in what degree remedies for international conflict actually can be applied. The present chapter deals with the structure or form of the system. The next one concerns the ways in which the system interacts.

The structure of the system is determined by four further factors: (1) the degree of stratification in the system; (2) the degree of polarity in the system; (3) the distribution of power in the system; and (4) the degree of homogeneity in the system.

SYSTEM STRATIFICATION

Stratification refers to the differential influence and access to resources which members of the system possess. At least four different situations can be conceived, shown by Figures 7-1 through 7-4. Figure 7-1 depicts a situation in which influence and access to resources are very unevenly distributed. The nations at the top of the influence pyramid have access to or possession of more than three-quarters of the resources in the system. In Figure 7-2 the influence pyramid still gives major status to a small number of nations. Their access to resources, however, is not as greatly disproportionate to that of

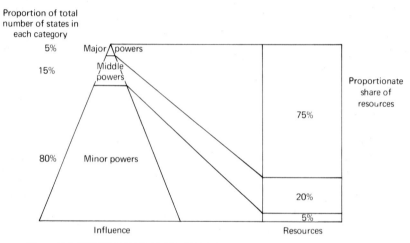

Figure 7-1 UNEVEN DISTRIBUTION OF INFLUENCE AND RESOURCES

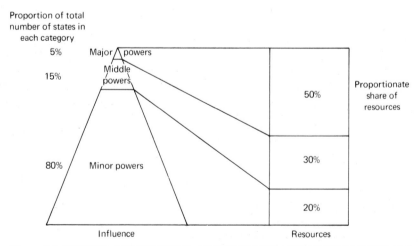

Figure 7-2 UNEVEN DISTRIBUTION OF INFLUENCE, RELATIVELY EVEN DIS-
TRIBUTION OF RESOURCES

states at middle and lower echelons as the access of major states in Figure 7-1. They control about half of the resources of the system, but do not enjoy the overwhelming leverage that is possessed by the major powers in the first diagram. In Figure 7-3 the influence pyramid becomes a trapezoid: status and influence are much more evenly distributed in the system.[1] However, the nations at the top of the trapezoid have privileged and discriminatory access to resources. The most equalitarian mode is that presented in Figure 7-4. Here

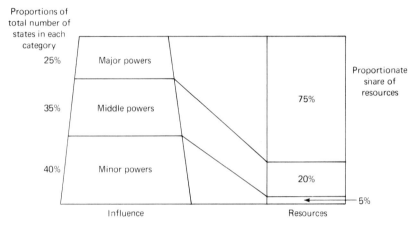

Figure 7-3 RELATIVELY EVEN DISTRIBUTION OF INFLUENCE, UNEVEN DISTRIBUTION OF RESOURCES

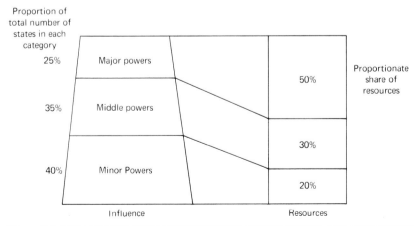

Figure 7-4 RELATIVELY EVEN DISTRIBUTION OF INFLUENCE AND RESOURCES

nations at the top are a much larger group and, in addition, their access to resources is much less preemptive.

At least two different considerations affect the success of regulation in such variant system structures. The first concerns the dissatisfactions that states may have owing to deficiencies in influence or control over resources. The greatest amount of resentment among middle and minor powers will occur in the situation pictured in Figure 7-1. Not only do they have limited access to resources, but their status gratifications are small. The major powers, on the other hand, have the best of all possible worlds. There are few such powers: they are on top, and have access to the great preponderance of resources in the system. Thus a situation of the sort described in Figure 7-1 would be likely to cause movements of reform to restructure the international system. The status and resource distributions outlined in Figure 7-1 are quite like those of the present international world.

Table 7-1 shows that less than 20 percent of the nations of the world have per capita Gross National Products in excess of $1,000 a year; more than eighty percent have per capita GNPs below that figure of which 70 percent are below $500. The powers with greatest influence in the system also possess disproportionate access to resources. The incentives to disruption in such a system structure are certainly high.

TABLE 7-1 **Gross national product per capita for 140 countries, 1963-1968**
(in United States dollars)

Afghanistan	80	Cameroon	168
Algeria	248	Canada	2997
Angola	71	Central African Republic	115
Argentina	739	Ceylon	151
Australia	2476	Chad	64
Austria	1544	Chile	569
Barbados	478	China (Taiwan)	312
Belgium	2154	Colombia	359
Bhutan	62	Comoro Islands	92
Bolivia	173	Congo, Dem. Republic of	79
Botswana	96	Congo, People's Republic of	188
Brazil	329	Costa Rica	456
British Honduras	335	Cyprus	704
Brunei	1075	Dahomey	80
Burma	78	Denmark	2545
Burundi	46	Dominican Republic	290
Cambodia	147	Ecuador	229

Source: Statistics are from *Yearbook of National Accounts Statistics 1969*, vol. II, *International Tables* (New York: United Nations, 1970), pp. 15-21.

TABLE 7-1 Gross national product per capita for 140 countries, 1963-1968
(in United States dollars) *(Continued)*

El Salvador	277	Malaysia, West	316
Ethiopia	63	Mali	83
Fiji Islands	334	Malta	575
Finland	1708	Mauritania	121
France	2537	Mauritius	220
Gabon	565	Mexico	566
Gambia	94	Morocco	208
Germany, Fed. Rep. of	2206	Mozambique	71
Ghana	238	Muscat and Oman	62
Greece	858	Nepal	75
Guatemala	315	Netherlands	1980
Guinea	99	Netherlands Antilles	1180
Guyana	298	New Zealand	1767
Haiti	91	Nicaragua	373
Honduras	256	Niger	88
Hong Kong	442	Nigeria	76
Iceland	2720	Norway	2362
India	80	Pakistan	140
Indonesia	96	Panama	609
Iran	295	Paraguay	229
Iraq	257	Peru	291
Ireland	1046	Philippines	301
Israel	1460	Portugal	529
Italy	1418	Portuguese Guinea	71
Ivory Coast	304	Portuguese Timor	95
Jamaica	496	Puerto Rico	1503
Japan	1404	Reunion	585
Jordan	263	Rwanda	39
Kenya	126	Ryukyu Islands	305
Korea, Republic of	194	Sabah	331
Kuwait	3738	Sarawak	286
Laos	67	Saudi Arabia	351
Lebanon	491	Senegal	225
Lesotho	88	Sierra Leone	153
Liberia	225	Singapore	723
Libya	1412	Somalia	69
Luxembourg	2277	South Africa	654
Madagascar	116	Southern Rhodesia	197
Malawi	58	Southern Yemen	167
Malaysia	314	Spain	773
Malaysia, East	304	Sudan	109

TABLE 7-1 Gross national product per capita for 140 countries, 1963-1968
(in United States dollars) *(Continued)*

Surinam	435	Uganda	96
Swaziland	167	United Arab Republic	186
Sweden	3315	United Kingdom	1861
Switzerland	2754	United States	4379
Syria	188	Upper Volta	49
Tanganyika	74	Uruguay	650
Tanzania, United Rep. of	69	Venezuela	944
Thailand	166	Vietnam, Rep. of	201
Togo	124	West Irian	56
Trinidad and Tobago	733	Yemen	48
Tunisia	225	Zambia	316
Turkey	380	Zanzibar and Pemba	111

Disparity of GNP per capita for 140 countries, 1963-1968

GNP per capita	No. of countries	%
$2,000 +	13	9.28
$1,000-2,000	13	9.28
$ 500-1,000	16	11.43
$ 0- 500	98	70.00
	140	99.99

The second consideration concerns the ability to regulate disruptive behavior by major, middle, or minor powers. It would be very difficult to regulate the behavior of major nations in Figure 7-1 for not only are they at the top of the status pyramid, they also have dominating access to resources. Even all the rest of the nations of the system would not be able to bring them to heel, or to prevent aggressive or disruptive behavior on their part. If disruption were initiated by middle or minor powers, however, the major nations would be in a good position to cope with it. It would be difficult for minor nations, for example, to mobilize enough resources to really transform the system. Thus, since the present system is not unlike that portrayed in Figure 7-1, it probably gives rise to considerable dissatisfaction; the major powers, however, have resources at their command to control the expression of that dissatisfaction by lesser states.

The other figures provide a much more equal distribution of the rewards of the system. In Figure 7-2 the middle and lower group of states have greater access to resources; in Figure 7-3 the middle and minor powers wield greater influence relative to the major states than they have done before; and in

Figure 7-4 the two lower groups have relatively more individual influence and greater access to resources. In Figure 7-4 middle and minor powers would appear to be least likely to mount a challenge against the structure of the system. Moreover, if major powers were to attempt to disrupt stability, the regulative forces that could be mobilized against them by middle and minor states would be much more varied and powerful than those that could be employed in Figure 7-1. On the other hand, if the middle and minor powers were to seek to change the established hierarchy, it would be much more difficult for the major nations to cope with their challenge.

Figures 7-1 and 7-4 are similar in that the states which would have the power to challenge the system are relatively satisfied; the states which are relatively dissatisfied with the system do not have the power to overthrow it. The major powers are relatively most satisfied in Figure 7-1; the middle and minor powers are relatively most satisfied in Figure 7-4.

In Figures 7-2 and 7-3 influence and access rewards are disproportionate. In Figure 7-2 middle and minor powers might be expected to seek a status position in the system more commensurate with their access to resources. Moreover, it would not be easy for the major powers to frustrate their challenge. In Figure 7-3 middle and minor powers might seek an access to resources that reflect their enhanced status positions. However, they would be unlikely to gain success in this endeavor. Under the conditions of Figure 7-3 major powers might be tempted to try to elevate their influence positions, to concede less status to middle and minor states. If they attempted to do so, they would be likely to succeed in some restructuring of the status hierarchy. In Figure 7-2 on the other hand, if major powers tried to improve their access to resources, they would be likely to fail. In both Figures 7-2 and 7-3, therefore, one might anticipate that challenges would be offered to the existing order that the system would not be able to regulate successfully.

This would not be true in Figures 7-1 and 7-4. The powers in both these diagrams that would be most dissatisfied, would be least successful in changing their lot. Those powers that would have the greatest ability to change their lot, would have least incentive to do so. Thus, the major challenges to successful regulation in the international system would be likely to occur when there is a disproportion between status-influence and resources-rewards. The apparent conclusion to be drawn is that a system which is uniformly stratified is easy to regulate; one which is uniformly equalitarian may not need regulation. But it will be difficult to regulate a system which is equalitarian on one dimension and stratified on another. In particular, disproportions between influence and access to resources are likely to produce demands that cannot be moderated.[2]

Differences in stratification may also affect the environmental supply of resources with which to meet national demands. If resources are entirely preempted, states which seek greater access to resources must come into conflict with states which are dominant possessors. If there is a pool of resources yet to be appropriated, however, states may be satisfied from this pool without coming into direct conflict with each other.

Even if resources are fully appropriated, there may be some variances in flexibility if there are different degrees of evenness in the distribution of resources. The more unequal the distribution of resources, other things equal, the easier it is to grant some measure of redistribution. This is partly because the marginal utility of resources to major states is less than their marginal utility to less developed nations. Yet less developed nations, almost by definition, cannot be in a position to force such a redistribution. They have essentially to rely on petition and appeal to effect a change.

The history of the eighteenth and nineteenth centuries affords numerous examples of these relationships. In the late nineteenth century European imperialists were able to conquer the rest of the world because of their monopoly of both status and resources. There was nothing that the extra-European territories could do to prevent conquest. Thus regulation by the middle and minor powers was ruled out.

While European powers expanded their empires, however, they did not immediately come into conflict with each other. For a time at least, the access to resources and influence of all major powers was roughly the same. Uncertainty began to develop, though, when prestige and influence began increasingly to be divorced from control of resources. Germany had increasing access to resources with her own powerful industrial development of the last half of the nineteenth century. She did not have, in her judgment, a proportionate status and influence in the diplomatic direction of the system. While in 1890 her diplomatic influence was very great, by 1914 it was far diminished, and her economic power had grown greatly in the interim. For Austria-Hungary a reverse process operated. Austria remained as a leading decision maker in the system until the eve of war in 1914; increasingly, however, she was losing her previous position of economic prominence. It was not surprising that the smaller, highly nationalist states on her southern frontier decided to challenge her. Once again influence and access to resources were developing in opposite directions.

The same phenomenon can be seen in regard to Victorian England. Once the most powerful nation in Europe, Britain's power had declined relative to Germany and Russia. But her diplomatic influence and political preeminence remained for a time unchallenged. It was not surprising that other nations would seek a greater share of status and influence in the system at the expense of Britain.

SYSTEM POLARITY

While system stratification refers to lateral or horizontal divisions between powers, system *polarity* refers to vertical divisions. How many blocs or groupings of states exert influence in the system? A number of different possibilities can be imagined. There may be a *bipolar* distribution of states (Figure 7-5), with all or most states at the major and middle power levels aligned into one of two camps. At an intermediate point, there might be a *quintipolar* system (Figure 7-6) with five great powers exercising predominant influence. Such was the case during most of the eighteenth and nineteenth centuries. At the opposite extreme there might be a *multipolar* system (Figure 7-7) in which fifteen or twenty nations possessed roughly equivalent influence and status. A true multipolar system could not take pyramidal form. There would be so many major powers exerting influence that the system would be trapezoidal. An ultimate form of multipolar system [Multipolar System (II) in

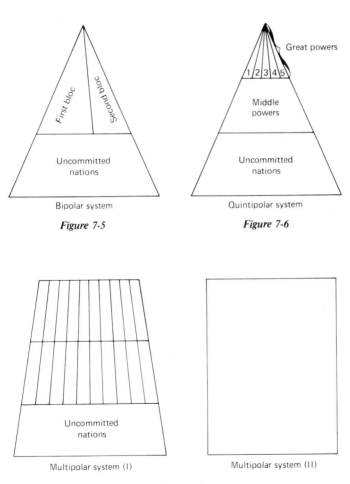

Bipolar system

Figure 7-5

Quintipolar system

Figure 7-6

Multipolar system (I)

Multipolar system (II)

Figure 7-7

Figure 7-7] would be a world in which there were no gradations between major and minor powers, and no bloc alignment of any kind, hence the absence of all vertical and horizontal divisions among states. All states would be roughly equal in strength and influence. Such a multipolar system can be disregarded, however, for its preconditions could not be met in the real world. Indeed, as we have seen, gradations in influence and access to resources now appear to make the world more stratified than ever before. The only realistic form of multipolar system would be Multipolar System (I).

These different forms of polarity create differences in the mode of regulation. A bipolar system is very difficult to regulate formally. All the uncommitted states together cannot impose a solution on the two major camps. International organizations cannot dictate their behavior. The two blocs themselves are the only two informal regulators, checking and limiting each other, balancing strength with strength. In a bipolar system there are no influences outside the two blocs capable of producing dependable regulation. One advantage of a bipolar system is that disruptive behavior and its consequences are clearly evidenced and clearly seen. If one of the blocs gains in strength, influence, and position, there can be no question against whom the increases are directed. The other camp will see its interests affected and therefore will quickly perceive the need for some offsetting gesture or accretion of strength. One bloc will not permit the other to engage in unregulated disruption.

A multipolar system offers almost exactly opposite benefits and disadvantages. Regulation, even formal regulation by an international institution, is physically easy to accomplish. Powers initiating disturbances can by definition have no greater strength than many other states. If they disrupt the system, that disruption may be countered by the action of other nations, either directly or through an international organization. Yet, in a multipolar system, it may be difficult to persuade other nations to engage in regulative action. Even though a single disturber may resolve upon actions which are inimical to at least one party and which might be the cause of violent conflict, other states may not be tempted to intervene. In a multipolar order it is not clear whose interests are primarily affected by a disruptive act. It is therefore possible for a whole series of disruptive events to occur without stimulating regulation. In the 1930s France, Britain, Italy, and Russia were led at various times to believe that Hitler's actions were not directed against them. Thus there was no need to attempt a serious regulation of Germany's conduct. In a fully multipolar order, many nations could believe that while a given state's actions were disruptive, they did not require counteraction by any particular nation, and a regulative coalition would not be formed.

In a multipolar system where no nation predominates, major ideological conflicts are unlikely. If these existed, international relations would be transformed into the competition of major camps for new ideological adherents, and the world would be split on ideological lines. Tripolarity or bipolarity would be likely to emerge. In a strict bipolar system all resources will be fully divided between two camps. Any attempt to reapportion them must develop into major war. A redivision of territorial spoils in a multipolar order would be less serious for the system as a whole, for its results would not necessarily affect many nations. Two states might fight it out on the periphery of the system.

In a multipolar order there is less temptation for one power to measure itself against others in relative terms. In a bipolar system relative measurements are crucial, for if one camp gets a slight preponderance over the other, the basic outcomes of the system might be altered. Relative measurements are less important in multipolar systems, for it is not clear whom to measure oneself against. The absolute position of a state in its access to environmental goods will be more important. If the absolute and not the relative position of a state is the critical question, there is greater hope of being able to satisfy a number of states simultaneously. If a state's relative position vis à vis others is crucial, however, there is no possibility of pleasing all nations at the same time. In this respect multipolarity appears to have the advantage over bipolarity: its resources are more likely to equal the demands made on them.

In between the bipolar and multipolar extremes, there might be a quintipolar (five-power) world, as was the case during important parts of the eighteenth and nineteenth centuries. In such an instance, it would be easier to compose a regulative coalition than under conditions of multipolarity, but informal regulation would be less automatic than under conditions of bipolarity. The ease of regulation under such conditions would be intermediate between multipolarity and bipolarity. The original notion of a great power in the eighteenth century was that of a state which could stand against the combined weight of all other major members of the system, and hence could not be coerced. But however difficult it might be to regulate a quintipolar order, it should be considerably easier than regulating a bipolar system. Four-fifths of the major powers of the world should have greater success in regulating the behavior of one-fifth, than one-half of the world should have in regulating the conduct of the other half.

A quintipolar system should also have certain advantages akin to those of multipolarity in that relative calculations of influence and position would be less important than in a bipolar system. If we assume a constant-sum game of the sort

$$A + B + C + D + E = K \text{ (any constant)}$$

and postulate that A increases its position, no one can immediately determine what the effect will be on other powers. The impact may be entirely confined to one power such as B:

$$\uparrow A + \downarrow B + C + D + E = \kappa$$

or all may be affected in some degree, each losing a small amount:

$$\uparrow A + \downarrow B + \uparrow C + \uparrow E = k$$

In the first case, if B is the only state affected and the others are satisfied with their position, there may be little that B can do to recoup her loss. In the second case, the other four states are likely to band together against A, striving to reduce his gains. Thirdly, and perhaps most importantly, the effect of A's gain may be imprecise:

$$\uparrow A + ?B + ?C + ?D + ?E = k$$

In this case, a number of states may think that their position is as before, and therefore remain relatively satisfied. This process, however, could clearly not go very far without some form of conflictual reckoning. Peace could be maintained for a time, but if A kept making gains at the others' expense, sooner or later they would turn against him. For an initial period, however, a quintipolar order should have a certain flexibility in accommodating small changes in national position that could not exist under bipolarity.

While the evidence is still not complete, it appears that multipolarity and bipolarity have inverse impacts on the probability and results of conflict in the system. As we look at recent international history, it seems that a multipolar order has had a wider variety of conflicts, simply because of the greater number of contending interests to adjust and advance. However, the consequences of multipolar conflict have not been greatly disruptive.[3] In the nineteenth century there were five wars between 1854 and 1871, but none of them fostered a permanent instability. The ultimately bipolar confrontations of World Wars I and II, however, completely transformed international relations. The results of conflict were far more pervasive and disastrous. In decision theory terms the expectation of any event is equal to its probability multiplied by its results or consequences. Under bipolarity, one would expect a small number of conflicts, because the issues would be confined to those between the two major camps. Since other powers would be part of one coalition or another, they would not follow individual and separate policies. But the bipolar conflicts which did occur would be likely to be very dangerous and have far-reaching consequences.[4] A war between bipolar camps is world war. In a multipolar system, war between two minor participants may have small impact on the system as a whole. Thus under multipolarity we would have:

Expectation of	=	Probability	X	Consequences
conflict		(high)		(low)

Under bipolarity we would have:

Expectation of	=	Probability	X	Consequences
conflict		(low)		(high)

Under quintipolarity the situation would be intermediate. Thus, the total expectation of conflict in the three cases might be about the same.

It is difficult to draw a trial balance on the influence of polarity on regulation and on environmental resources. Regulation will be difficult to perform in either strictly bipolar or strictly multipolar conditions. In bipolarity, as we have seen, the strength of either of the two main blocs makes regulation of its conduct very difficult. In multipolarity there may be no regulative coalition because no power feels threatened by a given change in the status quo. Considerable shifts, therefore, may occur without any countering regulation. A quintipolar system may derive the best of each extreme: powers are not so numerous that the impact of any disruptive change cannot be observed; powers are not so preponderant that one of them cannot be brought to heel by the concerted efforts of the remaining members of the system.

This does not mean that quintipolarity is to be approved under all circumstances. It did not keep peace in the 1930s; nor did it rule out the alignments which eventually led to World War I. Yet, during the eighteenth and nineteenth centuries, it held conflict to fairly minimal proportions most of the time. Only when bipolarity loomed, did the extremes of conflict among major powers follow. Since 1945 the rules of a bipolar system, together with nuclear deterrence, have been internalized sufficiently to permit a basic stability in international relations. But bipolarity is unlikely to remain stable if there is no intermediate group in world politics, and if there are no condominial ties between the two major powers.[5] Ultimately, such a system is more likely to transform itself into a version of eighteenth- and nineteenth-century constellations of power than to either strict multipolar or bipolar systems. Changes in international strategy will have to reflect the development of a new kind of balance of power environment. In principle, this system could be at least as stable as that which has prevailed since 1945, if nuclear technology does not prove a disruptive factor.

SYSTEM DISTRIBUTION OF POWER

In the previous sections we have discussed stratification and polarity. System distribution of power refers to the same dimensions that produce stratification; indeed, stratification is determined by power and influence. But we have used the term *stratification* to measure the difference between the top dogs, middle dogs, and underdogs. Distribution of power, in contrast, refers to the division of the spoils of power and influence among the major states themselves. It is similar to system polarity in that it marks a vertical, rather than a horizontal, differentiation among states. System polarity, as noted, refers to the number of states or blocs that exert influence in the system. Distribution of power refers to the way power is divided among those states or blocs. Neither bipolarity nor multipolarity must approximate a balance of power. If there are two main camps, one may be considerably stronger than the other, which has actually been the case since World War II. If there are many camps or nations, some may be larger or more powerful than others. The same is true for a quintipolar system. During the nineteenth century, five major powers determined the outcomes of international relations. They were themselves quite unequal in strength, with some powers going up, and others down the relative power scale. Whether a balance of power existed or not tended to depend upon who opposed whom, upon the coalitions at a particular historical moment. In the eighteenth century, France, Austria, and England were strong, and Prussia was very weak. In the latter part of the nineteenth century, Germany became very strong and Austria-Hungary weak. If peace depended upon equivalent strength among major powers, then, there was no period in the last two hundred years when a stable peace was possible.

Nor is it true that peace depended upon a balance of power between coalitions of states. On the whole, peace was preserved during the period of Germany's and Bismarck's diplomatic ascendancy, 1870 to 1890. Germany linked every major state except France in a web of entangling alliances and agreements under Berlin's aegis. But Germany was a satisfied nation and not interested in expansion. On the other hand, when power was more equally balanced between Triple Alliance and Triple Entente after 1907, there was a burgeoning hostility which culminated in World War I. The same was true immediately prior to World War II. Germany and Italy were not stronger than France and England in material or military terms. Yet an approximation to a balance of power did not deter Hitler from making demands and expansionist moves on the continent of Europe.

During the time of Napoleon, France was the largest and most powerful state economically and in terms of population, but she was not superior to the coalitions ranged against her which eventually included Austria, Prussia, Russia, and England. Napoleon embarked upon his last, fatal enterprise, the invasion of Russia, even though it was clear that the rest of the continent was aligned against him. At a certain point, it appears, states may be tempted to engage in conquest as a result of a succession of past victories, even when they are confronted by a balance, or even an overbalance, of power in the hands of their opponents.

It is impossible to find any one pattern in history on this subject, but at least there is a case to be made that the European peace has been most stable, not when there has been a balance of power, but *when one particular coalition enjoys a superiority of power.*[6] Periods of balance between coalitions have not been uniformly peaceful. Nor does peace follow when one state is superior to all others. France was stronger than other states individually in 1805, and a counterbalancing coalition was not organized against France until the waning days of the Empire. Europe was stable also between 1870 and 1890 because the imbalance of power resulted from the establishment of one preponderant coalition, not from the strength of a single state. One recipe for disaster develops when the single strongest state is not linked with a major coalition. It may then seek to act against that coalition. Thus, peace may possibly occur either when the strongest state is brought into a central coalition and prevented from acting disruptively because of its multifarious alliances. (This may partially account for the temporary constitutionalization of American power in the period 1945-1960.) Or peace may occur when the strongest state is opposed by an evidently and markedly stronger coalition. Peace by pacification or peace by deterrence may both succeed.

If it is true that predominant coalitions are not likely to be disruptive actors on the world scene, then the task of international regulation is facilitated when such coalitions exist. If power is more evenly balanced between coalitions or states, it may be more difficult to bring a disturber to heel. The Conference of Algeciras in 1906 did not succeed in settling an international dispute or regulating a quarrel; it merely registered the opposition between emergent blocs. The disputants were too balanced to produce a solution. International regulation was most effective when all great powers were in a European coalition, between 1815 and 1822. This supreme coalition served as the arbiter of European politics, both domestic and international, during its brief period of unity and ascendancy. The most difficult distribution of power from the standpoint of regulation apparently occurs when the single most potent state confronts a coalition of equal or lesser power. Then the single state is likely to be disruptive, and summoning the countercoalition is not sufficient to regulate his behavior effectively. Neither the Germany of 1910 nor the Germany of 1939 could be deterred by this method. To be effective, regulation requires a preponderant coalition, and it all too infrequently exists.

In the period since World War II the most powerful single state, the United States, has been a member of a predominant coalition. A less powerful state, the Soviet Union, has formed a slightly weaker grouping. The most dangerous period in post-1945 international relations occurred when the Soviet-dominated coalition appeared to begin to draw even with the American coalition, between 1957 and 1962.[7] Partly in response to the resolution of this world crisis, the bonds of both coalitions began to loosen, and divergent political policies emerged within each. No longer was international politics the encounter of two cohesive blocs.

The problem of international politics since that time has been that the two major actors, the United States and the Soviet Union, have paid less and less attention to erstwhile allies. Separate national actions have been and are now possible. Since the two major coalitions have partially collapsed from within, moreover, there is no countercoalition that can surely rebuff or deter action by either major state.

It may now be harder to regulate the international behavior of either the Soviet Union or the United States than it once was. Previously, United States behavior was regulated from within by its own coalition. Soviet behavior was regulated by a stronger opposing coalition. Presently neither situation is true, and everything depends upon the maneuvering of the two major states themselves. Fortunately, there has been a partial development of a third camp opposed to both powers. This serves the dual function of restraining them, while at the same time forcing them together. It reduces the possibility of major conflict between the United States and the Soviet Union. If the Soviets were to throw in their lot with the United States, however, there would be no force in the world which could stand against the two superpowers, but other powers could be certain to resent and to resist any such hegemony.

In this particular sense, therefore, one of the factors which restrains violence in the international system today is a delicate equipoise of cooperation and conflict. The Soviets and the United States are not fully allied; they still compete in many realms, not the least of which is the Middle East. However, they are not fully opposed to each other. They must in some degree jointly resist the pressure of third states. They both have certain conflicts of interest with China. Thus, they neither confront each other in bipolar antagonism, nor do they in some cooperative manner seek to aggrandize the rest of the world.

SYSTEM HOMOGENEITY

Other things being equal, homogeneous systems are easier to regulate than heterogeneous systems.[8] A system in which there are no divergent ideological issues and in which all nations take the same political and constitutional form does not usually tend to the extremes of conflict that are found in systems where ideologies and polities differ. There are a number of reasons for this.

If there are no divisive ideologies, all powers are equally ready to participate in regulation. They are not tempted to regulate only their enemies and to refuse to regulate their allies. A heterogeneous system, on the other hand, imposes rigidities upon the regulation process. States will be willing to regulate only for certain purposes, and to apply regulation only against certain states. They will not wish to restrain their ideological allies.

Since ideology is a disruptive factor in world politics, if there are no ideological differences, there will be fewer conflicts and those that exist will be contended less vigorously. As we have seen, conflicts in the international system of the eighteenth century, before ideological differences emerged, were much more limited than those which occurred after revolutionary liberalism mounted a frontal challenge to the old regime. Ideological homogeneity therefore assists regulation.

It is also true that the environmental supply of resources to gratify objectives is insufficient where there are competing ideologies. If one state gains its objective, another is frustrated. And even where ideologies do not clash, if states are differently organized internally, they are likely to seek different objectives in the external realm. There was no overt ideological conflict in the period immediately preceding World War I, and the Triple

Alliance and Triple Entente were by no means organized on ideological grounds. Still, differences in the internal political organization of states occasioned differences at the external level. Differences in social and political structure thus helped to undermine the consensus that had prevailed a hundred years previously.

There will always be divergences in the objectives of states at the international level: a nation formulates its position in a field of partially competing states. If major internal or ideological divergences are added to these, it is more difficult to reconcile state objectives. There is a chance that environmental supply of resources may be adequate when states are pursuing the same goals in ideological and political terms. It is unlikely that all can be satisfied simultaneously when the triumph of one state is also the defeat of another.

CONCLUSION

The international system is not easily regulated, nor is it simple to provide an adequate environmental supply of the goods that states demand. System structure has much to do with whether regulation or environmental supply of resources can hold conflict within bounds. A system in which influence and access to resources is highly stratified is easy to regulate, but is likely to stimulate demands for a more equitable division of the spoils of the system. A system which is equalitarian in the distribution of influence and resources may be very difficult to regulate, but it probably gives rise to few disruptive demands. Most difficult to regulate are systems where access to resources and influence are differentially distributed.

It is not clear that multipolarity is superior to bipolarity in facilitating regulation. A multipolar system is easy to regulate in that a disturber can easily be brought to heel, but it is difficult to get a regulative coalition together to coerce him. Bipolarity provides an automatic countercoalition but cannot guarantee that one camp in a bipolar world will submit to the regulation of the other. It seems that some combination of the features of bipolarity and multipolarity is necessary for there to be genuine and effective conflict control in the system. States must be willing to compose a regulative coalition, and that coalition must be truly capable of disciplining the disturbing powers. Such a situation is more likely to exist under quintipolarity than under either of the other two forms of system.

Neither an imbalance nor a balance of power offers the key to peace. Rather, it appears that there must be a preponderant or even predominant coalition before peace is secure. If the most powerful state is part of this coalition, it is disciplined by its allies. If the most powerful state stands against this coalition, it must be deterred from action against it.

System homogeneity is preferable to system heterogeneity. If the system is heterogeneous, two powers on opposite sides of the ideological or political fence cannot gain their objectives simultaneously. A heterogeneous system is likely to be harder to regulate because there will be desperate and perhaps violent international issues to be contended.

In more general terms, any system in which the immediate impact of the action of one state upon the interests of another is vague or ambivalent is likely to defuse conflict. As long as relative positions are not directly in question, states can believe that they can achieve their objectives simultaneously. From this point of view, a strict or tight bipolarity would appear to be the most intractable form of international system.

NOTES

1 At a theoretical extreme, one might even conceive of an absence of hierarchy in the system and a disappearance of stratification. In practice, however, such a result does not occur. Although more nations may become major powers and new middle powers may develop, differences in influence persist.

2 This argument is similar to Galtung's in "Rank and Social Integration: A Multi-dimensional Approach" in J. Berger, M. Zelditch, Jr., and B. Anderson, *Sociological Theories in Progress* (Boston: Houghton Mifflin, 1966). Galtung argues that rank incongruency (between achievement and ascriptive status) will lead to disequilibrium. See particularly pp. 172-177.

3 See Michael Haas, "International Subsystems: Stability and Polarity," *American Political Science Review*, pp. 116-121, March 1970; R. Rosecrance, "Bipolarity, Multipolarity and the Future," *Journal of Conflict Resolution*, pp. 318-19, September 1966.

4 On this point see particularly Haas, op. cit., pp. 118, 121.

5 See Rosecrance, op. cit., pp. 314-316, 322-324.

6 For contrasting views see F. H. Hinsley, *Power and the Pursuit of Peace* (Cambridge: Cambridge University Press, 1963); and A. F. K. Organski, *World Politics* (New York: Knopf, 1968).

7 See W. H. Riker, *The Theory of Political Coalitions* (New Haven: Yale University Press, 1962).

8 For similar views see Raymond Aron, *Peace and War* (Garden City, N.Y.: Doubleday, 1966), chap. 5.

CHAPTER EIGHT

System Interaction

The international system succeeds in preventing large-scale instability only if it can regulate disruption or if it can directly satisfy the desires of nations through provision of environmental resources. If the supply of resources is inadequate, regulation is required. Whether regulation can be successful, however, depends on the structure and interaction of the system. Certain structures are easier to regulate than others. How easy it is to regulate disruptive behavior or to assist states to achieve their objectives also depends upon the system's interaction: how tightly or loosely knit is the system? In what areas is it most fully interactive? What kinds of links do states have with one another?

In this chapter we shall consider a number of different aspects of interaction. First, states may be isolated or highly participant in the international system. If they are participant, they may express their involvement in different realms. A nation may be economically involved without being fully involved politically. If a nation has political involvements they may be global or geographically limited.

Nations that are involved with one another may have different kinds of social and cultural contacts. Links and interactions may proceed across boundaries of social differentiation, or they may exist between homogeneous societies. They may exist among societies which are fully nationalized and mobilized, or among populations which are increasingly adopting an international orientation. The contacts which states may have reflect high or low transactions among them; they may reflect high positive or negative inter-dependence, or low interdependence. In addition to environmental supply and system structure, the success of regulation will depend upon the type of interactions which take place.

NON-INTERACTION: ISOLATION

It is of course a truism that states cannot fight with one another if they are entirely out of contact. In this sense a complete and final isolation would be the answer to all international problems. But the very term *international relations* presupposes some form of contact or relationship among states. Technically, peace or stability is a condition which exists when there are relations among nations, but those relations are not conflictual. Still, there are degrees of participation or involvement in international relations. Some states are fully involved: they accord large diplomatic representation, they participate in a wide range of international organizations; they maintain security and defense as well as economic ties with many other nations; they spend a large proportion of their Gross National Product upon defense, international, political, or economic matters. Others are much less involved: they may exchange diplomats with only a few states; they participate in a minor way in the international organizations to which they belong, and they belong only to a few; they develop few trade or alliance ties; they may depend much more on regional than upon general international contacts. The Maldives, Nauru, and Tonga participate less in the international system than the United States and the Soviet Union, to put it mildly.

PARTIAL INTERACTION

Total isolation is not possible in our present international world, so peace cannot be obtained by placing states out of each other's reach. Total inter-action and total interdependence have, as yet, also not been possible. Tech-nology has fostered nationalism and national independence as well as international interdependence. Unless communications among nations and peoples become more frequent and intense than they are now, or seem likely to be, complete interaction will not be achieved and peace cannot be gained. In practice we are left with an intermediate situation: partial interaction or a more complete interaction which yet fails to bring about full cooperation.

There are various forms of partial interaction. Partial interaction may be complete in certain realms but deficient in others; or, interaction may be partial on a geographic basis. The first form of partial interaction is economic, the second is spatial.

Economic or Political Interaction?

Partial interaction of an economic type is likely to occur when states are in the initial stages of developing relationships with each other. States have often sought economic relations with each other without restrictive political ties. In the early years of the American republic, the United States policy of "no entangling alliances" was accompanied by important trade links to Europe and Britain. At various stages in European history, England had crucially important financial and trade relations with Europe without participating in continental pacts or alliances. In medieval Europe and among the city-states of ancient Greece, economic or trade ties often took place in the absence of political relations or conflicts.

Historically, economic ties have sooner or later given rise to political connections or conflicts. Renaissance economic links soon led to Renaissance political and military intrigue. By the fifth century B. C., trade contacts among Greek city-states had fomented important political rivalries. The United States was drawn into the War of 1812 because of trade with Europe, and it was involved in World War I because of a desire to protect neutral trading rights against infringement by a belligerent power. In the latter part of the nineteenth century, European political imperialism followed upon commercial efforts to open up trade and investment with new territories in Asia, Africa, and the Near East. Polities engage in trade with one another; then they seek to police trade routes, to maintain access to sources of raw materials and markets. Eventually political contacts and conflicts arise with other trading units. Thus it appears, at least historically, that economic contacts burgeon into political relationships. These relationships may contain the seed of international conflict.

Today, it is probably even more difficult to restrict ties to the purely economic level. Nations which have economic relationships will develop political relationships in a shorter period than was the case previously. But if the development of political contacts from economic contacts may bring conflict, economic contacts when added to political relationships may, under certain circumstances, reduce conflict. Economic relationships are more consistent with a variable-sum game than are political relationships. If economic contacts and commitments proliferate and intensify as they have done, for example, in Western Europe, where integrative economic institutions have been created, they may reinforce political solidarity. States may become so enmeshed in the web of economic organizations that independent political action against other participants becomes less likely. Here, of course, interaction extends beyond mere economic links and comes to embrace a panoply of new political and administrative agencies. The lesson seems to be, nonetheless, that one cannot reduce conflict by trying to limit interactions to economic realms; economic interaction will give way to political interaction.

Global or Spatial Interaction?

If limited interaction cannot be attained economically, it may be more easily obtained spatially. A state can decide, within limits, whether it wants to be a central participant in all geographic areas of the world. It may opt for a pattern of limited involvement on a geographic basis: some areas will be of central importance, others of only peripheral significance. Even when a state is participant in an area, its participation can be of many types. It can vary from the most minimal formal diplomatic relationship, to a profusion of political and military contacts at all levels and throughout the bureaucracy. The United States has a much more limited relationship with Senegal, albeit political, than it does with the United Kingdom.

Nor does it appear that economic power dictates involvement, in the way that economic ties generate political ties. America became the most powerful nation on earth before it entered into global international politics on a continuing basis. After the Bolshevik Revolution, the Russians remained limited participants in European and world diplomacy at least until the eve of World War II, despite the considerable increase in their economic and military power in the interim. England, on the other hand, continued to be a major participant in all global system events long after its relative power position had declined. The Empire, the Commonwealth, and Britain's history of involvement in worldwide international relations kept her as the premier participant at least until World War II, long after she had been surpassed economically and militarily by the United States, Russia, and Germany. Equally, Spain and Austria continued to be involved in general international politics, well after they had declined in relative power. This tends to suggest that a nation's involvement in world politics (which may be at least partly volitional) may be a more subtle predictor of participation in war than relative power. The more commitments a nation has, the more dependencies or colonies, the more alliances, the more spheres of interest—the more likely is it that it will have to defend those interests in military conflict. In this sense worldwide empire has been correlated with involvement in war, and it has done so even when we exclude wars between sovereign nations and dependencies. Of the sovereign or near-sovereign conflicts in the past two hundred and ten years, England has participated in more conflict pairs than any other state. The top ten participants in war over the past two centuries are shown as a percentage of England's participation in these pairs of conflict (Table 8-1). Considering that there were about fifty potential sovereign or near-sovereign participants in international politics during most of this period, the fact that England was involved in seventeen percent of all conflict pairs and France fourteen percent is very striking. On a pure probability basis a null model would have found each of the fifty political entities engaged in two percent of the conflicts.[1] Of course, this conclusion must be modified by the type of international system in which the states participated. A bipolar or quintipolar system would make the two major (or five major) actors much

TABLE 8-1 Participation in war (1750-1960)

(Percentage participation in conflict pairs, with England at 1.00)

Entire Period		1750-1820		1821-1890		1891-1960	
England	1.00	England	1.00	England	1.00	England	1.00
France	0.80	France	0.79	France	0.92	Germany	0.87
Russia	0.65	Russia	0.68	Russia	0.66	France	0.70
Germany-							
Prussia	0.52	Spain	0.65	Turkey	0.63	Russia	0.62
Turkey	0.49	Austria	0.47	Spain	0.50	Italy	0.57
Spain	0.49	Prussia	0.38	Italy	0.42	Turkey	0.53
Italy-							
Piedmont	0.40	Turkey	0.26	Austria	0.34	U. S.	0.43
Austria	0.35	Holland	0.26	U. S.	0.26	Austria	0.28
U. S.	0.30	Poland	0.24	Mexico	0.24	Spain	0.26
Holland	0.24	Sweden	0.21	Holland	0.21	Holland	0.21

Source: F.H. Denton, *Factors in International System Violence–1750-1960* (RAND Corporation P-4216, October 1969), p. 12.

more likely to be involved in conflict than lesser states. Holding these factors constant, however, one can observe that if nations can minimize their participation in international relations on a geographic basis, they may also be able to reduce their involvement in conflict. Nations with fewer military ties or political commitments, other things being equal, are less likely to be involved in war than nations with a heavy burden of commitments, alliances, and spheres of influence.

From an individual state's point of view, this is a heartening finding. But from the standpoint of the system, it is not helpful unless the amount of system violence overall can be reduced. While not unambiguous, however, the data do not suggest constant levels of violence in the international system. There have been lulls in international conflict. The lulls, moreover, appear partly to coincide with diminished involvement of at least some of the major powers. It is therefore conceivable that the sum of conflict in the system can be reduced by lessening the participation of major states.

It is also conceivable, however, that diminished involvement could lead to power vacuums which in turn would provoke increased involvement and greater conflict.[2] Much would presumably depend upon the common restraint of major states; if only a few tried to minimize their commitments, the others would be likely to take advantage of their abstention. Still, given various favorable conditions of this kind, it is possible that regulation and environmental supply could be more adequate in a system in which connections are loosely knit, than in one in which interaction is both more complete, more frequent, and more intense. This would be true, not because of the greater effectiveness of regulation, but because of the greater scarcity of disruptive actions on the world scene.

If some kinds of overparticipation and overinvolvement can cause unnecessary conflict on the international scene, it does not follow that all types of participation present equivalent problems. As we have seen, economic and social involvement may later cause political and military involvement. But nations have often extended the contours of their political, military, and strategic interests far beyond the scope of prior economic relationships. The United States had few if any economic relationships with Vietnam or Korea before its participation in those conflicts. Britain in the nineteenth century was ready to defend its lines of communication with the empire, even though many of the political strong points on those lines of communication were valuable only in strategic terms. If nations confined their political and strategic interests to those states or regions in which they had great financial or economic interests, every major state would be obliged to contract its spheres of influence and interest far beyond their present extent. From the standpoint of limiting overinvolvement, economic, financial, and cultural ties do not appear to present a problem. But military, political, and strategic ties not only are likely to be more widely extended, they are also more likely to cause conflict. A nation may still decide if it wishes to fight over economic interests; but military pacts, guarantees, and strategic bases are particularly likely to be fought over, because they are thought to be important.

One of the ways in which military participation or involvement can be limited geographically is to reinforce the social distance between states. After all, geographic distance tends to imply social distance (although the relationship is far from being one to one), and social distance, though nations have not always been aware of the fact, places limits on any state's power.[3] Historically, of course, the English Channel and the Atlantic Ocean tended to protect Britain and the United States from invasion by European states. Continental states could not exercise power at such a distance. Today, the intercontinental missile and strategic air transports have made nuclear or conventional war feasible even across great distances. But technology has not eradicated cultural, ethnic, and political differences. It is still harder to exert power at a distance than it is nearby, where cultural diffusion of common traits has occurred to a high degree.

Cultural diffusion is not a simple function of geographic space. For example, Australia and New Zealand remain "closer" to Britain in cultural terms than do France or Germany. However, no cultures have diffused to worldwide limits. At some point a nation of one culture or social origin finds it difficult to exercise dependable and continuing authority over a nation of a different culture and social composition. Failures of American foreign policy in Asia, Latin America, and the Middle East illustrate this principle. No nation can expect to have equivalent influence in all areas of the globe—with increased space and social distance, a nation's influence declines.

Cultural and linguistic diversity, then, have probably made national expansion more difficult. States may be less tempted to aggrandize a region, when they believe they cannot govern or control it. Thus while a nation's military power is no longer strictly geographical, its influence still is.[4] Indeed, it is even more so. As populations in the developing countries are mobilized to political activity, it is ever more difficult for them to accept foreign influence or rule. Karl Deutsch refers to this as "the rising cost of foreign intervention." Nineteenth-century imperialism was successful not because of the absence of cultural differences, but because the European imperialist encroached upon inert and inactive local populations in Asia, Africa, and the Near East. With the mobilization of popular sentiment in these regions, the European imperialist has suffered an unending series of defeats since 1945. To exert political force at a distance is even more difficult and dangerous than it once was.

Superficially, this conclusion might appear to conflict with that reached in the preceding chapter on the desirability of homogeneous international systems, involving states with similar ideologies and political structures. As we noted earlier, heterogeneous systems, reflecting social and spatial differences, have been more difficult to regulate. Nations of different cultural or ethnic backgrounds are likely to misunderstand one another at the international level. In the past two hundred years about one-third of the major military conflicts have occurred in imperial-colonial wars where participants were of differing ethnic backgrounds. States embodying different cultural traits are likely to have varying, and perhaps even clashing, objectives in world politics. Further, a world of disparate ethnic and cultural types may not be able to furnish a powerful regulative coalition when disruption occurs. Nations will be too disunited politically and ideologically to join together for regulative purposes. Thus cultural distance may offer deterrents to offensive or aggressive action, but it also may be a major cause of international rivalry and misunderstanding. It is difficult, moreover, to observe a net trend. Certainly the obstacles which cultural and ethnic differences pose to expansion are better understood today when they were in the nineteenth century. Historically, however, differences of political form, culture, or ideology have been at the root of many of the world's wars. It is nonetheless true that the most disastrous wars have not been between members of differing civilizations. They have tended to be between nations embracing fundamentally the same civilization or cultural background, which nonetheless have had important differences in governmental system and ideology. If this is true, it is just possible that cultural differentiation is today a net contributor to peace and stability, though the margin would be a narrow one.

Assuming this, partial interaction on a spatial basis may hold the clue to a modest reduction in conflict among nations. If nations cannot contend successfully in other geographic-cultural regions, they may be less tempted to become involved in them politically and militarily.

FULL INTERACTION: PARTIAL PARTICIPATION

A fully interacting system usually develops out of a partially interacting system based upon trade and functional contacts. Economic relations lead to political relations. But even when interaction is more complete in the sense that contacts among states burgeon beyond the economic and functional realm, states are still not equal participants in the system. The United States has diplomatic relations with more than 100 nations, more than any other country. Even where minimal diplomatic representation exists, there may be no additional network of economic, political, or security relationships. If we were to graph the relationships of a single state in the international system, we would find that it had complex and multiple relationships with only a few other nations (Figure 8-1).

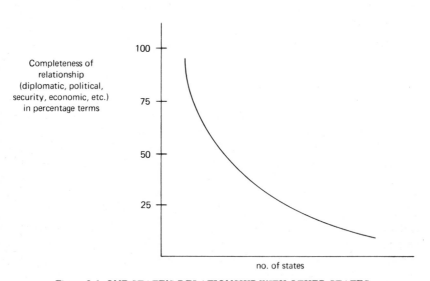

Figure 8-1 ONE STATE'S RELATIONSHIP WITH OTHER STATES

While there is an increasing proliferation of economic, financial, trade, and communications contacts among states, it is by no means certain that the world has become a less nationalistic place as a result. For the crucial question is not the *absolute growth* in international communications and transactions; it is the *relative growth* of international versus intranational transactions. If intranational transactions have increased more than international transactions, the world may be a more nationalistic place.[5] There is some evidence that this is precisely what has happened. Rapid growth in literacy, increases in urbanization, expansion in governmental expenditure, and rises in political participation are all measures of national and social mobilization. They incline the citizenry to focus more upon political and economic happenings at the national level. After leading to demands for national governmental action, they engender increased governmental response and expenditure. The urban population particularly looks to national government for the solution of its problems.

The more the population directly or indirectly participates in government, moreover, the more identified it is with government decisions. In many Western countries the development of popular sovereignty in the eighteenth and nineteenth centuries was the major stimulus to nationalism. Perhaps surprisingly, as major nations have grown economically, particularly in the industrial sector, their dependence upon foreign trade has eventually declined. It is possible, therefore, that the net impact of economic and political modernity has been to resuscitate and strengthen national, as compared with international, loyalties. Table 8-2 gives figures for five countries which point to such a nationalizing effect.

It is, of course, true that modern political life places demands upon domestic political systems. If these demands are met, there is greater satisfaction with the nation-state. If they are not met, there may be appeals to extranational standards and loyalties. There may also be, however, demands for smaller governmental units, and more controllable, smaller bureaucracies. It does not follow, therefore, that doubts about the performance of the nation-state will necessarily lead in a more internationalist direction.

Moreover, despite contemporary political protests and discontents, there are some reasons for believing that the nation-state has at least tolerably satisfied the majority of its citizens in economic terms. Basic demands for governmental economic policy performance have previously reached peaks while supplies are still being increased. In Table 8-2, urbanization, literacy, and political participation (as expressed in percentages of adults voting) can be regarded as providing mobilized political demands. Populations have grievances, but their demands only become politically relevant when they can be articulately expressed and can make their weight felt in political outcomes. Governments neglect at their own peril, therefore, the urban, literate, and politically participant population. Of the indices which measure these factors, only urbanization has shown any significant increase since the 1930s. The basic structure of political and economic demand is probably not greatly different today from what it was forty years ago. Yet, national fulfillments in terms of governmental expenditures and a rising per capita Gross National Product are now substantially greater than they were even in the 1930s. In

TABLE 8-2 Comparative development of five countries
1890-1965

YEAR	GNP PER CAPITA (in 1965 U.S. $1,000s)					URBANIZATION (% of pop. in cities of 20,000 and over)					LITERACY (% of literates over 10 or 14 yrs., or among recruits or newlyweds)				
	U.S.	U.K.	Fr.	Ger.	U.S.S.R.	U.S.	U.K.	Fr.	Ger.	U.S.S.R.	U.S.	U.K.	Fr.	Ger.	U.S.S.R.
1890	0.9	0.8	0.4	0.5	0.18	22.2	56.6	19.3	21.9	11.9*	86.7	91.0	85.0	99.5	31.5
1913	1.3	1.0	0.7	0.7	0.23	32.2	62.1	26.3	35.8	13.4*	92.8	96.0+	88.8	99.9+	45.0
1928	1.7	1.0	0.9	0.8	0.25	39.8	64.4	30.0	41.3	17.9*	95.4	96.0+	—	99.9+	57.0
1965	3.5	1.9	2.1	2.3	1.5	45.4	67.2	38.9	49.6	53.8* / 35.5†	97.7	96.0+	97.0+	99.9+	95.0

Sources: K.W. Deutsch, *The Analysis of International Relations* (Englewood Cliffs, N.J.: Prentice-Hall, 1968); Abram Bergson, *The Real Nation Income of Soviet Russia Since 1928* (Cambridge, Mass.: Harvard University Press, 1961); S. Cohn, *Economic Development in the Soviet Union* (Lexington, Mass.: Heath, 1970); R.W. Goldsmith, "The Economic Growth of Tsarist Russia 1860-1913," *Economic Development and Cultural Change*, April 1961; *Statesman's Yearbook—1889, 1890, 1891, 1892, 1913, 1914, 1915, 1928-1929, 1929-1930, 1965-1966; Encyclopedia Britannica—1898, 1926, 1929, 1965 Yearbook*, 1968.

* Urbanization in these instances is the % of population in cities of 3,000 and over.

† This figure represents the % of the population in cities of 20,000 and over.

TABLE 8-2 Comparative development of five countries *(Continued)*

	ADULTS VOTING (as % of total pop.)††					GOVERNMENT EXPENDITURE (as % of GNP)					FOREIGN TRADE (as % of GNP)				
	U.S.	U.K.	Fr.	Ger.	U.S.S.R.	U.S.	U.K.	Fr.	Ger.	U.S.S.R.	U.S.	U.K.	Fr.	Ger.	U.S.S.R.
1890	18.6	11.4	20.7	15.5	—	6.9	8.9	13.1	13.2	9.4	12.1	44.9	32.8	32.3	11.1
1913	15.8	11.7	25.9	33.5	—	8.0	12.4	13.1	17.7	16.8	10.5	49.2	39.6	38.1	13.1
1928	30.5	49.6	22.3	49.9	—	11.7	24.2	15.8	29.4	—§	9.3	42.4	37.4	50.4	4.5
1965	36.9	51.2	40.8	56.6	—	30.5	39.1	40.0	46.9	—§	6.8	33.9	21.8	31.7	2.6

††There are no reliable voting statistics for Tsarist Russia. After the establishment of the Soviet Union they have no meaning.

§Statistics on government expenditure have no meaning in an economy in which there is no private sector.

terms of these structural categories, supplies have increased relative to demand for the bulk of the population in major nations in recent years. Even those who have suffered relatively, or even absolutely, in the age of affluence turn to the nation for a solution to their ills. Thus one must expect a continued reliance on the nation-state for the solving of crucial social and economic problems. There appears to be no agency at the international level which can better meet these needs. It is perhaps not surprising then, that with all the technological interdependence of the world, the nationalizing trend of popular loyalty, which started with the French Revolution, has not yet been broken.

INTERACTION BALANCES:
CONTACT AND INTERDEPENDENCE

It may be possible at this point to elaborate a tentative approach to desirable balances of interaction in the international system. One dimension of importance is the frequency and magnitude of international transactions and communications. If nations and peoples are communicating very intensively with outside populations, they will be less likely to be hostile to them. At the extreme, such communications could attain a multiplicity and depth which would counterbalance domestic communications. States would then develop international orientations, and nationalism would decline.[6]

Interaction, however, is not simply communications and transactions. It has another aspect. There is also the interaction that flows from the relationship among state interests. How much interdependence is there, compared with independence? If states pursue the same objectives, and there is a constant-sum game, the achievement of goals by one state will interfere with the ability of another to attain its ends. This will be true regardless of the communications balances between states.[7]

In addition there is the communication transactions balance itself. Below a certain threshold, states have often had increasing communications links while their interests were contrary. Contact and communication with Germany probably went up in a range of categories after Hitler achieved power. Such an increase, however, did little to mitigate the differences in concrete interest. Nations may be in a constant-sum game when their communications balances are improving. They may be in a game of increasing sum when their communications networks do not foster an atmosphere of cordiality. In the case of the easing of the cold war after 1963, it may have been that the concrete interests of the United States and the Soviet Union moved closer together even though there was scarcely any visible increase in communications contact.

When the two factors operate inversely, it is not clear which will win out. Sometimes, as in the case of the Suez war of 1956, interest gives way at the behest of favorable communications balances. In that instance, the United

States and Britain had conflicting concrete interests, but communications and sentiment effected a rapprochement nonetheless. In other cases, like that of the Franco-Russian alliance of 1894, interest was governing. On grounds of sentiment and communications links, Russia would have much preferred to have had an alliance with Germany. After Germany declined to renew the Reinsurance Treaty with Russia in 1890, however, Russia had to find another ally. Eventually she turned to France even though ideology, communications, values, and governmental form tended to separate France and Russia. Interest prevailed over traditional communications patterns.

The relationship between interest interdependence and communications contact may be seen more concretely in Table 8-3.

TABLE 8-3 Stability, contact, and interdependence

	High interdependence		Low interdependence
	Positive	Negative	
High communications contact	Stability	Instability	Instability
Low communications contact	Temporary Instability	Instability	Stability

The most favorable situations from the standpoint of stability appear to occur when there is high communications contact and high positive interdependence of interest between two states (High, High: Positive). Alternatively, where there is little contact and no relationship of interests or interdependence, peace may occur by default (Low, Low). Nothing that one state does impinges upon another state. The difficulties appear to be intermediate: where there is low contact and still great interdependence (Either: Low, High: Positive *or* Low, High: Negative); or where there is relatively high contact and low or negative interdependence (Either: High, Low, *or* High, High: Negative). In the first instance, because of low contact nations will not cooperate to maximize joint positions in an interdependent game. Because of attention to unfavorable contacts with another state, nations may not even perceive how interdependent their interests are. This case is one causing temporary instability, since the mutual interests would become apparent as contact increased. For the moment, in addition, it appears that we are experiencing something akin to this situation (Low, High: Positive). While intranational messages have increased relative to international messages and therefore have reduced net contact, there is an even greater factual interdependence of interest than ever before. In economic, technological, trade, financial, and military terms, there are greater common interests than existed previously. Thus, because of interdependence, the world is in fact tightly knit; because of deficiencies in relative contact, it may not be perceived as such. The net effects of modern technology and popular sovereignty may be inverse. They may actually create an interdependent world, while at the same time making people focus more and more on the individual nation-state.

Putting aside military variables for the moment (whose positive interdependency at the thermonuclear level is obvious), the growing financial interdependence of the developed world cannot be denied. How much of a policy of internal development and inflation one nation can try to maintain is a function of the willingness of other states to follow basically similar policies. If one of the developed states seeks to follow a policy of inflation and others do not, it will only worsen its international payments position. If all nations pursue basic policies of growth and development, however, they will be less likely to suffer payments reverses which could force the adoption of domestic contractionist measures. If one or more nations strive to improve their balance of payments positions when others are inflating to stimulate economic growth, they may force contractionist policies upon other states, hindering their growth and development.

Thus in some measure developed states tend to go up and down the scale together. If several major trading nations suffer, the danger to others becomes very great. For this very reason it was essential in the postwar era to safeguard the position of the pound sterling and the United States dollar. If the United States and Britain had been forced to take ultimately restrictive and contractionist measures to preserve their balance of payments, the welfare of the rest of Western Europe and Japan might have been affected. In economic realms there is a high interdependence among developed states.

Table 8-3 shows, however, that high positive interdependence may often occur in a context of low or lagging contact. Nationalistic introversion does not provide a desirable context for positive interdependence.

A second unstable situation emerges where there is a low contact and high, but negative, interdependence. In this case, where one state goes up the scale, another goes down. The relationship between American and Japanese interests immediately prior to World War II was certainly one of interdependence, but it was a negative interdependence. American policy was to prevent further Japanese expansion in the Pacific and in East Asia. The Japanese, however, calculated that they could not even maintain their position in 1940-1941 without additional expansion to secure the necessary raw materials from Southeast Asia. While Japan and the United States had important economic contacts, they had few cultural and no political links. The United States had already acted to limit Japanese immigration to the United States. The combination of differences in interests, and lack of communications and understanding eventually led to military conflict.

Thus there may be relationships of interest which are constant-sum or even zero-sum. If there is also a low net balance of contact, the international situation is very serious. If, on the other hand, there is a variable-sum game in which players go up and down the scale together, but communications contact balances lead states to take increasingly nationalist perspectives, the result is still undesirable. Today, the world is in fact more positively interdependent than ever before but may be being perceived more in nationalistic terms. There may be high positive interdependence, but low net contact.

This statement seems to be true of the developed world. Among the less developed states, and between the less developed and modern nations, there is far less clearly a real and favorable interdependence of interests. Even in economic terms, some constant-sum game aspects appear to prevail. The richer developed states are getting richer, while the poorer states (in relative but not absolute terms) are getting poorer. The gap between them is increasing. Thus there is a much more limited harmony of interest than exists among developed states. Johan Galtung puts the point even more strongly: " ... there is a disharmony of interest between the Center nation as a whole and the Periphery nation as a whole."[8] In addition, there is no balance of favorable contacts. Many less developed states are in immediate pre- or post-revolutionary situations in which nationalistic identification takes on great importance as a kind of domestic cement. Neither in regard to each other nor toward the developed world are they likely to adopt favorable attitudes. This lack of favor, moreover, is strengthened de facto by the real contrariety of material national interests. Here then lie the seeds of a really virulent conflict. As in the case of United States-Japanese relations before the Pacific war, there is negative interdependency and insufficient contact. Were it not for the resources which the developed nations possess to prevent disruption by the developing states, a major conflict might follow. (Note here the similarity of situation with that discussed in the preceding chapter: highly stratified influence patterns conjoined with highly stratified access to resources.)

Just as one difficulty is presented by high interdependence and low contact, another is offered by low interdependence and high contact. There have certainly been periods before the technological developments of the past century in which states had high communications contacts, but relatively low interdependence of interest. During the eighteenth century there was a great deal of social communication across frontiers in Europe. French was the language of diplomacy for many countries. There was considerable geographic mobility for the nobility and higher bourgeoisie.

The relationship of state interest was such that great powers believed that they could engage in constant jockeying for power, position, and territory. A great power was supposed to be able to hold its own against the combined weight of other states. It was not supposed to have to defer to opposition from the rest of the system. Technologically, nations could not proceed very far in their attacks on other states, but neither could they be eliminated or humiliated. Thus in the period 1740-1763 we have a succession of wars, based partly on the presumption of self-sufficiency and independence of great powers. Only after 1763 did they begin to recognize the limitations placed on their action by the system and their newly found interdependence with other nations.

Germany in the 1930s evinced aspects of the same situation. Hitler saw no interdependence in Germany's relations with other states. Germany believed she could expand virtually without limits without provoking decisive opposition from other powers. German propaganda manipulation could always rationalize Germany's moves so that other powers would not see them as expansionist or threatening. Germany could follow a policy of unfettered independence and autonomy because, from Berlin's point of view, there were no intrinsic French or British national interests which would require Western nations to oppose Germany by force of arms. These moves, of course, took place on a world stage in which all nations were paying more and more attention to Germany, and in which communications and transactions were on the rise following the economic and social dislocations of the Great Depression.

From a slightly more theoretical vantage point, one can see why these two intermediate situations of contact and interdependence should hold problems for peace. Where relative contact is low and negative interdependence high, states might act as if they were in nationalistic isolation, but they would rapidly come into conflict with others in terms of concrete interests. Where contact is high, but interdependence low, states would have considerable freedom of action, even though they might not be tempted to exercise it to the full. Nations would be likely to proceed so far on the assumption of independence that they would eventually cause the world to become more interdependent. Such a recognition, however, would only dawn after an aggressive power had already made major gains. If the interdependence turned out to be negative, war might be necessary to redress the balance.

In the future another problem of this sort may possibly emerge. It is conceivable that as more and more nations acquire nuclear weapons and delivery capabilities, they may think of themselves as more self-sufficient. They will feel less need to rely on allies, or upon major power guarantors. It is possible that they will then be tempted to engage in actions that were proscribed to them when they possessed no such weapons. The underlying interdependence of the system would not be seen by them until it was too late. Some smaller nuclear states or potential nuclear powers unquestionably look upon nuclear weapons as a great leveller, implicitly conferring great power status on their possessors. If they attempt to act upon such presumptions, conflict may be the result.

CONCLUSION

In this chapter we have surveyed several types of interaction and their impact upon war and peace. Total isolation is today ruled out for most states. But complete and full interaction, in terms of total participation and communication, is also not a realistic prospect. Partial interaction of an economic sort is likely to eventually extend to political and military interaction, possibly causing hostilities. Partial interaction of a spatial or geographic sort is more stable.

If states could recognize that social and geographic distance really present a formidable barrier to expansion, they might be less tempted to engage in it. However, social and cultural differences and divergences are themselves a partial motivation for conflict and expansion.

Even if states are more completely involved in the international system, they need not participate in the entire spectrum of relationships, ranging from economic to political-military in every area of the globe. Imperial, colonial, and other types of commitments lead to greater involvement in war. States, within limits however, can decide to define the contours of their interests more narrowly.

Where there are imbalances in favorable contact and interdependence, one can work either to reduce or increase one of the variables. If contact is high and interdependence at least apparently low, one can seek to point to the consequences which unfettered expansionism will have in creating a greater negative interdependence, one that in the end may lead either to war or to denying the aggressor the fruits of his military and political ventures. In the end, moreover, the recognition of the negative military interdependence that war would represent might, in turn, foster some form of positive interdependence in the mutually recognized need to avoid war.

If interdependence, is high and contact low, one can strive to increase relative contact, focusing more messages and communications internationally, and fewer intranationally. The lack of success of modern nation-states in meeting many contemporary problems can be used as a justification for reorienting communications outward.

On the whole, the international experience since 1945 has not borne out the arguments of the internationalists against the isolationists. It is not transparently clear that nations which participate energetically and fully in all dimensions of international politics are in some sense better off or more secure than those which do not.

If we consider to what degree international involvement has caused conflicts, as well as perhaps helping to regulate them, it is not easy to draw a trial balance. Since it is very difficult to get nations to perceive others as friendly through an expansion of international versus intranational messages, it may be necessary to try to reduce their points of interaction. (In more formal terms, if contact cannot be increased, interdependence should be reduced.) National interests should be defined more narrowly. At the same time, interests should not be defined so narrowly that power vacuums develop, leading to increased intervention and negative interdependence. Figures 8-2, 8-3, and 8-4 demonstrate that overly expanded interests lead to conflict, that overly contracted interests lead to power vacuums and subsequent conflict, and that properly defined interests avoid the excesses of either.

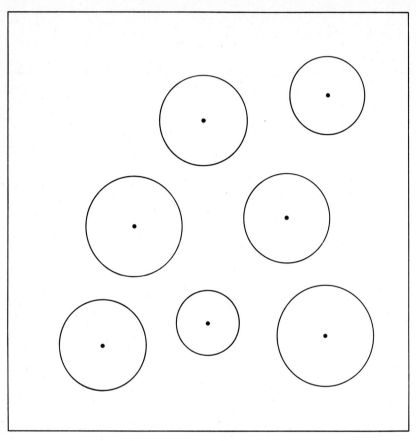

Figure 8-2 CONTRACTED INTERESTS (Interests do not collide, but power vacuums are created.)

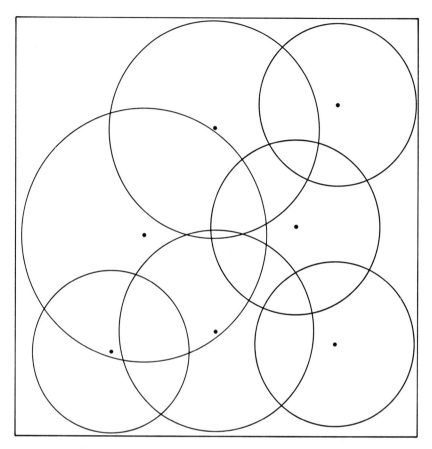

Figure 8-3 EXPANDED INTERESTS (Interests collide.)

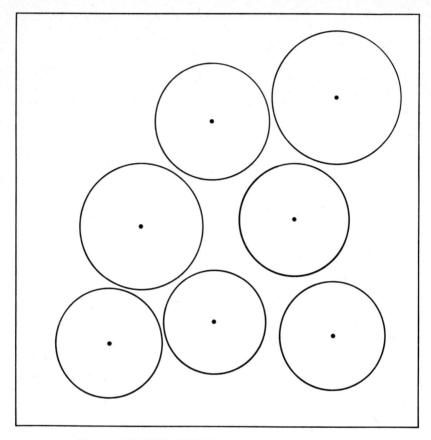

Figure 8-4 PROPER INTERESTS (Interests do not collide.)

NOTES

1 F. H. Denton, *Factors in International System Violence—1750-1960* (Rand Corporation, P-4216, Oct. 1969) p. 12.
2 I am indebted to Jeffrey Hart for this point.
3 See K. W. Deutsch, "Nation and World," in Ithiel Pool (ed.), *Contemporary Political Science* (New York: McGraw-Hill, 1967), p. 218. Deutsch argues (p. 219) that, owing to the increasing mobilization of the masses, we are entering an age of "rising costs of foreign intervention. For the next half-century at least," he says, "the world is becoming irremediably pluralistic."
4 For two contrasting views see Kenneth Boulding, *Conflict and Defense* (New York: Harper & Row, 1962); and Albert Wohlstetter, "Illusions of Distance," *Foreign Affairs,* January 1968.
5 Karl Deutsch puts it this way: "What counts is how many people spend how large a proportion of their total time and attention on . . . globe-girdling messages, against the time and attention they are spending on national or local ones." Deutsch in Pool (ed.), op. cit., p. 215.

6 Deutsch writes: "If . . . the flow of messages across group boundaries is much larger or more salient than the communications flow within the group, then a larger code, common to both the group and its outside partners is likely to prevail and to be maintained more or less uniformly for at least as long as this prevalence of cross-boundary communications lasts." Deutsch in Pool (ed.), op. cit., p. 213.

7 This point does not conflict with the one above. At extremely high levels of interaction and transaction (communication), two states will not adopt contrary objectives. Short of such complete interaction, however, communications can be increasing between states which have divergent interests. Thus communication balances do not necessarily override differences of objectives.

8 "A Structural Theory of Imperialism," *Journal of Peace Research*, no. 2, p. 84, 1971. Italics in the original.

3

Objectives

As we have seen, the systemic determinants of international war and peace are external to the perspective of any given state. Systems refer to relationships among states and are outside the control of individual states. *Objectives*, however, refer to the goals of particular states. Nations cannot control relationships with other states, but each nation can specify the goals it will seek. As we have also seen, the need for regulation and environmental restraints will depend partly on the objectives which states have chosen. Some types of objectives are more conflictual than others. In the next six chapters we shall examine the domestic decisional process, the development of objectives, the determination of objectives by external and internal influences, the nature of objectives, and possible means for transcending conflictual objectives in international politics.

CHAPTER NINE

The Arena of Goal Formation: Domestic Politics and Decision Making

The foreign policy objectives of nations have their origin in the domestic arena. The views, and to some extent the actions, of decision makers are influenced by domestic opinion. This opinion is in turn subdivided among various sectors. The public sector constitutes the overwhelming majority of any society. The opinion which it expresses, tapped by polling organizations, is the least differentiated and the most ill-informed influence upon foreign policy. Since its informational base is slender, government policy and pronouncements can greatly affect its position. The record shows that public opinion on a variety of international questions has varied greatly from one foreign policy episode to the next.

The media sector is composed of the press, radio, television, and opinion journals. It represents a more sophisticated understanding of international policy and is less susceptible to sudden change. It does not follow, however, that media opinion has decisive influence on the governors of a country. During most of his four administrations, newspapers and news media opposed the policies of President Franklin D. Roosevelt. This did not deter him from pursuing policies which he believed a majority of Americans would support. President Harry S. Truman also was vehemently and continually criticized in the press of the United States. There is no evidence, however, that this opposition led him to change his policies. In a number of subsequent cases both Presidents Lyndon Johnson and Richard Nixon followed policies which the press, television, and the newspapers largely condemned.

The nongovernmental elite sector includes members of the social, economic, and legislative elite: business and labor organizations, congressional groups, interest groups with well-defined attitudes toward international questions. The nongovernmental elite sector, in short, includes all the politically relevant strata which are not in the immediate coterie of the decision makers themselves. Their influence upon policy and goal formation is much greater than either of the two other sectors. In recent years particularly, the influence of legislative bodies on foreign policy formation has probably increased.

The governmental elite sector refers to that group of government officials, not actual authors of high policy, that serves as advisors, implementers of policy, and sounding boards for the policy notions of the governing group. The governmental elite sector offers views and opinions that influence government policy more directly than those of other sectors. This sector is likely to share the fundamental policy orientations adopted by the governors themselves. Changes in policy are most likely to be foreshadowed by changes in the opinion of this governmental elite.

INFORMATIONAL AND ATTITUDINAL FLOW

There are three types of informational flow. First, the attitudes of all four sectors are continuously transmitted upward to the governors: do they support the policies currently in effect? Second, information specifically released by the regime to engender support for its policies proceeds downward. Third, all sectors and the governors themselves have sources of information grounded in reality. They judge not only in terms of what they are told, but what their appreciation of reality is. Credibility gaps develop when the information proceeding downward from the regime in power is contradicted by the apprehensions of reality held by the sectors. Credibility gaps will also affect support. If the information sectors receive from the regime is contradicted by information from reality, they may lessen their support for the regime. This in turn may cause a regime to modify its policies and to refresh its own sources of information from reality. These processes are depicted in Figures 9-1 through 9-4.

This model of the informational process applies broadly to both democratic and to authoritarian and totalitarian states. In the first case, but even more critically in the last two cases, it may become very important to prevent reality information from reaching the various sectors, thereby preventing the development of credibility gaps. If there is no outside information to contradict the information provided by the regime, credibility gaps, diminishing the authority of the regime, cannot emerge. Of course no regime, however powerful, can entirely prevent contact with the outside world. Nor can it obliterate the divergence between its domestic promises and its performance.

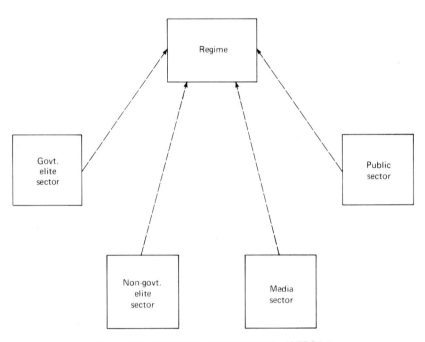

Figure 9-1 FLOW OF ATTITUDINAL SUPPORT

The support rendered to all regimes in all polities is thus limited to some degree. Where organized opposition to the regime is impossible, cynicism and even passive resistance may occur.

It was formerly believed that the internal form of the regime would make a great deal of difference in the type of policy pursued at the external level. Immanuel Kant argued that a republican, as contrasted with a despotic government, would not be likely to go to war. More recently, others have claimed that totalitarian or monistic polities would be more likely to wage war or to risk international instability rather than to give up their basic goals. Democratic or pluralistic polities, on the other hand, were more likely to accept a compromise of their objectives.[1] In 1972, however, these judgments are far from certain. Pluralistic democracies, in particular the United States,

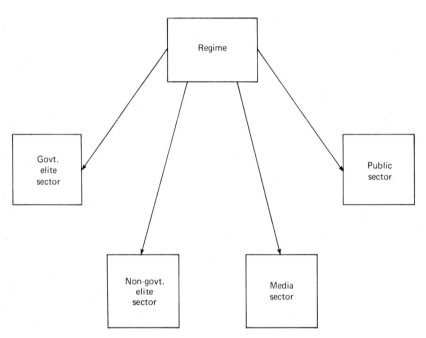

Figure 9-2 FLOW OF REGIME INFORMATION

have often found it harder to compromise their objectives in world politics than totalitarian polities. In the Cuban missile crisis of 1962 it was the totalitarian polity which offered compromise. Yet on Vietnam and other cold war issues, it has been very difficult for the United States to change its policy. The adoption of Vietnamization as an American strategy seems to suggest that the United States would only leave Vietnam if it could win the war through strengthening its Vietnamese allies.

In more analytical terms, as Thomas Schelling has shown,[2] democracies have certain inflexibilities of strategy that are not matched by totalitarian states. If a democratic regime commits itself publicly to a given course of action and rallies popular support to justify its policies, it is very difficult for it to extricate itself from that commitment. Compromise and adjustment,

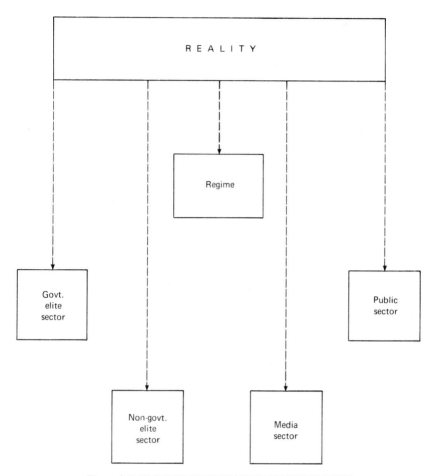

Figure 9-3 FLOW OF INFORMATION FROM REALITY

therefore, may even be more difficult for such polities. Authoritarian states possessed of the ability to reshape internal public opinion, may more easily "rationalize" changes in their courses of action. Democracies, in short, may find it difficult to commit themselves to a position or strategy: once committed, however, change is very difficult. Totalitarians find commitment easy, but withdrawal from the commitment is also easy.

THE DECISIONAL PROCESS

Basic decisions of democratic and authoritarian polities, moreover, are not so different. Even in democratic states, the information possessed by outside

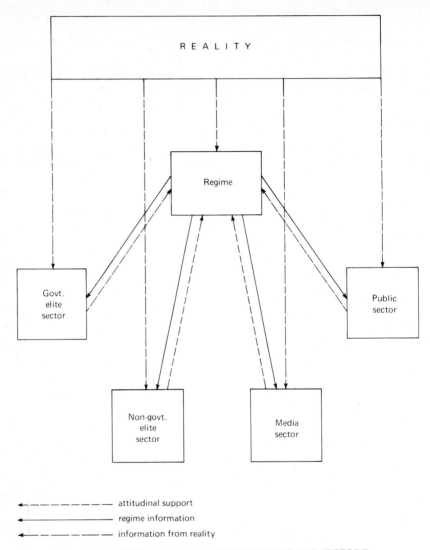

REALITY

Regime

Govt.
elite
sector

Public
sector

Non-govt.
elite
sector

Media
sector

- - - - - - - - attitudinal support
——————— regime information
- - - - - - - - information from reality

Figure 9-4 COMBINED FLOW OF INFORMATION AND SUPPORT

sectors is not sufficient to enable them to judge the likely efficacy of policy. In the choice of fundamental policies, therefore, regimes are likely to operate without great impediment. Only after the implementation of these policies begins to require major commitments of men, resources, and financial support, do sector opinions and attitudes become relevant. The basic process may be depicted as in Figures 9-5 and 9-6. In democratic polities the procedure is as follows: (1) sectors determine basic values for a regime; (2) regimes set objectives, hopefully in accord with the values prescribed; and (3) they also set policies or techniques to realize these objectives. If the policies are relatively costly in terms of their absorption of resources and manpower, the sectors may eventually intervene to interpose a limitation or veto on the use of such policies. This will particularly be the case if the policies and techniques distort the objectives of the regime, and cause those objectives to develop in ways that are out of harmony with the fundamental values prescribed by the sectors. This in turn will cause the regime to set new objectives and new policies which will be in greater harmony with sector values, and which will minimize costs. As a general rule in foreign policy, however, regimes may proceed quite far with a given policy and objective before sector restraints are called into play. Sector limitations or vetoes are called into operation only after policies have egregiously violated basic values of the nations or cost restrictions. Both democratic and totalitarian regimes have a good deal of latitude in setting foreign policy objectives and in determining means of implementation. In democratic states policies are most likely to be changed by conflicts with a basic value structure and assessments of cost; in totalitarian regimes policies are likely to be changed by cost considerations alone. Limitations on policy operate only after a considerable time.

This point reinforces that made in the previous section. Sectors are likely to see credibility gaps between information received from the regime and from reality only after the claims of the former have become exorbitant or the conditions of the latter are particularly patent. In the American case, so

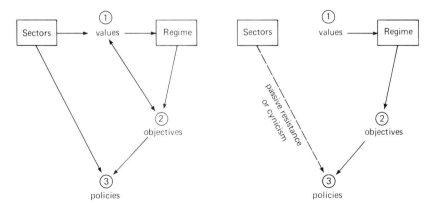

Figure 9-5 DECISIONAL PROCESS IN DEMOCRATIC SOCIETIES

Figure 9-6 DECISIONAL PROCESS IN AUTHORITARIAN SOCIETIES

long as people could believe that the United States government was "winning" in Vietnam, no credibility gap could emerge. It was only after years of optimistic government statements which clashed with the need to pour more and more troops and firepower into Vietnam, both North and South, that sectors were willing to conclude that the governments informational claims were exaggerated and could not be sustained. The values to be gained by pursuing the war were shown to be minimal compared to the costs of fighting it. Hence it was only after some time (at least seven years), that judgments against the United States government's Vietnam policy could be made by the sectors.

Both pluralistic and monistic regimes, in this respect, therefore, have considerable latitude in foreign policy decisions. They do not have unlimited sway, however, even in the initial choice of objectives and policies. Now that states have become nationalized units, the limitations upon foreign policy choice are much greater than they were, for example, in the eighteenth century. What regimes do must be in accord with a sense of loyalty to the national public and advancement of national interests. It is no longer possible for leaders to pursue essentially private goals. The leader of the regime cannot think of creating his own foreign policy; rather he is responsible for the creation of a national foreign policy which serves national interests. Private or pecuniary objectives have to be eschewed. This was not true in the eighteenth century because it was not clear that princes and aristocrats were supposed to be loyal to the nation. They had only to be loyal to themselves.

THE POLITICS OF DEMOCRATIC DECISION MAKING

The record of United States behavior in foreign relations since 1945 reveals some additional factors which influence decisions in democratic states. First, and as we have already noted, regimes can carry on in power and make foreign policy with much less than majority support. From early 1951 until March 1952, less than 30 percent of Americans approved of President Truman's conduct of the office; yet he did not change his policies.[3] Second, the approval expressed of presidential actions is likely to vary with time in office after an election. "The longer the man has been in office, the lower his popularity."[4] Thirdly, presidential popularity will also vary with wars and with major events on the world scene in which the President is seen as the spokesman for all Americans. In the last category would fall major crises, like Cuba or Berlin, major meetings with foreign states, major new departures in foreign policy, and even major defeats (like the Bay of Pigs defeat in 1962). It appears that even unfavorable major events have a positive effect on presidential popularity, President Kennedy having achieved his highest rating after the disastrous CIA-sponsored invasion of Cuba in 1961. Wars, however, are likely to create greater unpopularity, President Truman having suffered greatly on this score.

If these conclusions are capable of being manipulated by Presidents in office, they would suggest an avoidance of large-scale participation in war, together with a fairly frequent participation in major events on the world scene. Crises are tolerable to American public opinion in a way that wars are not.

DECISION MAKING FOR WAR OR CRISIS

A number of crises and wars in modern history illustrate the operation of the decision-making network in contemporary states. In 1914, a crucial move toward war occurred when German Kaiser Wilhelm gave Austria a "blank check" to humiliate Serbia. It is interesting to note that the Kaiser had not always supported his Austrian allies in their quarrels with Serbia. In 1913, for example, he had supported the Austrians when it appeared that the Serbians, in their acquisitions of Turkish territory, were seeking gains beyond those allotted in the Treaty of London. He had not supported the Austrians, however, when Serbian aggrandizement did not impinge upon the Treaty settlement. In 1914 it was by no means certain that Germany would support Austria. The first two German officials whom the Austrians consulted after the assassination of Austrian Archduke Franz Ferdinand recommended a policy of caution and restraint. Not until the German emissary was able to see the Kaiser on July 5, 1914, was the green light signaled for Austrian preparations against Serbia. In this instance the Kaiser seems to have acted not on the basis of any popular consensus or agreement of his immediate coterie, but partly because of his own outrage at the assassination, presumably with Serbian complicity, of a brother member of the family of European royalty. He "personalized" the insult, though he could clearly rationalize his position in terms of German national interests. His advisers, moreover, did not advocate restraint on the part of the Austrians until it was too late. In the Austrian case the basic decision to humiliate Austria was not personalist. All members of the Austrian regime except Count Tisza were for action against Serbia within a few days of the assassination. They awaited only the go-ahead from Berlin.

In contrast, the Japanese decision to attack the United States had great support not only in the regime and its immediate coterie, but also among Japanese outside the government. In the waning days of the crisis, the Japanese leaders were afraid of what might happen if they did *not* take military action: they feared assassinations or a coup from extreme nationalists outside the government. The consensual basis of the Japanese decision was well established.

In the Cuban missile crisis of October 1962, President Kennedy might have rationalized the presence of Russian missiles and avoided the crisis. That is, he might have convinced himself that the presence of these missiles did not enormously affect United States security and that the Russian development of intercontinental ballistic missiles stationed in the U.S.S.R. would soon give the Russians the same strategic strength against the United States that they would gain by stationing missiles in Cuba. Secretary of Defense Robert McNamara even used this argument in his discussions with the President. President Kennedy, however, had to take into account a wider range of factors. He had the problem of the November elections in which his Republican critics were likely to fare well unless he adopted a strong stand on Cuba. He had officially denied the presence of such missiles, and he had warned the Soviets on September 4 not to establish them in Cuba. But the Soviets had done so anyway. More important, perhaps, the Russians had "lied" to the United States about their presence. President Kennedy looked upon this as a personal insult, one which he could not brook. His advisers came around to this view, though Adlai Stevenson and Robert McNamara took more conciliatory stands.

In 1939 British Prime Minister Neville Chamberlain changed the policy of appeasement of Nazi Germany to one of seeking to deter German expansion. This change was the result of the Nazi absorption of Bohemia (a non-German territory) in March 1939. Initially, however, Chamberlain was disposed to rationalize the German aggrandizement. He saw no immediate reason for changing the appeasement policy, and still hoped for a broader Anglo-German accord. It was not until Parliament and influential advisers like Lord Halifax could not stomach the continuation of appeasement that Chamberlain was forced to change, and to give guarantees to Poland and Rumania. German action against Poland, as we know, brought on World War II. In this case, Chamberlain took no personal affront at Hitler's action; he could even explain and partially justify it. It was the change in the consensual basis of his policy that made him alter his stand.

The same factor seems to have been present in President Johnson's *volte-face* of March 1968. Until then, it had been assumed that he would run for office in 1968, and that he might intensify the United States bombing and ground force commitment in Vietnam. Presumably, it was the change of attitude of influential advisers like Clark Clifford and others that helped to produce the shift in policy. After the North Vietnamese Tet offensive, the coterie surrounding Johnson could no longer accept a policy of increasing United States commitment as being likely to bring success. Even an increase of bombing or an invasion of North Vietnam did not hold the key to a successful outcome from the United States point of view.[5] Consensual aspects finally prevailed in reducing and ending (during the Johnson Administration) the bombing of the North.

The conclusions that one may draw from these crisis episodes show that at crucial junctures, what is most important is not the outside attitude of nongovernmental, media, or public sectors, but rather that of the governmental sector itself. When that consensus alters, it is likely to have great impact on foreign policy decision making. The immediate coterie around the regime then may be very influential indeed. In some cases, however, what is most important is not a consensus of advisers and lieutenants, but rather the feeling of personality challenge or humiliation that the leader of the regime himself senses. Nothing in the Kaiser's Germany forced World War I upon him; yet he readily accepted the challenge, when his own feelings of right and wrong were outraged. The United States governmental sector did not mandate a response to the emplacement of missiles in Cuba; rather, it was President Kennedy's own sense of wrongful treatment that led him to take a strong stand against those missiles and to precipitate the only potentially nuclear crisis since World War II.

Further, and somewhat pessimistically, decision making on either a personality or consensual basis does not guarantee rationality. The Japanese attacked the United States because they were not willing to give up their position in China, and because they needed access to the Southeast Asian raw materials to carry on their conquest of the Chinese. Since the United States fleet stood in the way, it was attacked at Pearl Harbor. But the Japanese had no plans for victory over the United States. The best they could anticipate was to win a few stunning victories in 1942 and then hope that the United States would be willing to sign a compromise peace. In one sense the Japanese knew that they would lose, yet they still attacked.

In 1962 it was far from clear that United States strategic or national interests dictated provoking a major world crisis over the presence of strategic missiles in Cuba. The United States, after all, already had such missiles in Turkey and in Italy which presented an analogous threat to the Soviet Union. On October 27, 1962 the world was nearer to nuclear war than at any time since 1945.

In 1914 the conflict which ensued was the most devastating war in world history to that time. If statesmen could have known the full consequences of their actions in July 1914, they presumably would have compromised and avoided the war. Even the winners of World War I were far worse off after the war than they had been at its inception.

Statesmen and regimes, therefore, often make irrational decisions in questions of crisis, war, and peace. Because of the imponderables of the personalist or consensual bases of decision, it is never possible to fully control such irrational acts. Nonetheless, we can search for those types of situations and those variables which may make decisions for war more likely. How can the objectives of nations be tailored and refined so that they are less likely to cause conflict? This is the fundamental question we will be dealing with in the next five chapters.

NOTES

1 See among others: Morton A. Kaplan, *System and Process in International Politics* (New York: Wiley, 1957), chap. 2.

2 See Thomas C. Schelling, *Arms and Influence* (New Haven, Conn.: Yale University Press, 1966), chap. 2

3 See John E. Muller, "Presidential Popularity from Truman to Johnson," *American Political Science Review,* p. 19, March 1970.

4 Ibid., p. 20.

5 See Townsend Hoopes, *The Limits of Intervention* (New York: McKay, 1969), chap. 9; and Roger Hilsman, "Must We Invade the North?" *Foreign Affairs*, vol. 46, no. 3, pp. 425-441, April 1968.

CHAPTER TEN

The Formulation of National Objectives

International systems determine outcomes in the sense that once the size and nature of an international disturbance is known, regulative forces and environmental supply decide whether outcomes will be conflictual or cooperative, whether outcomes can be held within stable and acceptable bounds.

International systems, in other words, are the arena in which the forces of disturbance and regulation contend. Given this contest, systems indicate the direction in which international politics will proceed—toward conflict or toward cooperation.

But systemic determinants depend in part on antecedent factors. National objectives and techniques have to be set before we can know the strength of disruptive and regulative forces. Do they add up to a zero-sum game, a constant-sum game, or a variable-sum game? Once objectives have been chosen, an important part of the game of international politics has already been specified. They are thus an independent determinant of international outcomes. This chapter and the next five focus on the nature of objectives and their evolution over time.

HISTORICAL DEVELOPMENT OF OBJECTIVES

Despite occasional argument to the contrary, the objectives of states are not the same at all times and places. Some states may not have international objectives at all, since they may not recognize that they are engaged in international relations. A state which is, or believes itself to be, perfectly self-sufficient, which is not impinged upon by other states, may not have any distinctively international objectives. It will tend to prefer isolation in order to advance its domestic purposes.

If a state begins to participate in the international economic and trading system, however, it will gradually be drawn into political relationships. These may not come immediately. The American experience, for example, suggests that a state can participate in an international economic system for some period of time without becoming engaged in day-to-day political involvements and commitments. Yet the United States was drawn into two major wars by virtue of trying to protect its trading position: the War of 1812 and World War I. Once economic relations were established with China and Japan, these civilizations were opened to political influence and international contact. Increasingly, as economic relationships take on political significance, it will be impossible for states to try to limit their connections with others to a purely economic dimension. At this point, nations must formulate international objectives. They must decide what forces or features of the international environment they wish to foster and which they wish to restrict.

Even this, however, does not mean that states formulate national objectives en bloc. States have existed much longer than nations. Distinctively national interests and national diplomacy began to appear only with the French Revolution. The nationalization process which the French Revolution represented, moreover, was not fully worked out in the body politic of Europe until the end of the nineteenth century. Prior to that time, the diplomacy of a state at least partially represented the particular interests of those who were immediately in charge of policy. Until then, there was no nationalized and politically participant public to influence or determine objectives. There was no necessity felt, even from a single state's point of view, that German interests, for example, be prior to French interests, or that Russians yield to English interests. Leaders did not define objectives in that fashion. In this sense, Stanhope, Talleyrand, Metternich, Castlereagh, and even Palmerston and Bismarck had much more scope than do statesmen today. They could reach agreements, conclude treaties, exchange favors, and wage wars without worrying overmuch about the dictates of national or popular interest. Their own interests, and their own concerns about good policy for their state, were sufficient to guide them. Until the 1830s and 1840s at the earliest, statesmen did not have to consider public opinion in the policies they pursued, nor would the public have understood their policies.

Two stages in the historic development of objectives can be distinguished. In the eighteenth century at least, it was not clear that foreign ministers or princes were supposed to pursue collective objectives—that is, objectives that represented more than the sum of the personal concerns of those who governed policy. Louis XV would not have conceived of a disembodied

French diplomacy or of abstract French national interests. Rather, he thought of the policy of the French monarch. The diplomacy of France was his own personal diplomacy. His predecessor, Louis XIV, regarded the French state as an incarnation of himself: "L'état, c'est moi!" It was some time, therefore, before the recognition dawned that the policy makers were not simply acting in their own behalf, but in behalf of the collectivity which they governed. As late as the end of the eighteenth century, diplomacy remains tinctured by this personal element.

Even after objectives were seen to bear some relationship to a national collectivity, it was still not clear in which order of priority they would be pursued. Alexander I of Russia probably thought in terms of serving Russian national and legitimist concerns, but he was unclear what specific objectives should be put first. In 1820-1822, he was content to advance the ideological solidarity of Europe against revolution. Thus he did not help the Greek insurgents against Turkey. By 1827, however, he had changed his tune and was seeking Russian territorial expansion at the expense of the Ottoman Empire; he was thus prepared to intervene to help the Greeks. Russian national interests were being served in both cases, but it was not clear which interest was primary. Thus for a considerable period in the nineteenth century, diplomatic virtuosity had its uses. A foreign statesman or prince could be persuaded to change his priorities. He could be convinced to alter his objectives at the behest of international imperatives. As late as 1878, Bismarck, Andrassy, and Gorchakov could exercise their sway by persuasive arts. And they could often succeed.

FUSED AND DIFFUSE OBJECTIVES

These considerations lead us to recognize a distinction between fused and diffuse objectives. Diffuse objectives characterized the old regime. No clear hierarchy had been established among goals. It was not clear which were central and which peripheral interests. Territory could be regarded as the prime goal in one encounter, and prestige or glory in the next. Military strength could take priority in one situation, and allied solidarity take precedence in the following one. Since priorities were not established once and for all, they could be altered by diplomatists. And since rulers were not accountable, or accountable only to a small group, international policy and the priority of objectives could be changed without great difficulty.

This flexibility meant that there was a greater armory of devices to reach accommodation among states than there is today. With the development of fused objectives, and the establishment of fixed hierarchies in the ranking of objectives, diplomatic *savoir-faire* can no longer hold the preeminent role. Today the threat or use of military force plays a much more important part in the international system than it did even a century ago. Since one cannot change national objective priorities by negotiation or diplomatic persuasion, it is difficult to produce accommodation without the invocation of dire military threats. States do not tend to change their objectives voluntarily or through persuasion, but only when they are forced to the wall, and a major military crisis is underway. And even then objectives may not be fundamentally altered, but only postponed. Since the costs may be excessive relative to the gains in a particular crisis, policy makers may have to wait to resume their normal priority of goals. But in the next crisis as well, events will proceed by threat and counter-threat, perhaps involving the use of military force before an accommodation is reached.

The development of fused objectives took considerable time. European nations had finally achieved them by the eve of World War I, but the process had taken more than a century to complete. As long as nationalism, national interests, and patriotism were not the most important values, scope was left to the diplomatist. He did not always have to advance a solidified interest of his own state against that of others or risk being deposed from the seat of power. Provinces could be transferred without a hint of disloyalty or disgrace attaching to those who presided over the cession.

One salient example of this practice was the transfer of Alsace-Lorraine from France to Germany at the close of the Franco-Prussian War in 1871. In the eighteenth century, such a change in frontiers would not have constituted a blot on the national escutcheon of France. France actually lost more important territories in the final settlement at Vienna in 1815 after the Napoleonic Wars. The trouble was that by 1871 all French lands had come to be regarded as part of the French patrie. Alsace-Lorraine could not be alienated without sacrificing the nation itself; according to the nationalist pantheon, they had to be reclaimed. Even after 1871 the issue of *revanche* against Germany was never far from patriotic French minds. It was not an insignificant issue in fomenting the hostility which led to World War I. And yet, the error was essentially that of regarding objectives as diffuse when they had already become fused. One could not give away territory in an age of nationalism. According to patriots, French diplomats should not have agreed to the terms of the peace of Frankfort. They allowed themselves to concede a German demand as if it were peripheral to France, when it was really central. Diplomats themselves were powerless to alter these priorities. They could only reflect and adhere to the priorities laid down by the French people and by the French nation. Diplomacy no longer had untrammeled sway.

The problem, of course, is that the more clearly the priorities of state objectives are worked out, and the more firmly they are set, the more difficult it is to realize the objectives of states without conflict, unless all states attach priority to complementary goals. If there is a limited supply of one international good, and if two states desire it with high priority, they cannot both be satisfied. Only if it is possible to rearrange the objectives of at least one state can conflict be avoided. In the eighteenth century, and to a degree even in the nineteenth century, such rearrangement was possible at the behest of diplomatic pressure. But it is becoming less and less possible today. Thus there is, as a result of fused objectives, less flexibility in the system than there was even a hundred years ago.

The lessening of flexibility is due not only to the rigid hierarchy of objectives, but also to the disappearance of purely personal approaches to statecraft. Notions of treason or disloyalty were unknown in the eighteenth century. There was no nationalized public to whom diplomats were held accountable. Their loyalty was given to the sovereign, and even then it was not unlimited. As a result, a convenient corruption, bribery, and a willingness to serve alternative masters had a much greater role in the old regime than it did in the nineteenth century. If strictly national interests could not always be accommodated, sometimes it was possible to pay a reward to an opposing diplomat and thereby secure agreement.

In addition, there was an international corps of diplomats, soldiers, and statesmen in the eighteenth century who were available and willing to work for different states. Many countries had chancellors, foreign ministers, ambassadors, or military men whose national background was different from that of the state they served. The *ancien régime* was in this, as in other respects, an internationalist age. Loyalties were much more likely to be a function of class than of nation. Again, therefore, there were tools in the hands of diplomats that are simply not available today. Bribery, corruption, and subornation were not only possible, but widely practiced. Indeed, the terms themselves had no pejorative connotation. A diplomat was not less moral for having proposed a monetary settlement of a dispute than if he had firmly stood on national principle and abjured compromise. From the standpoint of war and peace, an age which diminishes the virtues of national patriotism is more likely to bring agreement and accommodation among states than one which does not. It is one of the tragedies of the contemporary period that the establishment of fused national objectives has greatly reduced the importance of diplomacy and raised military arts to a new and perilous importance. Today war has become more of a *prima ratio* than an *ultima ratio.*

CHAPTER ELEVEN

External Determination
of Objectives

We have seen that the objectives of states have become more collective, and that they have been organized in rigid hierarchies as a result of the forces of nationalism unleashed by the French Revolution. We have also seen that within the limits imposed by nationalism, both authoritarian and democratic regimes have some leeway in choosing the initial directions of foreign policy. Popular checks are likely to be administered when credibility gaps become excessive, when policies appear to violate basic values laid down by democratic sectors, and when they impose disproportionate costs. These checks are most likely to be applied after a policy has been in force for a considerable time, after its deficiencies have gradually become apparent.

In general terms, regimes chart initial policy objectives. They then seek popular support for the course of action they have chosen. Once they have received this support, however, it becomes more difficult for them to deviate from established policy (Figure 11-1). In the eighteenth century, in contrast, it was easier to change policy and objectives once they had been formed. Public sector support was lacking for policy. Thus policy could be changed without violating public trust or confidence. Today, if statesmen retreat from objectives which have popular support, they may jeopardize their national positions. There is insufficient flexibility in the international system.

It is therefore true that objectives are now shaped by internal forces to a greater degree than before. In the inception of objectives, regimes have considerable latitude in finding objectives which accord with democratic

Figure 11-1 CONTEMPORARY POLICY FORMATION

values. If they wish to *change* objectives in midstream, however, they can expect to encounter opposition. The rough difference between the eighteenth and late twentieth centuries might be described as follows: eighteenth-century regimes had great discretion in choosing and changing objectives but they were unable to implement objectives with great force and continuity, because they had little popular support; in the third quarter of the twentieth century regimes can choose policy objectives relatively freely, but they cannot change them easily. They can, however, pursue objectives with great persistence and energy because of substantial popular support. In an age of democratic regimes and nationalized publics, objectives are more internally determined than externally determined. Internal determination refers to considerations of maintaining the regime in power domestically. External determination refers to considerations of maintaining the state's position in a field of competing nations internationally. The internal determination of objectives will occupy our attention in the next chapter. In this chapter we shall look at some of the ways in which objectives are still externally determined.

External influences derive from the fact that a nation-state exists in a field of other, at least partially competing, nation-states. It can never ignore the field of competitors, for if it does so, it risks its own survival. Not only does the nation have to find protection against other states directly, it must also secure access to resources for which other states may be competing. It follows that no state can afford to adopt altruistic perspectives. To seek the welfare of all nations may be to sacrifice the individual state interest.

PARTICULARITY

Another way of saying this is to observe that since there are particular, individual state-units, there will be particular interests and perspectives. The interest of any particular unit, even defined in terms of enlightened self-interest will not be identical with the general interests of the collectivity of all states. Jean Jacques Rousseau noted this tension between the individual and the group in his famous parable of the stag and the hare. In the state of nature, a number of men agree to try to catch a stag. If caught, it will provide ample food for all of them. Also, because deer are difficult to apprehend, it is assumed that the stag cannot be captured unless all dedicate their energetic

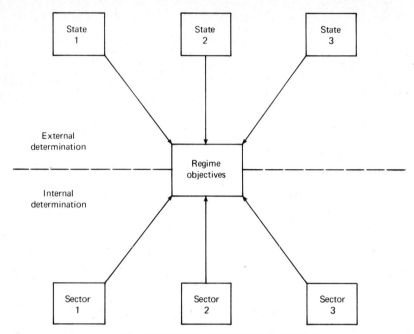

Figure 11-2 DETERMINATION OF OBJECTIVES

efforts to its pursuit. As they are engaged in the hunt, one of them sees a hare and deserts his position to catch it, allowing the stag to escape. A hare is sufficient for one person's needs, but cannot assuage the hunger of others. Essentially, therefore, one has advanced his position at the expense of the group.[1]

It does not follow that the possessor of the hare is irrational, that he is failing to pursue his enlightened self-interest. It would have been irrational from the standpoint of his particular interest to let the hare escape. His fellows would have made the same choice if they had had the opportunity to catch the hare. In international relations where a partial state of nature also obtains, states will generally make the same calculus, pursuing their own advantage as against that of other nations.[2]

In decision theory terms we can see the hare and stag example in the following way:

If U_s is the utility (for one person) of catching the stag

          P_s the probability of catching the stag

          U_h the utility (for one person) of catching the hare

and P_h the probability of catching the hare

then:

$$P_h \times U_h > P_s \times U_s$$

The expectation of catching the hare is clearly higher than that of catching the stag because the probabilities of catching the hare approximate 1.00. In this episode we have another illustration of the cliché that a bird in the hand is worth two in the bush. Suppose, however, that the other hunters may turn on the hare catcher and punish him. Then any advantage in the previous calculation must be modified or reduced by:

$P_p \times U_p$ where P_p is the probability of punishment and U_p is its disutility.

If $P_s \times U_s > P_h \times U_h - (P_p \times U_p)$

then the hare would not be caught.

Our hare catcher would refrain because of the probability and disutility of punishment he would receive. Actually, a good argument can be made that Rousseau picked a bad example to illustrate his principle. In a face-to-face situation of the sort assumed, it is very likely that the other hunters would turn on our hare catcher and at the minimum deprive him of the fruits of his self-interested action. In any other situations in which the probability of punishment for such antisocial behavior were high, there would also be major deterrents to its performance. These will not generally be characteristic in international relations, however. If there was a common rule to the effect that any participant who deserted a mutual cause in order to benefit his own position would not reap the benefit, then few would seek to act against the group. But agreement to such a collective rule would be out of harmony with what we usually mean when we talk of an international system. It would reflect the prior installation of an *integrated social system*, one in which national interests were subordinated to common interests. If all antisocial actions were punishable, one would have something approximating aspects of a domestic social order.

One characteristic of an international system then, is that actions which are not in the general interest may nonetheless be performed when they benefit individual nations. Aside from the hare-stag case, this phenomenon can be seen in many facets of international activity. A nation, for example, can improve its terms of trade for exports and imports by putting on a tariff. It can improve its supply of foreign exchange and its balance of payments by depreciating its currency relative to other currencies, thus making its exports cheaper and its imports more expensive. In each of these two cases, a nation improves its position at the expense of other states, whose trade will now be hurt. Of course, other nations may decide to cancel the benefit through competitive devaluations or tariff wars, but they will not certainly do so.

Devaluations or import surcharges have by no means routinely led to retaliation. The initiating state often ends up in a better position.

What is rational for one state, however, is not rational for the system as a whole. If all states simultaneously depreciated their currencies, no state would benefit. If all put on simultaneous tariffs, the level of international trade would fall precipitously, and all would be worse off. Thus measures that benefit individual states can be chosen only because it is assumed that other states will not respond. Who is to say that a single tariff hike will call forth retaliation? Who can be sure that a single devaluation will cause competitive devaluations by other states? In any given case there is a very good chance that there will be no retaliation. Hence for any given state there is a good rationale for separate action. But for all states to follow such rationales at all times is a recipe for disaster.

Immanuel Kant's "categorical imperative" does not operate among nations.[3] States quite often perform actions, the maxim of which could not be willed to be a universal law. If Kant's moral theories applied, no state would ever engage in action which could not simultaneously and successfully be engaged in by all other states. If it were found that certain categories of action could not be performed successfully by all states together, then one state would not engage in them. Kant's notions may have some limited application within civil society, but they certainly do not restrain states in international relations from acting to further their individual interests as against the general interest.

On a probability basis, since all states will not simultaneously engage in disruptive actions, one nation may do so and derive independent benefit. Given the particular interests and perspectives of nation-states, perfectly rational decision makers can undertake such actions (which if all states performed them would be self-defeating) because they know that not all states will perform them. Indeed, an increase in the background level of cooperation in the system, paradoxically, may actually make separate national action easier, since it may reduce the probability of retaliation. Since World War II there has been a much greater cooperation and reciprocity among the developed economies of Europe and the world. International financial institutions show great understanding of the fiscal problems of debtor countries. Because of this more supportive financial environment, French devaluations, English import surcharges, and American depreciation may be accepted in ways they would not have been in the 1930s when economic nationalism was at its height. Surprisingly, therefore, an intermediate level of cooperation may actually advantage protagonists of the fait accompli. If there is little or no cooperation and states recognize the law of an eye for an eye and a tooth for a tooth, credible deterrence of hostile action may obtain. If a state acts against its peers, it may expect to be punished. If there is a great deal of cooperation, there will be no reliable punishment for antisocial acts, but neither will there be incentives for such behavior. Habituated to cooperation and the observance of social rules, nations will not be willing to act against the framework of international solidarity. Intermediate cooperation may be less satisfactory than either of these polar alternatives, in that there is no deterrence of separatist action, and the nationalist initiator gets what he wants.

The problem of an intermediate level of cooperation has become particularly relevant in recent years. Adolph Hitler was able to make great gains in such a framework because other nations were willing to bend over backwards to advantage the German position. Other states were more concerned to preserve the apparently peaceful international system than to retaliate against German expansion.

Since World War II the strategic environment has offered a measure of deterrence to aggressive initiatives in political-military areas. In economic realms states have been more cooperative, however, the nationalist economic gains have often been made on the structure of underlying agreement and solidarity.

EXTERNALITY

The particularity of state-units is at least partly responsible for national, as distinct from international, action. National perspectives incline states to national action. They put their own interests ahead of collective or general interests. In this sense the external determination of objectives is inimical to cooperation. But if particularity makes for conflict, there are other aspects of the external field in which states interact that moderate nationalist policy. States are aware that they operate in a field with other states. Thus no nation can afford to attend only to domestic imperatives while pursuing policy in the external realm. National decisions are taken on the basis of particular perspectives, but they are not taken with purely internal factors in mind. In the final analysis, a state's activity is dependent upon its survival in the external system. It must make its way and ensure its existence. This need is independent of domestic or internal determinants of policy. Thus the international or external constituency of a state becomes important along with its domestic constituency. A decision-making elite which ignores its domestic constituency in the contemporary period is not likely to retain power. A decision-making elite which totally neglects the impact of the external world may ensure the demise of the nation itself.

Historically, there has been a limited international socialization of nation-states. Indeed, for good or ill, what has happened since World War I has been the extension of an essentially European system of international relations to the entire world. One of the impacts of this extension has been a partial circumscription of the latitude which states possess. Prior to the extension of this system to worldwide limits, states outside Europe could and did deal with one another in a highly irregular manner. There was chronic, but not highly organized, violence. Indeed, one of the standard justifications given for European imperialism was the need to put an end to endemic disputes and conflicts overseas—warring tribes, feuding pashas, conflicting religious, political, or ethnic factions. Local violence was chronic. Standards of external behavior were primitive. Warlordism was prevalent. Kipling was wrong when he characterized overseas peoples as "half devil and half child" but he did understand aspects of the regional social order which permitted untrammeled political behavior. Thus the extension of an essentially European system of international relations probably did restrict the previous behavior of sheikdoms, emirates, tribes, and contending feudalisms. Once states were consolidated and drawn into lawlike relations with one another, it was somewhat more difficult to continue the earlier, unfettered violence. Feuds were difficult to explain or justify at the international level. The support one got externally depended at least in part on the case one could make. As terms like *self-defense, aggression,* and *collective security* came into currency, it was harder to rationalize a stab in the back. Thus a modest regularization and circumscription of the violence previously expressed by unorganized territories has probably occurred with their admission to a general international system.

But just as it was true that the extension of the European system has tended to restrict and modify the objectives of new polities, it is even more true that the extension of the European system has tended to moderate the behavior and objectives of European states. European nations had already made a distinction between states within and states outside the system. Originally, it was a narrow distinction. Europe stopped at the Vistula River, and Russia, a barbarian power, remained outside it.[4] Poland was certainly outside the system, and therefore could be partitioned, whereas no central European actor could have been divided and absorbed. In the nineteenth century, of course, Asia, Africa, and the Middle East were also conceived to be outside the pale of the European system. Hence the behavior, the decorum which one had to observe toward such regions was much less restricted and civilized than one had to follow in Europe. Imperialism of the old variety was distinctly an extra-system phenomenon. As the international system, the League of Nations, and the United Nations opened membership to new states, it restricted the behavior which European states could express toward them. The juridical equality of each state under the League and the UN entailed a respect which had not previously been accorded. The new nations were not tributaries, feudatories, vassal states, or fiefs: all were equal in legal terms. Hence the extension of the international system has probably restricted behavior in both directions. It is an interesting example of partial international socialization—the establishment of international mores for nations to follow.

This does not mean, of course, that aggression or uncivilized, wanton behavior no longer occurs. European states, even in respect of each other, had engaged in serial wars during the seventeenth and eighteenth centuries. The nineteenth and early twentieth centuries saw a ninety-nine year period of general peace in Europe, but even that period of calm was interrupted by five wars between European states between 1854 and 1871. Some wars, like the Franco-Austrian War of 1859 were provoked for trivial, even frivolous, reasons. There were no irreconcilable issues between France and Austria. Louis Napoleon merely needed a war with Austria to consummate the unification of Italy.

On the whole, however, states did not resolve lightly on such campaigns. European sovereigns accorded a basic respect and deference to each other. They did not humiliate one another. In the eighteenth century, wars were often fought, but they changed little. They were limited encounters which did not affect the social or domestic orders of European states. In the nineteenth century, wars were a much more serious matter, but they were not frequent. Wars in Europe were not fought to "civilize" a recalcitrant, they were disputes among gentlemen. Outside of Europe, however, behavior was much more untrammeled. Primitive races were considered inferior. They were backward in technology and manners. They deserved to be conquered and reformed. The British, French, Germans, Dutch, Belgians, and Portuguese ran roughshod over their new denizens. They treated them as inferior peoples and were not hesitant to use force and repression.

After 1945, however, when the erstwhile colonial territories began to win their independence, the trappings of sovereignty and international legal recognition made European or Western intervention harder to justify or to engage in. Members of the United Nations could not be as easily attacked as those outside it. In this connection it is perhaps interesting to note that the contemporary war in Indochina would have occasioned less comment and opposition if it had been carried out at the end of the nineteenth century. Today, legal concepts like *aggression*, *territorial integrity*, and *nonintervention* are applied because one is now dealing with internationally recognized state-units. Further, as difficult and as agonizing as the war in Indochina has been, it would surely have been fought with fewer limitations if it had been part of nineteenth-century imperialism. Neither side would have recognized any restraints in its conduct of the war. Public opinion in imperialist countries would not have offered resistance to the war because it could be rationalized in terms of "uplifting" backward civilizations. Of course, it would be absurd to claim that the extension of the international system has decisively hampered the waging of such wars: they have been and are being waged. But the limitations and the guilt attending such wars are surely far greater now than they were seventy years ago.

SECURITY

The previous section showed that external influences force a state to recognize that it exists in a field of partly competing national units. In some respects this heightens individual nationalistic perspectives and objectives; in others, it limits and restricts national desires and goals. Inevitably, the existence of an external world forces states minimally to consider their own security and survival. A nation operating in a field with others must safeguard its own position in a context in which the danger of conflict is not negligible.

Historically, the concern to protect a nation's security from attack has increased greatly since the French Revolution and the Napoleonic Wars. During the old regime, there was no challenge to the existence of a member of the European system. Regimes were not subverted from within or without. National capitals were not occupied. Armies waged limited, even ritualistic, wars of maneuver and position. Civil populations were not involved in war, and princes and aristocracies ceded provinces rather than accept a major defeat. Since personal and not national loyalties held states together, diplomatic or military encounters were never carried to extreme lengths. Under these circumstances, it was clear that a state's security would not be easily undermined. Wars or conflicts would not proceed far enough, either in length or in intensity, to undermine it.

The French Revolution changed all this. States began to rely on the patriotism of their subjects to sustain the regime in war. They could make exactions of the citizenry, who could be forced to serve in conscript armies or to lend economic substance to support the government's wars. People fighting for their fatherland endured more sacrifices than the subjects of prince or aristocracy. With the extension of a popular role in government, moreover, people came to believe that it was *their* government. They therefore became identified with its successes and failures. They would no longer brook their government's humiliation in diplomatic or military struggles with a foreign adversary. Compromises among governments became harder to arrange.

Security became endangered. Now capitals could be occupied. Conquered regimes could be revolutionized by a foreign invader. Mass slaughter in military combat became a real possibility. The economic fibres of national strength were tied to the war effort. Once victorious, a nation-in-arms would demand punishment of a foe. After Napoleon's defeat, France was greatly reduced in size and her internal institutions reformed at the behest of foreign victors. During the Napoleonic struggles Prussia and Austria were so badly humiliated that it appeared they might not recover. War now held all the potentialities of revolution. A state could be revolutionized by domestic strife, but, as Napoleon's conquests of the German states showed, it could also be revolutionized from without. And where Napoleon's armies moved, he installed French institutions and French liberal reforms. He extended the revolution by military might.

A nation, therefore, could no longer be sure of maintaining its external territorial integrity, nor of protecting the political character of its internal regime. A state might be eliminated, or its government revolutionized. If this were true, a nation might not have enough strength to maintain its own position. While in the eighteenth century the protection of security had been a modest task, after 1800 it loomed as a much larger problem. One had now to cope with a much wider variety of possible threats. Desperate expedients might have to be resorted to.

At least three means have been found for coping with recognized deficiencies in security. The first is to reduce national involvements and commitments so that existing resources will suffice to meet those demands that remain. This is a difficult business, for it may threaten the existence of a state, depending upon the responses of other nations. A nation can try to regain security by partly opting out of the game of international politics. It may adopt an isolationist stance. It may reduce its commitments. The success of these techniques, however, depends ultimately on the willingness of other states to permit a reduction in involvement. It was easy for the United States to remain isolated so long as it was not a preponderant factor in international political and economic affairs. Once it became the greatest power in the world, however, other states did not leave it alone. A nation like Belgium, Switzerland, or Sweden may find security through neutrality if it is not likely to be the object of some other power's designs. In 1914, however, Belgium found that she could not remain aloof from the conflict between Germany and France and was forced to abandon her neutrality. Turkey tried to play a neutral role in World War II and afterward found she had to align herself with Western European nations. In other words, if a state tries to play a more inactive role in defense of its own security, it runs the risk of being attacked or of becoming a helpless pawn in the pattern of international rivalry.

This does not mean, of course, that a reduction in the involvement of large numbers of states would not be beneficial to the system, limiting international conflict. But states may have to make certain sacrifices of their preexisting security boundaries if this goal is to be achieved. Nations may have to decide not to be interested or involved in the affairs of certain other states or continents. If they can maintain this attitude, changes in the position of these realms should not bother them.

A second, more threatening tactic is to reduce the demands of security by eliminating the enemies which create them. Just before the outbreak of World War I, several nations became convinced that they could not ultimately sustain the burdens and challenges which other nations forced upon them. They were therefore ready to go to war to eliminate major antagonists, hoping thereby to reduce once and for all the demands on their security position. If one believes that one will lose in the long run unless one makes war, one may be tempted to wage it. In the June 1967 war, Israel could not tolerate the maintenance of Egyptian troops in the Sinai peninsula and felt obliged to attack to protect her security. If she had waited, the Egyptian air force as well as the Arab armies might have been able to get in the first blow. Since Israeli plans depended upon air superiority, Tel Aviv could not risk postponing an attack on Egyptian planes and airfields. In 1941 Japan decided she had to eliminate the United States role in the western Pacific if she were to have access to the necessary raw materials with which to carry on her campaign in China. She attacked Pearl Harbor, believing that initial defeats might cause the United States to sue for peace. Her attack was irrational in one sense at least, in that she had no plans which could guarantee victory over the United States. If the war went beyond 1943, she knew that she would lose. Yet the Japanese saw themselves as losing in the long run anyway, and believed their only hope lay in eliminating the United States position in Asia. In World War I Austria felt that she could not live indefinitely with the political challenge of a nationalist, Slavic state (Serbia) on her southern frontiers. She was resolved to end that menace at any cost. This in turn brought the Russians into the war in defense of Serbia, the Germans in defense of Austria, the French in defense of Russia, and finally the British in defense of France and Belgium.

A third means for coping with security deficiencies is to acquire new resources, internal or external. Generally speaking, this is the least hazardous method of bringing about an equilibrium between demands for and supplies of security. Two general techniques of increasing resources are to seek aid from other powers through alliances or alignments, or to aim at a long-term increase in economic or technological capacity which will compensate for an existing deficiency. Which of these two techniques will be chosen depends in part on the nature of present threats. If security must be increased in the very short run in order to ward off an immediate challenge, economic and technological development is not likely to provide the answer. Allies will be needed right away. If, on the other hand, the threat to security is in the future, and if economic and technological prospects for a breakthrough in rates of development or in new military systems are good, nations may decide to seek equilibrium in this fashion.

Both of these tactics have been used in the past. During the old regime nations often had allies, but allies were not crucial for the maintenance of essential security. In the Seven Years' War Prussia, with minimal help from England, stood alone and finally emerged unscathed in a military struggle with Austria, France, and Russia. In the eighteenth century, however, states were not in a position to carry warfare to an extreme. Powers could neither be devastated nor revolutionized.

After the Napoleonic Wars, however, both changes could occur, and nations began to see the need for allies. The Quadruple Alliance of Britain, Russia, Austria, and Prussia was one of the main results of these wars. A half-century later, states were so unsure of their security that they were willing to conclude long-term alliances in peacetime. The Dual Alliance of Germany and Austria-Hungary emerged in 1879. This was followed by the Triple Alliance of Austria-Hungary, Germany, and Italy in 1882, and the Franco-Russian Alliance of 1894. As a result of the Anglo-French Entente of 1904 and the Anglo-Russian Entente of 1907 England joined the Franco-

Russian combination and European international relations were divided into two blocs: Triple Alliance and Triple Entente. During the last quarter of the nineteenth century, states were aware of their need for security and sought to make it up through alliances with friendly powers.

The recourse to alliances as a means of gaining security is perhaps even more characteristic today. Only a few of the greatest powers can maintain their security entirely by their own efforts, if indeed they can do so at all. For others, allies have been a typical recourse. When the international system was essentially confined to Europe, there was little hierarchy in the ranking of powers. The five great powers were about equal. But as the system extended, it admitted states who were far stronger—the United States and the Soviet Union—and those that were far weaker—the less developed countries of Asia, Africa, the Middle East, and Latin America. Lacking technical military skills, many of these latter nations have found security through diplomacy, through the establishment of de jure or de facto alignments with stronger powers. Some nations have formally joined alliances. Others have sought friendly relations with all sides, so as to be sure that if military help were needed it could be provided multilaterally. These states have required even greater diplomatic skill to maintain their positions of accord with both Communist and Western nations.

Alliances, however, are only one means of increasing resources to meet security demands. In recent years resort to new military technologies has been made by states to substitute for or to supplement alliance guarantees. This is particularly true where the threats to a nation's security are conceived as long-range in character. Alliances have the disadvantage of imposing political restrictions. They may cause difficulties in domestic politics. They limit a state's independence. Today states whose security concerns are long term have begun to turn to the development of nuclear technology and nuclear weapons as a means of gaining security resources. If alliance arrangements decline in solidarity and cohesion, nuclear weapons are a likely alternative.

Oddly enough, the impact of the increased need for security in international relations has been to heighten both cooperation and conflict. Alliances have become more characteristic as security needs have become precautionary. Preemptive war and arms races, however, have also been more frequent. States appear to be more ready to attack, but also more ready to cooperate than they were before.

CONCLUSION

The influence of external factors on the determination of national objectives is ambivalent. On the one hand, a state maneuvering in a field of many will be bound to set its objectives on the basis of particularistic perspectives. When its interests and those of the group conflict, it will pursue its own goals. On the other hand, a state which is attending to the outside world will moderate its objectives in comparison to a nation which sets its international policies and goals solely on the basis of internal imperatives. Total focusing upon external imperatives will emphasize external security and survival. Total focusing upon internal imperatives will emphasize the internal survival of the regime. The first goal is likely to be less disruptive on the world scene than the second.

There has probably been a modest international socialization of nations in the past two hundred years as the European system has been extended to worldwide limits. This does not mean that rapacious and belligerent actions no longer occur. It probably does mean that the distinction, previously made, between civilized and barbarian nations is no longer found. Further, it seems likely that present wars would be even more vicious and unlimited had it not been for the inclusion of new states in the formal international system.

One of the greatest quandaries concerns the externally determined objective of security. If security is sought through war, it brings ultimate insecurity. If security is sought through alliances (particularly if alliances are not crosscutting), it may divide the world into blocs, and this in turn creates insecurity. We have already seen that in a world in which nations have large numbers of alliance commitments, there is likely to be conflict; involvements are likely to be too high for the general peace. Here we see individual and general welfare in conflict: a given nation may improve its own security position through alliances, but if all states did so (unless a single world alliance were formed), international conflict would be likely to increase. The search for alternative means of gaining security (through development of economic and technological resources) appears to be preferable. Yet, even here, if all states develop nuclear weapons, it is scarcely to be imagined that conflict will decrease. Unless the world can find new means of coping with the problem of deficient security, war and tension are likely to become more chronic.

NOTES

1 See Jean Jacques Rousseau, *Discourse on the Origins of Inequality among Men,* trans. Roger D. Masters (New York: St. Martin's, 1964), p. 145.
2 See K. Waltz, *Man, the State and War* (New York: Columbia University Press, 1959), chap. 6.
3 See Kant's essay, "Eternal Peace," appendix in Carl J. Friedrich, *Inevitable Peace* (Cambridge, Mass.: Harvard University Press, 1948).
4 See Hajo Holborn, *The Political Collapse of Europe,* (New York: Knopf, 1951), chap. 1.

CHAPTER TWELVE

Internal Determination of Objectives

In the preceding chapter we saw how external determinants influence national objectives and perspectives. Inevitably states think first about their own interests, only secondarily, or not at all, about what is desirable for the entire international system. States exist in a field of other states. Minimally, they must assure their own survival against attack. This protection has become more difficult since the eighteenth century because new methods have been found to undermine security. In certain respects there are greater limitations upon state action now than there were previously because of the extension of an essentially European international system to the rest of the world. Where formerly many territories had no such standing, all states now enjoy legal status under international law. On the other hand, more states are insecure today than were insecure two centuries ago. Coincident with the new techniques of undermining security has come the need for greater resources to protect it. Some of the ways of overcoming the problem of deficient security have been disruptive, both domestically and internationally.

It remains true, however, that regimes which attend particularly to their international security position are at least cognizant of what is happening in the outside world. They choose policy on the basis of whether it assists or detracts from their position in international relations. They presumably take into account the likely international reaction to their policies. They are at all times concerned to protect their state interest in the external field, and they may even be willing to subordinate domestic considerations to the well-being of the state in foreign affairs. Regimes which emphasize external determination of objectives are likely to put the imperatives of the international system ahead even of the need to cultivate support in domestic affairs. This can be done if the domestic public imposes no limits on foreign policy goals or techniques, as for example was the case in the eighteenth century. It can also be done if the leadership, through manipulation of the information it passes to the domestic sectors, manages to build support for any policy it chooses to adopt. In some less developed countries the charismatic leadership of a Nehru, Nasser, or Nkrumah has permitted the leader of the national revolution to change his course in foreign policy with bewildering rapidity. In other cases as well, largely external determination of objectives has occurred. The West German people under Chancellor Konrad Adenauer bowed to the necessity of subordinating German policy to the overriding needs of Western unity and resistance to the Soviet Union.[1] For years East European puppet states were so completely dependent on the goodwill of the Soviet Union for economic and technological assistance that they had to bend to Soviet pressures in foreign policy, almost without concern for domestic opinion.

Merely to cite these examples, however, is to indicate that many or even most regimes do not pay exclusive attention to external factors in setting their objectives. They have to take into account the internal demands of their populations as well. Under conditions of complete internal determination, moreover, regimes will tend to neglect events in the international system. Objectives are formulated in response to domestic needs and demands, almost without regard to what is going on in the external world. When objectives are internally determined, they may force a regime to adopt different policies and stances in international affairs from those which would be mandated by external concerns alone.

DOMESTIC LIMITATIONS

The first point to be made is that international objectives which are set or influenced by internal considerations are likely to be more rigid, less flexible, and more definitely prescribed than those stimulated by external factors. One would expect a measure of internal determination to exist in typical democratic societies, where popular opinion is very important. Domestic impulsions surely have been very important in the record of American diplomacy. In the early days of this country they tended to favor isolation and to rule out contamination by European influences. Much later, in the late 1940s and 1950s popular anti-Communism made it impossible for any regime in power to compromise with China or Russia. Those who appeared to advocate doing so were accused of having perpetrated "twenty years of treason." In the 1970s it will be very difficult for any Presidential regime,

Republican or Democratic, to commit the United States to participation in future conflicts of the Vietnamese type, or even to involvements that might lead to such conflicts. In the 1930s, the U.S. Congress, through a succession of Neutrality Acts, made it very difficult for President Roosevelt to undo the American tradition of isolation. Only after the United States itself was attacked, was this sentiment finally laid to rest.

In the case of other democratic polities, the record is similar. Popular sympathy for the Greek revolutionaries made it impossible for the British government to support Turkey in its effort to put down the rebellion in 1827. The British "khaki election" at the end of World War I tied Lloyd George's hands and made him insist on a punitive peace against Germany in 1919. In many other instances, popular opinion has interposed a mandate or a veto on a course of action in foreign affairs.

Democratic societies, however, are not pure cases of internal determination of objectives. Despite concerns for internal welfare and stability, democratic regimes do not neglect external affairs. Democratic leaders have a considerable latitude in initiating policy and a considerable role in moulding popular opinion to support it. The checks on democratic foreign policy tend to emerge when failures on the international level become manifest; then the electorate will demand a change. Short of this, democratic elites can chart foreign policy with relative freedom. In doing so, they can try to take into account the external determinants of policy.

A purer case of internal determination emerges when a regime, beset by opponents or afraid of revolution, resorts to almost any expedient to prevent a fall from power. Elites which have only a precarious hold on popular sentiment may try desperate expedients to reinsure their domestic position. Examples can be found in a wide range of political contexts—conservative, liberal, and authoritarian—where a regime is losing popular favor and needs to regain it. In these circumstances, international objectives and policies will be charted solely in terms of their domestic impact. As we shall see in the next section, such regimes are a very disruptive factor on the world scene.

INTERNAL IMPULSIONS TOWARD
EXTERNAL INTERVENTION

There is of course no one-to-one relationship between internal and external instability, and various studies have given contradictory evidence on this score.[2] Nevertheless, where insecure regimes exist, there is often external conflict. The French revolutionaries in 1792 sought to extend their revolution to other areas of Europe in order to consolidate it at home. If they had not attempted to do so, they might have lost power in France. But this was not exclusively a liberal tactic. The conservatives in Prussia and Austria after the revolutions of 1848 saw that they could not resist liberal reform unless they found other means of gaining popular support. They sought to win adherents by supporting German national unification. But the difficulty was that Prussian and Austrian conservatives had different conceptions of the ideal German union. Austrians wanted a large Germany in which they would be the predominant state by virtue of the inclusion of their non-German territories. Prussia wanted a small Germany with Austria and her non-German territories excluded. The issues at stake were vital since it appeared that whichever group lost would also lose its domestic position. In the end, as a result of the Austro-Prussian and Franco-Prussian Wars, Prussia triumphed. Germany was united without Austria, and the Austrian Germans were only able to reinsure their position by conceding equality within the empire to the Hungarians. The Dual Monarchy of Austria-Hungary was born in 1867. The lesson, however, was clear. The conservatives, facing a deficiency of popular support, decided to seek nationalist expansion and grandeur to refurbish their tarnished public image. In large measure they succeeded. Domestic opinion was pleased by national unification, and the Prussian conservatives won a new lease on life.

The same tactic was used by ruling elites in other countries. By the third quarter of the nineteenth century, liberals in power in France and England were facing new demands from radical working-class movements, both for an extension of the franchise and for social and economic reform. In Germany, Austria, and Russia, ruling conservatives had not offered liberal reforms and were confronted as well with demands for social legislation and a much greater participation in government. Both groups of nations found that imperialism was a means of submerging social discontent. They were so successful that liberals and even socialists willingly supported imperialistic policies.

The imperialist phenomenon of 1880 to 1914, however, was quite different from the period of liberal revolution of 1789 to 1814. The French revolutionists and Napoleon had sought to reinsure their positions *after* they had gained power. The conservatives and liberals of the late nineteenth century used imperialism and nationalism to *prevent* reform or revolution.

After World War I the domestic insecurity issue arose once again, though in altered guise. The war had discredited the upper middle class, the class that inevitably had profited from its economic activities during the war. The businessman could adjust prices to keep pace with the rampant wartime inflation. But the wage earner could not raise his wages, and those who lived on fixed incomes saw their savings wiped away. The tragedy of post-World War I Europe was that political liberalism had its first real chance and failed. Conservative regimes were destroyed in Germany, Austria, Russia, and else-where in Europe. World War I appeared to have completed the process begun with the French Revolution and the revolutions of 1848. If all states were now to be liberal and national, there would be no ideological conflicts. State frontiers would finally be drawn on national lines. If so, what would nations fight about? Regimes would be popularly supported; they would not have to seek external aggrandizement to win popular approval.

At the very time when the international conditions were favorable to liberal democracy, however, the domestic conditions for its success were being undermined. The upper middle class was no longer trusted in many European countries. Thus even in France and England there were strikes, political tensions, and labor troubles. In Germany and Italy, the middle class failed to keep its hand on power. But the discrediting of the middle class did not lead to socialism; rather, it strengthened unappeased nationalist grievances. The lower middle classes did not want to be proletarianized, to go socialist or communist. They wanted to avenge German defeat in World War I and erase the infamous "stab in the back." The German defeat, the Italian failure at the peace conference—these made nationalism an even more potent threat. It was a fusion of the lower middle class with rampant nationalism and a working-class acceptance of national socialism that brought fascism to power in Italy and Germany. Mussolini and Hitler took control. Once again, however, there was no overt revolutionary violence that preceded international crisis. Nationalist expansionism in Germany and Italy submerged domestic discontent without revolution. Populations supported the dictators in their attempts to undo the Versailles settlement.

Thus it appears that in some instances there is a link between domestic and international instability. In some cases, domestic revolutionary instability may lead to external expansion to legitimize an internal regime. In other cases, the threat of revolution may cause an ultranationalist regime to hide internal division in a welter of patriotism, racism, and external aggression. In either case, however, domestic demands are reduced or suppressed by concentration upon an external foe. Hence, there is in revolutionary or prerevolutionary periods a very important internal determination of objectives. National elites, worried about their domestic position, may be more influenced by the internal balance of forces than by the international constellation of power. They may sometimes choose policies on domestic grounds that they would not pick if they had to think only about the survival and prosperity of the state in international terms.

DISJUNCTIONS BETWEEN INTERNAL AND EXTERNAL INSECURITY

While internal and external instability have often been associated, there is no uniform pattern. The Russian Revolution of 1917, for example, certainly did not initiate a period of international war akin to that unleashed by the French Revolution, even though it did prompt allied intervention in Russia itself. The revolutions of 1830 had no counterparts in international conflict.

Since World War II the world has been witness to a series of nationalist revolutions; many of these have *not* caused external strife. There is even some warrant for the view that when a state is totally paralyzed by domestic dissension, it can scarcely indulge in the luxury of foreign adventure. It must first place stress on knitting together the sinews of domestic strength.

How then, does one know whether or when domestic insecurity will burgeon into international instability? There are at least two polar cases where domestic instability does *not* lead to international conflict. The first occurs when revolutionary change is so profound and all-encompassing that regimes are too weak to engage in foreign adventure, however much they might like to do so for domestic considerations. In the case of the Russian Revolution, society had virtually been brought to its knees economically. It had lost all inner cohesion. After three years of war and social chaos, Russia could not continue to fight in World War I. She was simply not strong enough to use national expansion as a means of gaining social solidarity. Indeed, the Russian economy had suffered so grievously that only a respite from war could permit minimum social consensus to continue. Thus the very challenge of war and revolution was so decisive that expansion was impossible.

The Russian case, therefore, was quite unlike the French Revolutionary experience. In the French case, the Revolution did not impinge upon the basic constituents of French social strength. The Revolution, after a period of initial chaos, actually made France stronger. It did not reflect a prior collapse of the French economy but rather sought a redistribution of its product. Since the domestic challenge posed by the Revolution in France was less severe, it did not require major exertions to regain economic strength and cohesion. Thus after 1793 the French revolutionaries could intervene in other states without worrying about economic weakness at home.

The second case where domestic instability does not lead to international conflict occurs when revolutions are not profound at all, when little change results from them. The revolutions of 1830 were important, but they did not lead to any forceful revisions of the international status quo. Domestic insecurity was not great enough after the revolutions to demand a policy of external expansion. In this respect the 1830 revolutions were unlike the much more thoroughgoing revolutionary upheavals of 1848.

Similarly, typical "revolutions" in Latin America are not worthy of the name. Rather, they are usually a kind of political musical chairs in which elites from the same class exchange positions. Politics is not revolutionized; only the people who conduct it are changed.[3] Thus the less profound internal conflicts may not produce external hostilities.

To this point we have talked about situations in which a single regime is in power. It seeks either to support its revolutionary position or to prevent revolution from occurring. A third case emerges where there are two or more regimes in a single territory. Under conditions of civil war internal strife continues and localist nationalisms flourish. There may be no clear victor.

Domestic antagonists may then seek help from outside. There is no spillover of the revolution into international affairs; rather, international affairs spill into the domestic orbit of the country concerned. This is not a healthy phenomenon, for such conflicts, though they do not involve domestic attacks on the external world, form a kind of vortex into which outside powers are drawn, magnifying their antagonisms. In 1935-1937 the Spanish Civil War between General Franco and the Loyalist Republican regime brought German, Italian, and Russian participation. In Laos and Cambodia in the 1960s and early 1970s outside powers moved into a power vacuum in which feuding domestic factions could not gain the upper hand. It appears that this outside involvement will determine the outcome as it did in the case of the Spanish Civil War.

Vietnam, on the other hand, is not apparently such a case. Initially many believed that the Vietnamese participants were weak and the issue would be decided by outside intervention, by the stakes and resources committed by outside powers: Russia and China on the one side, and the United States on the other. But it appears that outside involvement is less potent than the strength of the domestic forces. Domestic strengths and weaknesses of the participants appear likely to decide the ultimate issue. The Vietnamese revolution may be like the Russian or French Revolutions: it may not be capable of being limitlessly reshaped by outside intervention, regardless of what great powers may have believed.

We have mentioned cases of revolution which have not led to war. There are also cases of the converse. War does not always lead to revolution; nor is there always domestic instability where there is international instability. Though Hitler's ideas had been shaped in a period of great domestic uncertainty and instability in Germany, his own rule was quite a stable one. He was a popular German leader. There was no necessity for embarking upon a career of conquest in Europe to maintain his domestic control. Merely overturning the Versailles settlement and winning a few prestige triumphs would have been enough. Hitler achieved the peak of domestic support with the union with Austria in 1938. There was no internal necessity for pressing further. He does not appear to have planned world war in the short run. He let his timetable, and to some degree even his own ambitions, be influenced by the actions of other European powers. He was responder as well as initiator.[4]

Aggression has often emerged from a context of reasonable domestic stability. The Indian seizure of Goa and the Chinese take-over of Tibet do not seem to have been connected with internal instability in either country. It is difficult to convince oneself that internal insecurity in Britain and France prompted the Suez invasion of 1956. Rather than salving a prior discontent, the Suez war tended to create divisions that had not previously existed. In 1740 Frederick the Great took Silesia from Austria, but not because of public pressure or internal insecurity. Israel invaded Egypt in June 1967 to ward off preemptive attack, not because of instability in Israeli internal politics.

It appears, therefore, that states fight for other reasons than internal pressure or insecurity. And internal instability, such as that manifested in some new states since World War II, does not always lead to foreign adventure. Yet historically, one of the means for coping with heightened domestic demands has been to seek to discharge them in the international environment. Regimes which are challenged domestically may opt for this position. If they do, they may reduce domestic demands only to find that they have imperiled the international position of their nation.

INTERNAL DETERMINATION AND CONTACT BALANCES

From the standpoint of maintaining peace, the chief disadvantage of the internal determination of objectives is that the outside world is relatively neglected in the calculations of such states. In this sense internal determination relates to the problems of contact and interdependence raised in Chapter Eight. If national objectives are set largely or preponderantly on the basis of internal impulses, there will tend to be a low balance of net contact with other states. Decision makers will not take into account, or not take into account sufficiently, the legitimate interests of other states. At an extreme, they may not even consider what the response of the system will be to their actions. Many, but not all, destabilizing actions in world politics have been taken for domestic reasons. Hitler tended to overlook or to slight probable system responses to his aggressive moves. Austria in 1914 made its decision for war largely on the basis of domestic imperatives, neglecting the possible responses of other powers in the system. Indeed, one of the fundamental reasons for tension in the international system is the formulation of objectives and policies on a purely domestic basis.

National elites in power operate in two arenas: domestic and external. They must stay in power domestically, but they must also protect their position internationally. To serve one purpose completely is often to slight the other. Except where international and internal mandates are completely complementary, choices have to be made that force an elite to advantage one realm at the expense of another.

NOTES

1 See Wolfram Hanrieder, *West German Foreign Policy, 1949-1963* (Stanford: Stanford University Press, 1967).

2 Rudolph Rummel found in 1963 that foreign conflict behavior was generally unrelated to domestic conflict behavior. Raymond Tanter concluded in 1966 that there was a small relationship between the domestic conflict behavior of one period and the foreign conflict behavior of the period following. Frank Denton found in 1969 that there was a strong relationship between domestic and international instability, assuming various time lags. Jonathan Wilkenfeld concluded in 1968 that

there was a definite relationship in terms of time lags between domestic and foreign conflict behavior if one controlled for type of polity. See R. Rummel, "Dimensions of Conflict Behavior within and between Nations," *General Systems*, 1963; Raymond Tanter, "Dimensions of Conflict Behavior within and between Nations," *Journal of Conflict Resolution*, March, 1966; Frank Denton, *Factors in International System Violence* (The RAND Corporation P-4216, October 1969); Jonathan Wilkenfeld, "Domestic and Foreign Conflict Behavior of Nations," *Journal of Peace Research*, no. 1, 1968.

3 One of the few recent exceptions to this proposition has been the Castro Revolution in Cuba.

4 For an amplification of this view see A.J.P. Taylor, *The Origins of the Second World War* (London: H. Hamilton, 1961).

CHAPTER THIRTEEN

Internal and External Determinants of Objectives

In the past two chapters we have discussed internal and external determinants of international objectives. In this chapter we shall try to put the two factors together and to consider some of the ways in which they may interact.

RECIPROCAL REINFORCEMENT

Under some circumstances, if rulers comply with internal demands and pursue goals that are internally set, a state's position in foreign affairs will be enhanced. Greater internal cohesion and support for the regime will often improve a nation's bargaining position in foreign affairs. Similarly, and reciprocally, if a nation's international position improves, this will frequently raise the level of domestic satisfaction with the regime. Under these conditions there is a positive relationship between internal political resources and external political resources (Figure 13-1). In Figure 13-1 if internal political resources increase from A to B, external resources increase from C to D, as shown by line LP. The solution of a regime's international problem is also the solution of its domestic problem.

Many examples of this type of situation exist. The strong domestic support which the Israeli government enjoys certainly enhances Israel's position in international affairs. Israel's successes in foreign policy in turn redound to the credit of its governmental regime. Prime Minister Indira Gandhi of India received an overwhelming electoral endorsement in 1971;

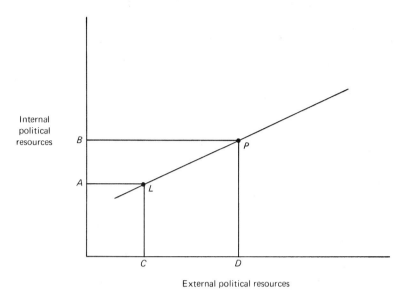

Figure 13-1 RELATIONSHIP BETWEEN INTERNAL AND EXTERNAL POLITICAL
RESOURCES: RECIPROCAL 'REINFORCEMENT

this considerably strengthened India's position in international negotiations.
And India's success in the war with Pakistan over Bangladesh in the latter part
of 1971 produced even more domestic support for Mrs. Gandhi.

Clearly, however, this result does not always occur. Sometimes the
attempt to improve an elite's domestic position may actually considerably
worsen its international position. A regime which seeks to rally domestic
support by staging a foreign war may end up losing the war or creating other
international security problems for itself. Conversely, a regime which devotes
all its attention to the solution of external problems may neglect domestic
issues. The United States in recent years has been preoccupied with international issues, such as Vietnam. The government's concern to win the
Vietnam war detracted greatly from its standing in domestic politics. In the
waning days of the Fourth Republic in France, the government's attempt to
maintain the French position in Algeria by force and terror finally alienated
many Frenchmen in France. Thus under some circumstances the attempt to
gain additional international resources may detract from domestic resources.
Equally, the attempt to gain additional domestic resources may hurt a state's
international position.

RECIPROCAL TRADE-OFFS

Under these conditions there is likely to be some trade-off between maximizing the internal and the international positions. Since resources are likely

to be limited, regimes may not be able to get as much support as they would like in both realms. Choices among relative balances, then, would have to be made. Under conditions of reciprocal trade-off, internal and external resources might have the relationship to one another that is shown in Figure 13-2. Under conditions of reciprocal trade-off a regime can maximize internal resources at A (with zero external resources), or it can maximize external resources at C (with zero internal resources). Alternatively and more likely it can seek a combination of the two, perhaps at L. Line ALC is curved because it is assumed that capacities are inefficient when they are devoted solely to the production of one set of resources. They are relatively more efficient when both internal and external resources are being produced. The regime will be most likely to choose a position like L in preference to either A or C. At L the regime provides for a certain quantity of both internal and external political resources.

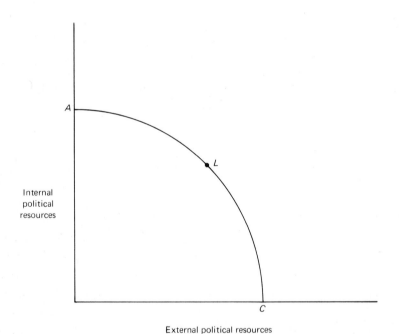

Figure 13-2 RELATIONSHIP BETWEEN INTERNAL AND EXTERNAL POLITICAL
RESOURCES: RECIPROCAL TRADE-OFFS

Point L will be satisfactory so long as the regime is able to meet minimum internal and external requirements for staying in power. Ideally, regimes would like to be in a position where their resources more than suffice to cover international and domestic requirements (demands). In these circumstances.

Total demand   is less than   external resources plus
(for external and   internal resources
internal resources)

or

$$TD < ER + IR$$

Under less favorable circumstances, however, the total demand for resources may exceed available supplies. Thus

$$TD > ER + IR$$

Let us imagine three types of total demand curves: one which is greater than the sum of resources; one which is less than the sum of resources; and one which is exactly equal to the sum of resources. These might be depicted as shown by Figure 13-3. The regime faces no problem if the need for internal and external resources is either TD_1 or TD_2. In the first case it has surplus resources; in the second its resources are precisely equal to total demands. A problem emerges only if the regime must have more resources than it commands, if demand is at TD_3. If it faces such a disequilibrium, it may seek to bring about equality between demands and resources in a number of ways.

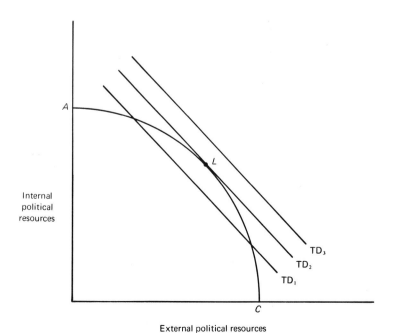

Figure 13-3 DEMAND AND SUPPLY OF RESOURCES

1. The regime may seek equality through a development of the resources production curve. If the demands which it faces are long-run in character, a development of internal economic and technological resources may make possible the eventual attainment of equilibrium between demand and resources. Imagine that a regime is facing domestic welfare demands which it cannot meet consistent with its international position. An increase in the domestic gross national product could, over time, finance a greater welfare bill and still maintain existing international commitments. Alternatively, imagine that the regime faces a major deficiency in its international security position—it may be surrounded by hostile and powerful enemies.

Israel has certainly confronted such problems. One of the ways of coping with them has been an emphasis upon new, technologically sophisticated weapons. For other powers and perhaps for Israel as well, nuclear weapons have often been seen as offering deterrence of enemies at a lower cost and thereby permitting the stretching of resources to cover both internal security and domestic welfare needs. The spread of nuclear weapons to additional powers, most recently to China, and afterward perhaps to Israel, India, and Japan is testimony to the reality of this situation. Powers have also frequently thought of greater economic strength as a means to security. The stronger and larger the economy, the greater the mobilization base for war. During most of the nineteenth century the United States did not raise large armies or navies; rather, she was content to develop her economy to the point where she could compete with and even surpass European states. Since the challenges which the United States faced were only long-term in character, economic development could be used to build her resource position. In Figure 13-4 the resources transformation curve has increased, making possible the attainment of equilibrium at P. Now the regime can meet demands at both international and domestic levels.

2. A second tactic which the regime can use is to try to reduce the total demand curve by an attack on its international antagonists. This alternative may be adopted if demands are particularly pressing and short-range in character. If its preemptive blow succeeds, the regime will have managed to reduce its demands for security. If it fails, its security needs will become even more acute.

Japan made these calculations in deciding to attack the United States in 1941. If she had succeeded, her resources would then have been more adequate to cope with international and domestic demands. She failed to understand, however, that the United States would not sign a compromise peace, and she knew that the United States could defeat her in the long run. In 1967 Israel made somewhat similar plans. By defeating the Egyptian army in the Sinai peninsula, Israel could reduce the threat to her international security position. She succeeded. In Figure 13-5 demand is reduced from TD_3 to TD_4 by defeating an international opponent. This makes possible the reestablishment of equilibrium of demand and resources at point L. The same

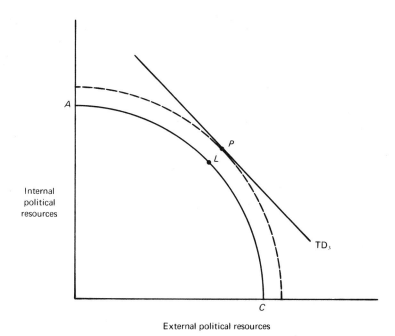

Figure 13-4 AN INCREASE OF RESOURCES TO MEET HIGHER DEMAND

result would occur if the cause of excessive demand for resources were to stem from internal sources. Suppose domestic grievances were very acute. A regime could not satisfy these grievances and still fend off its international opponent. Thus a defeat of the opponent would permit a transfer of resources to the domestic sphere, once again establishing equality between demand and resources.

3. A third means of producing equilibrium might be to coerce internal opponents. If external demand cannot be reduced, perhaps internal demand can be lessened. This might be accomplished in a number of ways. Emperor Louis Napoleon of France mobilized the peasantry to political activity and accorded it the vote. He knew that it would bolster his regime on the right, helping to counterbalance liberal and radical elements. A regime might also directly employ coercion against its internal foes. In Eastern Europe Communist regimes have often purged and imprisoned opposition elements. Hitler and Stalin both used terror and the secret police to intimidate their opponents. In Indonesia an unparalleled blood bath followed the attempted coup of September 1965, in which Communists and other enemies of the military regime were slaughtered. In each of these cases, after the defeat of internal enemies, more attention and resources were devoted to the external security problem.

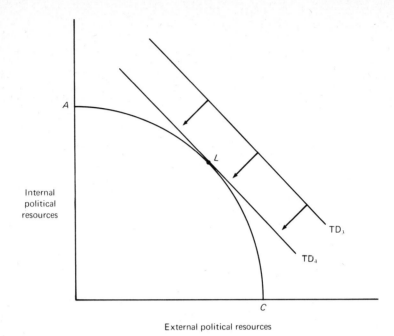

Internal
political
resources

External political resources

Figure 13-5 REDUCTION OF DEMAND THROUGH WAR

4. A fourth method of reestablishing equality between demand and resources is to seek cooperative arrangements. Internationally, a regime facing a deficit in its security requirements may try to enlist allies to help bear the burden. Imagine two countries with the resources transformation curve, each of which seeks to meet demands for external and internal security which are beyond its individual capacities. If they pool their resources (and if technological and geographic factors permit), they may be able to provide a joint defense of their two territories which requires fewer resources than each would need to maintain defense in isolation.

The United States and Canada have seen the logic of this situation. The defense of both Canada and the United States against nuclear attack constitutes a single problem. If the United States is to be defended, Canadian cooperation is required for radar stations and surface-to-air missiles. These in turn help protect Canada. The two nations can reduce costs and maximize their joint defense position by cooperating. In Figure 13-6 alliance between two powers reduces demand from TD_3 to TD_4. Thus, for each state, pre-existing resources are now adequate to bear the reduced burden. These conditions may be approximated where, for example, defense depends largely

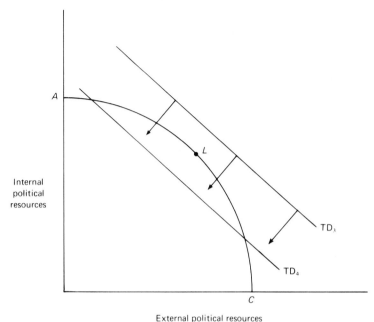

Internal
political
resources

External political resources

Figure 13-6 REDUCTION OF DEMAND THROUGH ALLIANCE

upon long-range strategic weapons of large-scale destructiveness. Under these conditions, the mutual security of two powers may be bought for little more than the expense of providing security for one.[1]

There are some disadvantages to relying upon allies to reduce demands for international security. Decisional latitude in foreign policy is reduced. Those regimes which have decided *not* to ally with others have on the whole concluded that the benefits they might derive from alliance in security terms would be less than the costs they would incur as a result of restraints on their international independence.

A somewhat similar phenomenon can be observed in the procurement of domestic security. A regime can strive to ignore its internal opponents and to pursue its domestic and foreign policies without constraint. The support which it musters domestically, however, may not be great enough to maintain its position. The regime may therefore decide to co-opt opponents or to broaden its coalition of supporters by adding some elements previously in opposition. This may solve its immediate problem of domestic support, but the result may be that the regime's ability to decide and act independently will be gravely limited. In a number of countries, the attempt to placate the opposition either by sharing power or by according a de facto veto to opposition groups results in a policy of immobility in both domestic and foreign affairs.

INTERNAL AND EXTERNAL RESOURCES: A CURVILINEAR RELATIONSHIP?

Enough has been said to indicate that the relationship between external and internal resources is complex. Under certain conditions, it appears that if a regime improves its position domestically, it will also benefit internationally. If it enhances its position in international relations, it may also increase its domestic support. Historically, many regimes have assumed that there is such a *direct* relationship between internal and external power: the increase of one seemed to be related to the increase of the other. During certain historical periods, regimes often acted as if the two could be maximized simultaneously. The French, the Germans, the British, and the Americans have occasionally assumed that greater domestic cohesion could be brought by a policy of national expansion; they have also hoped that national expansion would not risk the nation's long-term security in international affairs. Sometimes they were right, but not always.

Conversely, it has often been assumed that as a regime's external position improved, its domestic support would also increase. In the early years of the cold war, various United States administrations concentrated upon the external foe, believing that their domestic positions would not suffer, and that they might even be benefited.

Past history also makes clear, however, that international and domestic political resources sometimes bear an *inverse* relationship to each other. The attempt to gain greater support domestically may lead to neglect of the external sphere and to international insecurity. The attempt to solve external problems may create domestic discontent.

A combined assessment would stress the role of time factors. When a state begins to play a new role in international politics, or when a new regime comes to power domestically, there is usually a period in which domestic and international gains go together. A new regime may have more domestic capital, or it may be capable of using new means of increasing its domestic support. When new international policies are inaugurated, the other nations in the international system may adopt a wait-and-see attitude until the new policies have become fully clear. Only after the initial stages of success on all fronts are the hard choices likely to be faced. If a state has been following an expansionist foreign policy over a period of years, it may eventually encounter domestic costs. If a state has been pursuing purely internal aims without reference to the external system, it may eventually incur international costs. At this point the relationship between external and internal political resources will be seen as curvilinear. In Figure 13-7 the curve indicating the relationship between internal and external resources is depicted over time. At first, an improvement in one resource also involves an improvement in the other; later, however, any further expansion of one resource will have the impact of diminishing the other. The phase of direct relationship is followed by a phase of inverse relationship. Eventually, therefore, a point is reached where a regime must decide which value it wishes to maximize: its internal or its external position. Economic and technological resources may be inadequate to obtain minimum levels of internal and external security. This is the point at which regimes may be tempted to take risks: they may risk their domestic position and concentrate upon foreign affairs; or they may risk their international position and concentrate upon domestic affairs.

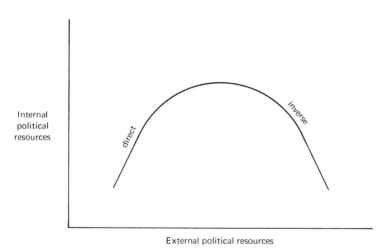

Figure 13-7 CURVILINEAR RELATIONSHIP OF EXTERNAL AND INTERNAL RESOURCES

One problem in contemporary politics is that internal security may seem more critical and yet be more difficult to attain than external security. Given new difficulties in ruling states in an age of differential affluence and political mobilization, regimes may be tempted to slight their external requirements. When this happens, there will be an increasing internal determination of international objectives. International affairs thereby becomes a by-product of domestic decision making. Whatever the outcome in internal politics, external politics is likely to be less carefully managed than before.

NOTES

1 See Mancur Olson and R. Zeckhauser, "An Economic Theory of Alliances," in B. Russett, *Economic Theories of International Politics* (Chicago: Markham, 1968), pp. 25-45. Olson and Zechkauser, using a *public goods* approach, argue that a smaller nation will tend to depend upon the defense expenditures of a larger state and can reliably do so since the larger state's demand for security is higher. See also A.L. Burns, "From Balance to Deterrence: A Theoretical Analysis," *World Politics*, July 1957.

CHAPTER FOURTEEN

The Nature of Objectives

In the previous four chapters we examined the factors which may determine objectives and possible interactions between them. Yet it is not sufficient to speak of internal and external influences on the formation of objectives. Because of internal impulsions, a regime may seek to solve its domestic problems through policies in external affairs. But we still do not know what precise objectives will be entertained in external affairs. Will a state aim at territorial conquest? At ideological conversion of nearby nations? At growing prestige? Or will it seek security against attack by potential foes?

TAUTOLOGICAL OBJECTIVES

Historically, many theorists have claimed that states sought power or tried to achieve a balance of power with other nations. The difficulty with asserting that the general or overriding objective of states is the pursuit of power, however, is that *power* is a very ill-defined term. If a very broad definition of power is employed, there is no action in international politics which could not be described as animated by a quest for power. Even such actions as those of President Eduard Beneš in 1938 in offering up large sections of Czech territory and fortifications to Hitler might be seen in power terms. After all, if Beneš had not given up the Sudetenland, he might have been attacked by Germany. States which resign their sovereignty and federate with others, as was the case in the unification of Germany and Italy, would not appear to be seeking the power aggrandizement of their particular unit. Still, it could be argued that they seek the greater power of the collectivity. In 1917 President Woodrow Wilson embarked on war with Germany because of German violation of American neutral rights on the high seas. Wilson clearly believed he was acting at the instigation of lofty principle. But a skeptic might ask if neutral rights for American trade did not contribute greatly to United States power in international politics. America wanted its peaceful commerce to be unhindered, and commerce clearly was a primary element in national power. Thus Wilson's idealism may really have been animated by pragmatic motives.

Using a broad definition of power, we cannot think even of hypothetical cases where nations would not seek power. Even the most apparently altruistic or self-sacrificial acts in international politics can be rationalized as evincing a power quest. Good will, cooperativeness, willingness to sacrifice traditional interests—all these can be explained in power terms. The self-abnegatory state actually seeks to improve its position in the long run by making concessions in the short run. Business corporations utilize this device: they often charge less than the market will bear in the short run, hoping to build up good will and a larger market for the future. One would scarcely suggest that they are not trying to maximize their profits. In international relations, as well, the most self-sacrificial, cooperative, and peaceful behavior can be rationalized as the pursuit of greater power in the long run. The meek, after all, were to inherit the earth.

Now if it is true that one cannot think, even hypothetically, of conditions in which the power theory would be false (presuming a broad definition of the term *power*), then the power theory is "unfalsifiable" and also unscientific.[1] For propositions to be seen as true or false, they must depend upon the contingent conditions of the real world. If they depend solely on definitions and not at all on real events, then they become definitional or tautological. It is as if one started out trying to formulate an empirical proposition about personal relations and ended up with a proposition like: "a brother is a male sibling" or "all nieces have either aunts or uncles." These two propositions are purely logical and definitional: they tell us nothing whatever about the empirical variety of human relationships. If no hypothetical exceptions exist to the notion: "international politics is a struggle for power" or to "all states seek power," then they, too, are rendered into logical formalisms, without empirical content. To say that states seek power in these terms is merely to list the logical attributes of states, not to offer contingent propositions which might be true or false in the real world.

If we are to give an empirical or historical account of the objectives states have held, we must use more narrowly and precisely defined terms. Those that we shall use—material objectives, ideological objectives, and security objectives—are more narrowly defined, at least as we shall employ them. Nor have all states pursued all three objectives at all times. Certain historical periods reflect one or more types of objectives; others evidence different objectives.

MATERIAL OBJECTIVES AND THE EIGHTEENTH CENTURY

The pursuit of material objectives was characteristic of the eighteenth century. By material we mean objectives like territory, prestige, glory, and influence in the international system. With the possible exception of Prussia's situation during the Seven Years' War (1756-1763) no power's security was really in danger. A state could lose territory, prestige, and influence without really endangering its security. Austria lost territory between 1740 and 1763, but her security was at no time placed in jeopardy. She managed to avoid the desperate plight that Frederick II found himself in as a result of territorial plunder during the Seven Years' War. In the vicissitudes of pursuit for overseas glory and empire, France and England improved their positions relative to Spain. In regard to each other, however, they oscillated back and forth. Yet a temporary setback for one was not a vital blow. Conflicts over material objectives were not really fundamental.

In one sense, the fact that eighteenth-century objectives were material was very beneficial.[2] It implied that wars would not be carried to unlimited extremes or fought for unlimited stakes. The consequences of military conflict were mostly tolerable. At the same time, since the impact of conflicts was limited, there was no deterrent to their occurrence. They therefore were not infrequent. When states can afford to pursue material objectives, it suggests that more fundamental issues have already been solved. And one of the cautionary tales of past international history is that states sometimes have resorted to war for insignificant or even trivial causes. When basic security is assured, and when ideology is not a problem, one can indulge one's material appetites. The imperialist phase of both the eighteenth and nineteenth centuries is partly explicable in these terms.

IDEOLOGICAL OBJECTIVES IN THE FIRST HALF OF
THE NINETEENTH CENTURY

If the dominant objective of the eighteenth century was material, then after the French Revolution the governing international concern was ideological. Liberals contended with conservatives, revolutionaries with partisans of the status quo. If the pursuit of material objectives in the eighteenth century had represented a variable-sum game (because shares of the territorial pie had not yet been fully appropriated), the pursuit of ideological objectives in the nineteenth century represented a constant-sum game. Given conflicting ideologies, if the revolutionaries succeeded in achieving their objectives, the *ancien régime* and the conservatives would everywhere be defeated. If the counterrevolution succeeded, the revolution would be expunged. After the French Revolution, regimes thought in terms of defending their own social ideas and practices against onslaught by internal and external enemies. They also sought to extend their political and ideological notions to other states.

The issues of ideological combat were much more serious and fundamental than those involved in material competition. Conflicts in the eighteenth century had been at the peripheries of state frontiers. Minor adjustments would not cause fundamental social or political change. Conflicts after 1789 had to do with the center; as a result of war, the political leadership could or would be changed. Since there was more at stake, ideological conflicts were contended much more desperately and carried to greater lengths.

It did not follow, of course, that ideological issues were the most fundamental. If the ideological and the security objectives were divorced, then a state could change political regimes without suffering an undue setback to its security. Ideology, by and of itself, did not challenge the very existence of states. It did not threaten their national and historic identities. France, Britain, the German states, and Russia—these would surely continue as national entities regardless of ideological orientation.

In the Revolutionary and Napoleonic period up to 1815, however, this point was sometimes obscured by the presence of both ideological and security concerns. The French Revolution not only injected an ideological dimension into foreign politics, it also posed the issue of the security or survival of the state itself. The new methods of leadership in France made possible the harnessing of the power of the entire social unit for purposes of warfare and defense. This meant that French armies would be that much more successful in coping with their continental adversaries. They could carry the war to the point where not just the ideological coloration of a conservative regime, but also the survival and security of conservative states were placed in jeopardy. The ideological objective was conjoined with a security objective. Given this conjunction it was not surprising that the Napoleonic Wars represented the most desperate period of social and international conflict since the Thirty Years' War of the seventeenth century.

It is also interesting to note that after the security issue had been defused and a military balance restored, the ideological issue alone (in the period from 1815 to 1856) did not greatly destabilize European relationships. The only war in this period which could be described as ideological was the Crimean War (1854-1856) which one historian described as a war in which "diplomacy was occasionally interrupted by battles."[3]

SECURITY OBJECTIVES AND THE LATER
NINETEENTH CENTURY

States came to seek security as their overriding objective when the arts of warfare, politics, and technology made possible the complete conquest of a foe in political and military terms. As we have seen, the problem of security was first posed in the Napoleonic Wars. With the total mobilization of a patriotic nation, it became feasible to conquer and occupy an opponent's capital cities, to redraw the map of Europe, creating large states from small ones, and paring large states down to size. The physical entity of the nation, then, was first challenged at the beginning of the nineteenth century.

It arose again after mid-century when military technology began to give primacy to the offensive, to the enveloping movement. From 1856-1871 the period of *Realpolitik* placed the existence of the nation once more in question. It appeared that warfare could be used to reforge new states or to submerge old ones. Warfare could be waged offensively, and one of the protagonists might be definitively defeated.

After 1871 the security issue remained but its force was muted. While it was true that offensive operations were even more likely to be central in a future war, it was also true that the deductions from the experience of the wars of 1866 and 1870-1871 were that wars were tolerable, even for the defeated powers. The Austro-Prussian and Franco-Prussian Wars seemed to convey the lesson that after limited indemnities and occupations, things would be restored to normal. The victors would be relatively generous to the vanquished. Thus threats to one's security were not all-important. The results of the Franco-Prussian War seemed also to show that nationalism had congealed the basic boundaries of Western and Central European states and that a conqueror could no longer transfer provinces at will. Even if a state had been defeated it had to be accorded roughly its own borders after the war. German Chancellor Bismarck's major mistake in international diplomacy was to agree to the demands of the Prussian generals for the seizure of Alsace-Lorraine from France. It was only the example of Alsace-Lorraine which made European regimes of the late nineteenth century fear for their security; otherwise there was little disadvantage to defeat in battle.

After 1871 the ideological issue between conservatives and liberals was no longer contended, which together with the submersion of security as an issue, fostered a return to the material objectives of the eighteenth century. After 1880 imperialism became the dominant issue of European international relations. Until the beginning of the twentieth century it was on the whole a benign issue, in the sense that it did not produce vital conflict between European states. It was only when regimes became insecure domestically and sought to use national expansion overseas as a means of distracting attention from the need for domestic social reform that imperialism became a desperate rather than a derivative urge, taking on ideological and security implications.

SECURITY AND IDEOLOGICAL OBJECTIVES IN THE TWENTIETH CENTURY

World War I totally disabused European populations of the notion that war could be painless and even fruitful. In addition to the cost in lives, its social exactions and depredations were such as to impoverish large sections of the middle and lower classes. Even more importantly perhaps, since World War I was indeed the Great War, its impact upon political leaders was decisive. However ready leaders were to forgive and forget after the wars of 1866 and 1870-1871, they demanded vengeance after 1918. Thus the victors decided to strip the defeated of his nationalist patrimony—to repeat the error of Alsace-Lorraine, but this time on an even more massive scale. This meant even more clearly creating an *irredenta* which would lead to continual recrimination and perhaps to future war. The Versailles Treaty sowed the seeds of World War II. Thus the fairly optimistic deductions about security that had been made in the third quarter of the nineteenth century could not be remade in the twentieth. As a result of World War I a concern for security as an objective became uppermost in the minds of many European leaders. The French enshrined this goal with a holy zeal, and the British, for all of their surface placidity, did not take it less seriously. For the French and the British, security was to be found in alignments or international arrangements—the French opting for the former, the British for the latter. Basically, what they both aimed to do was to defend their existing positions against *revanche*; this meant either hemming Germany in, or gradually sanctioning a relaxation of her obligations by means that would make her the passive servant of international comity. Neither wanted or considered another war.

The Germans, on the other hand, sought security through undoing the results of Versailles, which they considered a dismemberment of the German nation. If the nation were to be reconsolidated, a major change in the status quo would be required, a revision so drastic that it might not be accomplished peacefully. Under Hitler, at least some decision makers came to believe that the way to regain German security was through expansion to reunite Germany against Versailles. Their deductions were in favor of a military blow, and the doctrine of blitzkrieg or lightning war was devised to make it possible. This was a surprising result. One would have anticipated that the result of World War I would be to convince all military planners that the offensive could not be successful, that it would always be stymied by the defense and would involve incredible losses. Thus there should be no advantage to the first strike, the offensive blow. Defense would suffice. This indeed was the lesson absorbed by the French in their construction of the Maginot Line. Before World War II the Germans, however, guided by the theoretical works of the British strategist, Capt. B.H. Liddell Hart, were convinced that armored divisons utilizing the tank as the spearhead could break through even the most stubborn fortification. German Generals Guderian and Manstein were planning offensive blows aimed at the pivot of the Maginot Line at precisely the time that the French were thinking of countering another Schlieffen wheeling movement through the low countries. Thus the Germans put the offense paramount, while the British and French thought only of defense.

This difference in military strategy affected the entire conception of security held on each side. The French were afraid for their security, but they also felt that the German offense could not break through their fortifications. Thus the Germans should not start a war; French preparations should have deterred them. Thus in international diplomacy the French were passive, the Germans active. The Germans were ready to provoke issue, the French would wait. In one sense the result was the worst of both worlds. The French were willing to concede diplomatically because they had faith in their army. They did not realize how insecure they were. The Germans could threaten war (even though they hoped bluff would work) because they had a viable strategy of offense. If the Germans could strike quickly before the French could react, they were confident of victory.

The concentration upon security after 1918 did not exclude ideological objectives. When Hitler attained power in Germany in January 1933, a new ideological strand emerged in world politics. Hitler was not only the most violent nationalist the modern world has known, he was also animated by racist motives He believed that it was the destiny of Germany to rule "lower races" and to incorporate Germans in a thousand-year Reich. It was not surprising that he looked to Eastern Europe and Russia for room to expand: these Eastern peoples were deemed inferior. Thus in Adolph Hitler the chaos of Weimar Germany produced an ideological extremist.

Somewhat surprisingly, the ideological conflict was contended seriously only on one side. While the French and the British did not like Nazism, they were equally afraid of the revolutionary threat of communism. For some in Britain and in France, Hitler's National Socialism seemed a virile and successful alternative to left-wing revolution. Until the eve of war in 1939, many Britons and Frenchmen found the Hitlerian alternative more acceptable than the Russian option. They came to oppose Hitler and German ambitions with real reluctance. Thus the Germans took the lead in both ideological and security issues. In this context the French and the British were willing, until the end, to concede German demands and even to offer concessions.

After World War II, it appeared that a new ideological conflict would henceforth determine world relationships. It also seemed that the issues of military technology would insure the overriding primacy of security considerations. The first was true only briefly, the second has remained true. For a time after 1945 the ideological struggle was fought, but at no time did it have the virulence and force of the Napoleonic and Revolutionary periods. The Soviet Union was an advanced industrial nation; if it had to choose between ideological promotion and national security, it would always choose the latter. Looking back on the post-World War II era, what is surprising is not the depth of ideological combat but its tenuousness. The Soviets and the Chinese were very conservative in advancing their separate versions of Marxist ideology. The United States, in its vision of consolidating a "free world," was perhaps as animated by desires of ideological expansion as the Communists were. Where this vision contradicted United States security interests, as for example in the desired rollback of Soviet power in Eastern Europe, or the "unleashing" of Chiang Kai-shek to launch an attack in mainland China, the ideological preference was invariably subordinated to security considerations.

BEYOND SECURITY?

In 1972 security remains a primary goal. The complicated problems of nuclear weapons and strategy, together with concern over the maintenance of retaliatory capabilities, make it unlikely that these issues will ever decline in significance. They may even become increasingly important. It is also possible, however, that if security is tolerably well maintained, nations will concern themselves with other issues. One of these might be a return to material goals. If nations are secure enough, they may seek to indulge appetites for material or territorial expansion. Since World War II, this has not happened. It is difficult to identify a purely material objective in either American or Soviet policy. A general relaxation of tension, however, might facilitate a return to territorial questions. The Chinese would like to reacquire Taiwan. The Soviets seem to covet the Middle East. If the United States withdraws precipitately from major involvement in many areas of the world, other powers will think in terms of filling up the vacuum created. Weak nations in Asia and elsewhere might offer tempting targets for such expansion.

This view, of course, offers a pessimistic and perhaps relatively unlikely prospect. More hopefully, it is possible that a new set of goals are now in the process of creation. In years past, nations did not focus on welfare as an objective because it did not appear attainable and because other goals were deemed more critical. It is just possible, however, if goals of security and stability are already assured, that states will begin to seek welfare as an international goal. Welfare objectives would imply great emphasis upon expanding international trade, access to markets, and mobility of capital. Competition among states would be reflected in economic progress as much as in military forces. Economic strength and sufficiency would be measures of attainment. If welfare became a salient international goal, its achievement would cause less conflict than current objectives. We have already seen that Western and other developed states tend to progress together. It is in their mutual interests to expand markets in each other's countries. The implications for developing states are less clear, however. They would agree that a more equal distribution of welfare was desirable. There is a question, however, whether an unfettered quest for welfare among the developed states will speed the progress of the less developed. Unless the major developed countries are willing to open their markets to the less developed on preferential terms, the countries of Asia, Africa, the Middle East, and Latin

America will not benefit commensurately. Even with this limitation, however, if welfare were to emerge as a central goal of many countries, conflict in the system would diminish. The economic welfare of one country is more compatible with the economic welfare of another than the security of one is compatible with the security of another. To a greater degree than is true in the field of military security, nations tend to go up and down the economic scale together.

NOTES

1 See Karl Popper, *The Open Society and Its Enemies* (Princeton, N.J.: Princeton University Press, 1963).
2 See Walter L. Dorn, *Competition for Empire, 1740-1763* (New York: Harper, 1940).
3 See A.J.P. Taylor, *The Struggle for Mastery in Europe, 1848-1918* (Oxford: Clarendon Press, 1954), p. 79.

CHAPTER FIFTEEN

Transcending Objectives

THE ONION OF INTERNATIONAL OBJECTIVES

In one sense the three international objectives we have discussed—material, ideological, and security—constitute a hierarchy in importance and centrality. Material objectives are the most peripheral and the least important. A state may exist even though it does not expand territorially or gain new glory and empire. Normally, states do not seek territorial gain in order to assure national survival. If they do so, territory is merely a vehicle of enhanced security, and security is the objective being pursued. In 1940 and 1941 Japan expanded southward into the Pacific and Southeast Asia not because of a love of territorial aggrandizement for its own sake, but because she believed that Southeast Asian raw materials were essential to minimal national security. Russia wanted a buffer in Eastern Europe after World War II to protect her against a revival of German expansionism, but again the reason was concern for security. The material objectives of territory, glory, and prestige become vital only when they are critical to the achievement of some more central aim.

Ideological objectives are more important than material goals. States seek to protect the ideological character of their regimes and to resist external ideological encroachment or subversion. Under most conditions it is deemed more important to protect the ideology of the regime than to gain new territory.

Still more important than ideological objectives, however, is the overriding goal of state security. Under certain circumstances a nation may be willing to change its political ideologies and goals, but it will not wish to be invaded or attacked. The policies of the East European states since World War II illustrate this attitude. Though East European nations are in many instances traditionally anti-Russian and historically hostile to communist notions, they have usually been willing to sacrifice their historical ideological orientations in order to avoid wholesale Russian military intervention. Even during the turbulence of the French Revolution, the great patriot Danton was willing to negotiate with France's enemies when it appeared that France was on the verge of defeat. Yet at the very end of World War II Adolf Hitler did put ideology ahead of German security. He was ready to see the German people liquidated and Germany destroyed rather than compromise the Nazi ideology or sue for peace. At this point, however, other German leaders, reverting to traditional priorities, ceased to obey his instructions.

If objectives are ranked in this order, it becomes possible to think of an onion of international objectives, with an outer layer of material goals, an inner layer of ideological goals, and a core of security. Security is the most fundamental goal, and in most instances will be sought at the expense of other objectives. A nation may be willing to give up its territorial appetites and to reformulate its ideology rather than to risk its national security. In similar fashion the purity of a regime's ideology and the protection of the regime against political transformation tends to take priority over material objectives. If a nation has to choose between maintaining the ideological character of its domestic institutions and expansion abroad, it will be likely to sacrifice the latter.

PEELING THE ONION OF OBJECTIVES

Historically, the onion of objectives has in a sense been peeled. For most of the eighteenth century neither security nor ideology was in jeopardy; thus it was possible for European states to turn to material objectives. The century witnessed an overweening quest for territory, prestige, and empire. As revolutionary forces gathered momentum, however, the old urge for territorial aggrandizement faded, giving way to a much more desperate drive for protection against ideological revolution. Conservative states tried to prevent revolutionary contamination; France, the revolutionary power, had to guard against counterrevolution.

More important, with the French Revolution new military tactics became possible. The revolutionary mobilization of the *levée en masse* made it possible to overwhelm the archaic defenses of traditional monarchies. Soon the conservatives were fighting not only to protect their ideology, but also to stave off military onslaughts that might extinguish their distinct national identities. Napoleon was quite prepared to include parts of Switzerland, the Netherlands, the Rhineland, and Italy in the French Empire. He would have been satisfied with the collapse of Prussia and Austria. The challenge to the conservatives became so fundamental that glory and territory took second place to security and the preservation of conservative political structures against revolutionary infection.

For three-quarters of the nineteenth century security became an overriding concern precisely because it could no longer be taken for granted. In the period from 1848 to 1871 conservative states were even willing to modernize their ideologies, to include nationalist unification and universal suffrage in them, in order to safeguard national security. If the conservative states had not hummed the nationalist strain, they might have been overwhelmed in the liberal unification movements following the revolutions of 1848. Prussia and Austria might have been extinguished as separate identities in a new liberal and national Germany.

By 1871 security had been temporarily regained and along with it an equally temporary ideological stability. Owing to the progress of nationalist sentiment, states could no longer be eliminated by war, and war itself seemed tolerable. The Prussian victories of 1866 and 1870 seemed to indicate that losers did not suffer overmuch. Nor did these wars transform social structure or produce radical transfers of real estate. They were much more moderate in their impact than the revolutionary and Napoleonic wars at the beginning of the century. Statesmen, therefore, had less to concern themselves with; security was no longer the central issue. As a result, for a temporary period, the onion of objectives could be relayered. Once security was not centrally at stake, nations could turn to less fundamental questions like empire and glory. Imperialism, as we know, was the result.

Toward the end of the nineteenth century, however, security emerged once again. The pursuit of external territory which had once been seen as a derivative exercise, was now tied to security itself. Germany, in particular, believed she was encircled by the French and British empires. She could not, she believed, maintain her position as the greatest continental power without access to colonial raw materials and markets. Thus the imperialism of the turn of the century was much more desperate than the lackadaisical and intermittent incursions of the eighties. Territorial acquisition also became tied to ideology. If regimes could discharge social discontent overseas, they could maintain their ideological stance at home. World War I emerged when the dividing up of imperial real estate had brought nations into political and military confrontation. Further expansion would clearly imperil one or more empires. Yet, with the Darwinian emphasis of the age, many statesmen were led to believe that "if a nation could not expand, it could not live." Security therefore could not be attained by all nations simultaneously.

After World War I security emerged as the dominant consideration in one group of states, but not in another. Britain and France knew their security might be in jeopardy and were willing to use a variety of means to reinsure it. The French relied on their army; the British tried appeasement to put to rest the grievances that might lead to war. Nazi Germany, on the other hand, was not insecure militarily. The Nazis did not believe in the likelihood of aggression against them by either Western powers or the Soviet Union. In this sense, the Nazis were in a position to indulge in the luxury of material expansion and prestige triumphs.

Since World War II security, and security plus ideology, have been overriding goals. In the aftermath of the war, security and ideology were the twin goals of the two dominant powers. As the cold war developed, however, the threat of thermonuclear holocaust made security even more important, simultaneously reducing the need for ideological achievement. If an attempt to extend one's ideology to other powers were to make war likely, the risk could not be countenanced. Gradually the United States and the Soviet Union have come to see that the effort to make ideological gains must yield to a more elementary need for security. The Cuban crisis of 1962, as much as any other single episode, probably helped both powers to understand the fundamental need for security. It led them for a time to reject ideological expansion and risky military ventures in world politics. The aftermath of the Cuban missile crisis was quite fruitful in terms of new agreements and a relaxation of tension between the United States and the Soviet Union.

The emergence of China, Japan, and a major unification of Western Europe pose novel issues. While nuclear threats and jockeying for power cannot be ruled out, it seems unlikely that any great power can think in terms of dominating the rest of the world. The security issue is posed once again because of the interaction of nuclear forces, and the dangers of nuclear vulnerability. Tensions, however, have been diffused. It is no longer clear which powers are enemies and which allies. While security is likely to remain of primary importance, it is just possible that other values, like welfare, will come to the fore.

TRANSCENDING OBJECTIVES

If security remains fundamental, another problem is posed. The typical way in which particular objectives are transcended in international politics is to pass on to other ones. But the new objectives may also give rise to conflict. In the first half of the nineteenth century, material objectives were not normally sought. Nations were too concerned about maintaining their own ideologies and safeguarding their basic security to indulge in such appetites. Material objectives had, in a sense, been transcended. By the third quarter of the nineteenth century, however, security and ideology had been temporarily reinsured; it was possible to renew the imperial question and the pursuit of material gain.

Thus a real problem of public policy is posed. It is clearly crucially important that security objectives of states be minimally satisfied and that ideological claims be moderated. But once these issues are disposed of, a nation may press on to other realms of conflict in the area of material objectives. The onion relayers itself. Hence it seems that there is conflict whatever one does. If one solves central problems, derivative ones emerge. But if one fails to cope with central problems, they will remain major sources of hostility and conflict. Since the security problem is so important, particularly in the nuclear age, one certainly wants to provide minimal security to all states. But one does not want to produce so much satisfaction or overconfidence on security questions that a nation is tempted to turn to peripheral ones again.

Material Objectives

The problem of transcending material objectives is not difficult. If challenges to other, more important objectives are posed, material goals will give way. It is questionable if they can be transcended in other ways: giving nations what they want in material terms may not produce satisfaction or quiescence. The more material gains a nation makes, the more it may want to make. Since material territorial resources are limited, the endless pursuit of material gain ultimately fosters conflict with other states.

If material objectives of states could be refocused on other resources, such as economic growth, welfare, and development, the pursuit of material ambitions would be less conflictual. At this stage in history, it is difficult to hold out hope for such a prospect, but it should not be entirely ruled out for the future. In the eighteenth century, when material concerns were at their height, a nation's status and prestige in world politics tended to be measured in terms of territorial gain. Nations which were making such gains, such as Russia, Prussia, England, and France, were going up the scale while Austria remained relatively constant.

In the contemporary period, certain nations have gone up the material scale without gaining any additional territory or external resources. Since World War II, Germany and Japan, by almost any diplomatic estimate, have ascended to near the top of the scale of international influence and status. Their increase in position, however, has had little to do with military factors, and nothing to do with territorial acquisition. Their great rise has been due to what may be a coming currency in world politics: economic progress and stability. By this measure, neither the United States nor the Soviet Union has gained relative to these other two major nations since World War II.

This situation may reflect a considerable change in international relations since the 1930s. Forty years ago policies of economic protectionism and autarchy had made it difficult if not impossible for nations to trade across the high and rigid barriers to international commerce. If they wished to gain access to the markets and raw materials of certain areas, they needed political or even military influence in those realms. It was not surprising in this context that Hitler saw the need for military expansion to gain greater economic resources for Germany. The Japanese had been unable to gain access to the resources they needed in Southeast Asia through trade. When this was clear, they opted for military expansion. In the postwar period, however, the establishment of an approximation to an international free market in trade and commerce, with much lower tariffs and without resort to quotas and exchange controls has meant that nations could achieve access to external raw materials and markets without political influence or military pressure. Actually, Japan and Germany have done much better economically in the postwar period than they did in the prewar era.

It is possible that United States and Soviet stress upon technical military and space achievements may not ultimately be as important in the international system as stress upon those underlying economic processes which make military and technological development possible. If these types of material objectives could be pursued, the problem of international conflict might be ameliorated. Since economic progress for one nation, through expanding international trade, does not prevent similar progress for another, the size of the international pie and world GNP grows each year.[1]

Ideological Objectives

Transcending ideological objectives is more difficult. In the case of ideology it is not always sufficient to recommend attention to more central objectives. To be sure, ideological objectives often give way when central security is challenged. The United States and the U.S.S.R. limited their practical concern with ideological advancement when it appeared that nuclear war might be the result. The question of security took predominance. Even ideological maintenance may be sacrificed when security is at stake. President Eduard Beneš in 1938 allowed the Czech state to be dismembered, and eventually his own regime to be displaced, because he was thinking of the long-term security of the Czechoslovak population. If they had decided to fight Germany in 1938, they would have been defeated at terrible cost. It seemed better to submit peacefully, hoping to reconsolidate Czechoslovakia later on. In 1968, the same result emerged. The Czech regime of Dubcek was purged with the Russian occupation. The Czechs thought it would be better not to fight and to yield in ideology than to jeopardize their longer term security interests.

On some occasions, however, nations look upon the maintenance of their ideology as important to the maintenance of basic security. Ideology then becomes linked to the more fundamental objective of security. The conservatives in the late eighteenth century fought for ideological position as well as security against French attack. On their side, the French strove to protect the Revolution, as well as French security, from attack from without. Thus if one were to recommend a policy of threatening the security of another state in order to overcome its concern with ideological extension and maintenance, one could not safely predict the result. Sometimes a greater concern with security may make ideology more important: the population has to be rallied to protect the state. An actual or threatened attack upon the survival of a nation may heighten its ideological dedication. If the pursuit of ideology conflicted with the achievement of basic security, then ideology would be jettisoned under pressure. But if the two were compatible, external threats or pressures would be likely to bring forth extremely hostile reactions. In this instance, ideological and security goals could be reinforced.

When security and ideology are intertwined, new means must be found to reduce ideological claims. Paradoxically perhaps, one of the most successful means of transcending the demands of ideology has been a measure of fulfillment of ideological goals. Ideological claims tend to be most strident at their inception and to decline as gains are made. This is likely to be true in two senses: first, as a given regime succeeds in modernizing the political and economic structure of its country; second, as one regime succeeds in propagating its ideology to other states.

In regard to the first way, internal ideological achievement makes it imperative not to sacrifice the gains in external war. After mid-nineteenth century, liberal achievements were great enough to require policies of caution in foreign affairs. Conservative states had become more secure. Warfare between the two ideological camps might have ended decades of internal construction. The Soviet Union and the other socialist countries after World Wars I and II did not wish to hazard internal development in a resort to war. All the domestic gains since 1917 would be risked. Warfare emerges from the context of domestic ideological development only when that development is not secure. Then it may be necessary to stage a foreign war to build ideological strength. Where domestic ideological development is proceeding satisfactorily, a war might only jeopardize it.[2]

As successful internal ideological development helps to lessen ideological demands, so external ideological propagation also reduces ideological stridency. In historical terms, there is a fount of revolutionary ideology: France in the nineteenth century, Russia in the twentieth century. As revolutionary ideologies spread to other countries and territories, however, the control by the ideological fount declines. Initially, liberalism was a French doctrine; as it spread, however, liberals in other states declined more and more to act under the French banner. In the twentieth century, the spread of communism has not strengthened the Soviet Union (the revolutionary fount) because each new communist state insists on interpreting the doctrines of Marxism-Leninism in its own way. National communism has been characteristic. Today the schisms within the communist camp are greater even than conflicts between capitalist and communist states. Kenneth Boulding has enunciated the principle of "the further, the weaker" in describing the radii of a nation's military power.[3] In reference to ideology, the principle of "the further, the weaker," however, applies more than it does to military realms. In fact, in the contemporary world, military strength can be applied at great distance with little diminution of the efficacy it possesses at home. Ideological strength cannot, however. For nations to be *completely* agreed on ideological views, geographic contiguity may even be necessary. The further the distance from the source of ideological revolution, the less the agreement on ideological principles and practice. There is therefore a built-in limit on the desirability of ideological propagation and expansion. Success in transmitting the formal ideology to another territory by no means guarantees that the territory will see eye-to-eye with the ideological parent. National differences get in the way. From this standpoint, communist ideology is probably already too widely disseminated for the comfort of the Russian Marxists. The "spread of communist doctrine" has not enabled Russia to control more of the world; the spread of ideology may even have lessened her influence. Success, therefore, may be a dissolvent of ideological enterprise. Its urgency may fade as both internal and external gains are made.

Security Objectives

Perhaps the most important question is how the claims of security can be moderated, consistent with world peace and stability. In the case of material and ideological objectives, one possible solution is to aim at more fundamental objectives. But this device cannot succeed for security goals: no other goals are as fundamental. Thus security is a continuing problem and must constantly be attended to.

Thus one cannot technically speak of *transcending* security as an objective (in a world of particular states), but only of pursuing it in ways which do not bring conflict with other nations. In one sense an overarching concern with security is a good thing. Security does not usually require the acquisition of additional territory; it does not normally demand that other regimes be revolutionized. Rather, it focuses only on the survival of the state mechanism. Security is therefore typically a more minimal objective than either ideological or material aims. In terms of the involvements and commitments discussed in Chapter Eight, regimes pursuing purely security goals would have to make fewer commitments and could have fewer involvements than states pursuing other goals. Security should therefore be easier to achieve and demand less of other states to gain it.

A problem emerges, however, when security is taken to mean something *final* and *absolute*. If nations seek absolute security, they can get it only from the elimination of particularity in the international system: it can come only from world domination.[4] In the contemporary world, however, a final or absolute security cannot be attained. The attempt to get it, moreover, will almost certainly engender conflicts (domestic or external) with which even the strongest state cannot fully cope. Given the mobilization of national populations, it is now more difficult to reshape and reorganize the states of the world than it was a century ago. While national frontiers are now more permeable because of advances in military technology, states as social organizations are even more obdurate to external pressure.[5] Final security is harder to achieve, and a less realistic objective than ever before.

One of the problems of American policy has stemmed from an over-extended concept of security. Because the United States initially viewed international communism as a cohesive force, it seemed necessary to resist the threat of communist incursion wherever it might appear. Reasoning on such false premises, the United States was led to regard the outcome in Indochina as decisive for its own security. One of the great merits of the protest movement in many countries was that it exposed the shoddy logic behind such premises and helped to make clear the more narrowly circumscribed but more important American interests.

In Chapter Seventeen we shall return to the problem of gaining security in current contexts. We should state now, however, that the basic problem is one of accepting tolerable anxiety. A basic security can be attained, but nations should not be so confident of their security positions as to indulge the luxury of more inflated ambitions in world politics.

NOTES

1 This conclusion, however, must be subject to the warnings of ecologists that there may be a finite limit on world energy resources. If so, as that limit is approached, international economics also becomes a constant-sum game. Those nations which appropriate the major sources of energy prevent others from gaining access to similar sources.

2 M. Fainsod, *How Russia is Ruled* (Cambridge, Mass.: Harvard University Press, 1953), chap. 4.

3 See Kenneth Boulding, *Conflict and Defense* (New York: Harper & Row, 1962).

4 See A.L. Burns, "From Balance to Deterrence: A Theoretical Analysis," *World Politics*, July 1957; and Kenneth Waltz, *Man, the State and War* (New York: Columbia University Press, 1959).

5 Cf. John Herz, *International Politics in the Atomic Age* (New York: Columbia University Press, 1958).

PART

4

Techniques

Systems refer to relationships among states and are outside the control of individual states. Objectives refer to goals of particular states. Techniques are the means which states use to realize their goals. If a system is to be stable and peaceful, it either must have adequate regulative capacity or a sufficient supply of environmental resources to gratify national requirements. When states pursue extremely ambitious and ill-defined goals, it will be difficult to produce either regulation or an adequate environmental supply of the resources which states want. Even if states seek more moderate objectives, however, whether there is peace or war—stability or instability—will be a function of the techniques they employ. Some techniques, particularly certain military techniques, are much more likely to lead to conflict than others. In the next three chapters we consider the typical techniques used by nations in the contemporary system: diplomacy, military instruments, and economic transformation.

CHAPTER SIXTEEN

Diplomacy

We have to this point argued that systems and objectives influence or partly determine patterns of war and peace, stability and instability, in international relations. But systems and objectives are not the sole determinants of these outcomes. Techniques also play a critical role. Resort to extremely virulent techniques may be tantamount to war. This is not to say that techniques are the most important factor, but rather that no matter what type of international system or objectives states entertain, war does not occur until states have made recourse to particular techniques. Techniques, then, are the last preventative of war. If objectives and systems are very conflictual but nations compete in ritualistic and symbolic ways, without recourse to force, war does not occur. Different kinds of military technology also greatly influence the type and severity of war. The longbow and the stirrup (which permitted mounted shock combat) were no doubt major innovations in weapons technology in their time, but they did not make possible wholesale destruction of societies.

There is in fact a complex interaction of systems, objectives, and techniques producing international outcomes.[1] Not only do these three factors influence outcomes, but outcomes of one period react back on systems, objectives, and techniques, changing their form and content. This produces new outcomes at a subsequent period. For instance, after a major period of war and instability, nations will seek to fashion new systems, to seek different objectives, and to employ new techniques. These in turn will cause different outcomes.

Thus none of these concepts or categories can be viewed as unifaceted causes of war. If objectives and techniques are held constant and systemic factors allowed to vary, it will appear that systems are the cause of war. If systemic factors are fixed, and objectives and techniques permitted to change, the last two concepts will be seen as the proximate cause of conflict. If we look at international relations dynamically over time, outcomes at one time period may appear to cause outcomes at the following time period. In this special sense war is itself the cause of war. In our analysis up to this point we have tried to show how each factor, taken separately and by itself, can influence war or peace. Peace is most powerfully reinforced, of course, when several factors are pressing toward peaceful outcomes; war is most likely when more than one factor sanctions instability in the system. Our analysis of techniques takes the same point of departure. Regardless of the system and of the objectives pursued, techniques can disrupt peace or they can help to preserve it. It is to an investigation of techniques and their role in stability and instability that we now turn.

At a minimum, techniques embody diplomatic, military, and economic tools. In this chapter we shall look at the evolution of diplomatic techniques. In the next two chapters we shall treat military and economic instruments and their role.

ORIGINS OF DIPLOMACY

The role of emissary or representative goes back into ancient history. Even before states were formed, tribes sent emissaries back and forth to exchange information or to concert views. By the fifteenth century European states had developed the concept of permanent representatives stationed in each other's territory. The function of the diplomat was to obtain information, advise his home government on policy, and to protect the interests of his own countrymen in the host's territory. By 1815 gradations were introduced into the status of foreign missions. Embassies were presided over by ambassadors, legations by ministers. An embassy or legation without ambassador or minister would be run by a chargé d'affaires. These distinctions still exist today.

DIPLOMACY AND BARGAINING

The purpose of diplomacy is to persuade. For this purpose diplomats and negotiators can hint at serious consequences if negotiations are not successful. They have at their disposal, if supported by their home government, all the power resources of their nation. Successful bargaining, however, does not necessarily depend upon great strength. In some cases, the possession of a wide range of options actually hinders one's bargaining position. If two nations are in negotiations, and the range of compromise is uncertain, the nation which ends up compromising least may be the one with the fewest alternatives. Thomas Schelling has offered the following example:

> When one wishes to persuade someone that he would not pay more than $16,000 for a house that is really worth $20,000 to him, what can he do to take advantage of the usually superior credibility of the truth over a false assertion? Answer: make it true. . . . Suppose the buyer could make an irrevocable and enforceable bet with some third party, duly recorded and certified, according to which he would pay for the house no more than $16,000 or forfeit $5,000. The seller has lost; the buyer need simply present the truth. . . . This example demonstrates that if the buyer can accept an irrevocable *commitment* in a way that is unambiguously visible to the seller, he can squeeze the range of indeterminacy down to the point most favorable to him.
>
> The power to constrain an adversary may [therefore] depend on the power to bind oneself; . . . in bargaining weakness is often strength.[2]

For somewhat similar reasons, democratic states often have superior credibility in negotiations with totalitarian or authoritarian nations. Authoritarian regimes may always back down because domestic politics places little constraint upon them. Democratic regimes, however, once publicly committed, find it very difficult to back down. They may be repudiated by the electorate if they do. In the Cuban missile crisis of 1962, President Kennedy's latitude was much smaller than that of the Russians. Having presented his position in a nationwide television broadcast on October 22, 1962, he could not back down. The Russians, however, with greater freedom, were able to.

For this very reason, "negotiation from strength" seldom succeeds. A superior power might possess greater force, if an issue came to war. But the superior state is also likely to have more reasons to like an existing status quo. If he is willing to go to war, he may win. But he may not be willing. An inferior power, then, may be able to extract multiple concessions from a superior rival, simply because he has fewer alternatives and is more dissatisfied than his colleague.

STRATEGIC AND TACTICAL DIPLOMACY

Before embarking on a survey of diplomatic evolutions, it may be helpful to make a distinction between two kinds of diplomacy. The first, *strategic diplomacy*, may be described as diplomatic content in which the goals of statesmen are not fully set and in which there are no rigidly established priorities among objectives. In such circumstances, diplomatic persuasion is likely to be effective. In an age in which these conditions were met, one would expect to find diplomacy employed to effect significant and long-range outcomes; in short, to be employed strategically. The second diplomatic form may be called *tactical diplomacy*. It is characterized by diplomatic contact in which the goals of statesmen are rigidly set and in which priorities among objectives have been articulated and fixed. Under such conditions, diplomacy would be somewhat less effective, since the range of its employment would be circumscribed. One would expect that it would be used to influence less important and shorter-range outcomes.

STRATEGIC DIPLOMACY

In the eighteenth century there was an approximation to strategic diplomacy. Diplomacy not only helped to reshape and restructure the objectives of states, it also helped to set them. Since objectives were not hierarchically related en bloc, diplomatic virtuosity was at a maximum, and it is not surprising that the eighteenth and early nineteenth centuries are the ages of diplomatic *savoir-faire par excellence.* Talleyrand, Castelereagh, Metternich—French, British, and Austrian foreign ministers—these practitioners of diplomatic artistry have not been equalled since. The reasons for this of course have not merely to do with their own outstanding capacities. The age itself gave unlimited scope to practice and refine their skill. Since the objectives of states were unstructured, it was possible to persuade states to change their objectives or to seek new ones. Tentative hierarchies could be reversed. The gift of a gold snuff box could hold equal importance with treaties and territorial real estate. Personal and national rewards were not clearly differentiated.

The diplomacy of France, in this situation, was in part the personal diplomacy of the French monarch. The relations of France with other nations were in part the personal relations of Louis XV with Frederick II, Catherine II, and Maria Theresa. It was not surprising that the conflicts between these sovereigns were moderated by personal affection and loyalty. Personalization in one sense heightens morality. A person may hesitate to engage in very aggressive actions against another person, simply because of his awareness of the common humanity which binds the two. If, however, the enemy can be depersonalized, it is much easier to engage in violent and untrammeled behavior against him. This point can be observed in current domestic conflicts within Western society. When individual students can be dubbed "hippies" or "yippies," official repression and use of violence become easier. When leaders are dubbed "the establishment," and the police "pigs," violent protest activity becomes easier. To this degree, all ideological categories make the use of aggressive or violent tactics a more straightforward recourse. When individuals relate to each other without the intervention of conservative or revolutionary ideological categories, on the other hand, they are likely to be more tolerant and sympathetic of each other's position. Thus the personal quality of diplomacy in the eighteenth and early nineteenth centuries probably limited its excesses.

Immanuel Kant, the German philosopher, advocated republican rather than despotic government so that dynasts would not resolve on war for trivial or personal reasons. He wrote:

> ... in a constitution which is not republican, and under which the subjects are not citizens, a declaration of war is the easiest thing in the world to decide upon, because war does not require of the ruler, who is the proprietor and not a member of the state, the least sacrifice of the pleasures of his table, the chase, his country houses, his court functions, and the like. He may, therefore, resolve on war as a pleasure party for the most trivial reasons, and with perfect indifference leave the justification which decency requires to the diplomatic corps who are ever ready to provide it.[3]

The record of the century after Kant wrote, however, vitiated his claim. Republican governments were not more peaceful than personal-dynastic regimes. Moreover, because republican claims were more ideological and much more nationalistic, they were willing to go to greater lengths to subdue their opponents. Further, while moral obligations may be stated and understood between individual heads of state who are the authors of policy, greater numbers of individuals both inside and outside the government began to have influence on the policy process, causing the notion of "personal responsibility" to fade. Bureaucracy eroded personality. Professor Morgenthau comments:

> Moral rules operate within the consciences of individual men. Government by clearly identifiable men, who can be held personally accountable for their acts, is therefore the precondition for the existence of an effective system of international ethics. Where responsibility for government is widely distributed among a great number of individuals with different conceptions as to what is morally required in international affairs, or with no such conceptions at all, international morality as an effective system of restraints upon international policy becomes impossible.[4]

Kant's vision of a world of peace-abiding republican states, in short, could not be realized. The German philosopher was probably right in believing that warfare, though of a very limited kind, would be more frequent among dynastic, autocratic states than among republican regimes in which popular influences upon government were dominant. But the consequences of war among republican regimes were far more disastrous than those among their aristocratic counterparts. In modern history, mass killing originated with the French Revolutionary and Napoleonic wars and was perpetrated by republican and Bonapartist regimes which were much more responsive to public sentiment than those of the conservative monarchies of the old regime.

When nations were fighting for ideological principle or for their fatherland they were willing to go to much greater lengths to achieve their goals. The decline of the personal diplomacy of monarch and aristocrat, therefore, has probably had a baneful effect upon subsequent international relations.

THE TRANSFORMATION OF STRATEGIC INTO TACTICAL DIPLOMACY

At some point in the early nineteenth century, strategic diplomacy began to evolve into tactical diplomacy. This transformation occurred in two steps. First, the notion of personal responsibility and personal loyalty to the monarch was replaced by loyalty to the nation. As we know, the eighteenth century was an age of bribery and corruption. Since statesmen were not acting on behalf of nationalized peoples, but rather as an agent of the monarch or on their own authority, it was perfectly acceptable for international negotiations to be accompanied by pecuniary reward for their participants. All foreign ministers in the eighteenth century were offered payments for diplomatic services for foreign courts. They often accepted such rewards. Indeed, though from a modern standpoint the acceptance of bribes appears reprehensible, the passage of money and favors between statesmen provided a desirable lubricant for the diplomatic mechanism. If emoluments could be used, statesmen had another technique of accommodating conflicting interests. The had less reason to fight. One hundred years later, however, after patriotism had become well entrenched, diplomats could no longer accept rewards. There were, therefore, fewer means of reconciling or accommodating state interests short of war.

Personal diplomacy, of course, meant that there could be conflict or inconsistency between the personal goals of the prince or monarch and the interests of the state itself. National goals were an odd amalgam of objectives, fuzzy and ill-defined. When diplomats played upon this jumbled collection of aims, they could often change the objectives of chancellors or monarchs. In this way the diplomats of the old regime were able to mitigate conflict and to restrain its excesses.

Tsar Alexander I of Russia had traditional interests in expanding southward against Turkey toward the Straits of the Dardanelles. From one standpoint, anything that weakened Turkey was in accord with traditional Russian interests. When the Greek Revolution began in 1820, therefore, Alexander was initially tempted to support it as a desirable threat to Turkish territorial integrity. But Metternich, the Austrian Chancellor, was able to convince the Tsar that to support the Greek insurgents was to condone revolution and to upset the new structure of international legitimacy which had been erected after the Napoleonic Wars. Such support would loose forces of the kind that had caused the French Revolution and threaten the domestic position of a number of European countries. Alexander listened to these arguments and eventually changed Russian national objectives to conform with them. He gave up the idea of supporting the Greek revolutionists, at least for a time, and was willing to allow the revolutionary fires to burn themselves out on the fringe of Europe. In response to Metternich's argument, Russian objectives were transformed.

As personal objectives of monarchs were increasingly fused with national goals and interests, inconsistencies among objectives were gradually eliminated. At the same time, for an interim at least, national goals were not ranked in any determinate hierarchy. Even after the personal ambitions of the prince had ceased to determine state policy, it was still not clear which national objectives had the highest priority. After the French Revolution, states emerged with a number of goals, but ideological ambitions sometimes conflicted with security goals. While the forces of nationalism were developing rapidly in domestic politics, it was still not clear which objectives would be placed uppermost in the populist pantheon. As late as the third quarter of the nineteenth century, Chancellor Otto von Bismarck of Germany still had a remarkable latitude in adapting state policy to international requirements. He often changed his course, favored one nation and then another. He would bluster and threaten, then pursue a policy of docility and cooperation. The German public exercised little supervision of his actions, because popular will still had little influence upon the German bureaucracy. In this sense, for a period of time at least, the conservative autocracies of Germany, Russia, and Austria had more diplomatic flexibility than their liberal counterparts, England and France.

Thus the second step in the transformation of strategic into tactical diplomacy was not taken until national goals were ranked in some relatively fixed order of superordination and subordination. This occurred when popular influence made itself effective. The classic expression of popular limitations upon governmental diplomacy was the signing of the Versailles Treaty in 1918. Whether the diplomats thought better or not, the French and British publics demanded a peace of vengeance against Germany. The Versailles Treaty, of course, made it all the more difficult to readmit Germany to the comity of nations and to ease the discriminations against her. The consequences of the Treaty were disastrous. If the diplomatic settlement had been much more moderate in 1918, it is possible that Germany would have become a "good citizen" internationally. Domestically, discriminations against Germany could not have been used as an impetus to propel Hitler to power. When states have exceedingly rigid and well-defined goals, there is little play left in the system; there is therefore much less that diplomacy can do to avoid war.

Before the development of tactical diplomacy, there was a greater international agency in domestic foreign policy formulation. The policies of states had to be tentative and preliminary. Leaders had to be ready to restructure their goals at the behest of international influences. Indeed, the great failures of the international system, the periods of greatest instability, seem to have coincided with periods in which diplomacy had little or no influence. Of course, war is by definition the abandonment of peaceful means of adjustment in world politics. But in each of the major periods of world war, diplomacy had weakened as an instrument of international accommodation before the crisis occurred. Once objectives have become totally fixed upon aggrandizement or ideological expansion, diplomacy has spent its force and can no longer control events.

When diplomatic influences were at their height, on the other hand, nations could not proceed very far with aggressive policies. Indeed, as long as reformulation of objectives was a possibility, a state could not proceed very far at all. If effective objectives could be changed through diplomacy, firm commitments to any single set, or to any single ranking, could lead a state to undertake commitments or involvements that would eventually have to be jettisoned. Thus foreign policy had to stay flexible and loose; states could not adopt rigid stances.

In the days before foreign policy objectives took on an en bloc character, important transformations did occur. The British could not decide until the 1840s that they really wanted to maintain Turkey against the incursion of Russia. As late as 1827 they were acting with Russia to force the Turks to make concessions to Greece. The French started out as partisans of Egypt's Mehemet Ali, the Sultan's disobedient vassal, but they dumped him when other states intervened in 1839. No leader could decide whether and to what degree it was in the interests of the powers to permit a unification of the Italian or the German states. Issues were open; bureaucracies remained to be convinced one way or the other. There was a fluidity in international relations, and diplomacy existed to exploit that fluidity to the maximum possible degree.

TACTICAL DIPLOMACY

Certainly by the twentieth century, strategic diplomacy had been wholly transformed into tactical diplomacy. Not only had personal objectives of monarchs and aristocracies been forced to yield to national objectives, but national objectives were now organized in fixed orders of priority. Diplomacy could no longer change objectives or suggest new ones; nor could it propose a reranking of objectives. Diplomacy was limited to trying to find ways in which fixed objectives of states might be accommodated in some degree. As ideology has become important in the past century and a half, the diplomatic changing of national objectives has become even more difficult. When ideology is at the peak of its influence, it puts objectives into logical straitjackets. Thus to change objectives or to pursue them in different order is to commit a theoretical error. The more rationalized and theoretically codified a position, the harder it is to change. Certain ideologies, moreover, specify concrete programs of action by which ideological goals are to be attained. When these are in force, diplomacy can have little role. Negotiation with revolutionary ideological powers is necessary, but it may be a very unrewarding task. The tactical diplomacy of the present era seems to have its greatest influence either before ideological positions have been adopted and rationalized, or after an ideological crest has passed. Successful, more or less satisfied revolutionary powers are much easier to get along with than nations which are at ideological floodtide.

MODERN COMMUNICATIONS AND TACTICAL DIPLOMACY

The tactical character of diplomacy has been reinforced, somewhat surprisingly, by the revolution in communications. In previous eras in which communications were ineffective, slow, and cumbersome, the resident diplomat had a terribly important function to perform. He often had to make important decisions on behalf of his country. He could not consult with a home capital in time; he had to respond. In some ways this was useful. Certainly it reinforced the inconsistency of national objectives, because objectives could be partly reformulated by diplomatic acts of individuals who were not in firm and continuous communication with one another. Stratford Canning, the great British diplomatist, determined British policy in Turkey without great reference to the Foreign Office, and the same latitude was possessed by other diplomatic representatives in mid-nineteenth century.

Another one of the key features of the situation in which communications were rudimentary was that policy tended to be made on the basis of the local features of the situation. Diplomats responded to local imperatives, to the demands of powers in their region. This meant, probably, that countries intervened, both helpfully and unhelpfully, in situations they might never have gotten into if communications had been better. Local representatives, reflecting a local perspective, were perforce required to make the basic decisions. While local representatives could make the decision, however, it was clear that they could not commit the unified power of their government to long-term action. They could stage a military demonstration; they could write a sternly worded note; they might even get the fleet moved from one port to another. But they could not involve their country in war. Whether the demonstration would be developed into battles or campaigns—this would be decided by higher authority. In other words, the inadequacy of diplomatic communications meant that a resident ambassador could get his country to put its toe into warm water. But only the foreign office would decide whether to plunge in to the neck. The discoordination of policy which resulted was usually not serious, for one could always decide to pull one's toe out. The discoordination occurred, moreover, as a result of trying to respond to local imperatives. It was reflective of a high degree of international influence on diplomacy.

Today this is not the case. Diplomats are not diplomatists. They are not even negotiators. By and large they are transmittors of messages between governments. They do not *represent* their governments in the old sense. They merely carry out tasks specifically assigned to them by their superiors at home. They can recommend policy lines to their superiors, but they cannot initiate policy. Today, partly because of the communications revolution, policies are more firmly made at home than ever before.

The information that comes in from embassies overseas is taken into account in the formulation of policy, but it is not the first step in policy formulation. In one sense ambassadors in each country have become—more than they were previously—special pleaders for the country and area in which they serve. They would have the national foreign office be more responsive to the needs and requests of their assigned country and area. If he had the ability to make foreign policy decisions and chart policy, the ambassador would make his home capital respond more fully to the local imperatives of his area. He would force a more international stance. But since all ambassadors take much the same line, the special pleading for one area is cancelled by the special pleading for another. Foreign policy managers at home are left free to do as they wish. Thus, paradoxically, though the communications revolution has made possible a far greater flow of international information to home capitals, it has made possible a more national approach to policy making. National interests and national decisions are promoted much more rigorously than they were previously.

The U.S. Secretary of Defense under presidents Kennedy and Johnson was Robert McNamara. In many ways he was a model public servant—bright, self-effacing, and unremittingly loyal. And yet, the net effect of his approach to United States policy removed it farther than before from international and allied influence. Because nuclear strategy was of such great import, he decided that the President should possess all possible options in a crisis, to respond with whatever level or type of military force that seemed appropriate to the challenge. This meant centralizing even more stringently than before all the options of military and deterrent policy. In possession of all the information and with none of his options foreclosed, the President could then make the national decision. From the perspective of not allowing any of our other officials—military or civilian—to make such decisions, the new centralization was highly desirable. War should not be waged except after decisions by the highest authority. And as the weapons which the United States possessed became more and more destructive, the centralization which McNamara carried out was more necessary in its own terms. But the difficulty was that attempts to work out joint strategies with allies had to go by the board. The centralization of the decision, then, meant that it would be a national decision—the international context was thereby neglected. That is, paradoxically, why some of America's allies have thought of the desirability of putting a foreign-staffed bureau into the State or Defense Department.

Since the process of American decision making will be national, the allies must be represented in our national process of decision making.

These comments should not be understood as an attack on the centralization of American nuclear decision making. But the centralization in this case is typical of the centralization which has occurred in other areas as well. The United States now responds to its own imperatives, and in so doing has reduced the foreign impact upon its decision making. Diplomacy has become internalized. The result has tended to be that the United States intervenes less, becomes involved less than it did before, but that when it does so, as the Vietnamese case demonstrates, it does so intensively, as the result of policies which were wholly worked out within the national framework. Considering the net impact of such policies in the international system, it is possible that the United States might have been better off with bumbling and uncoordinated policies in many areas. It might be better to use the British tactic of "muddling through," acknowledging the false starts and *faux pas* that might be involved. In such an instance, at least America would be more fully responding to international influences upon its policies.

Of course the problems that beset current American foreign policy are not unique to the United States. All foreign offices operate in ways that devalue the role of the local representative. The establishment of hierarchically ordered national objectives also reduces diplomatic scope for many powers. It is therefore not surprising that over the past one hundred years or so nations have come more and more to rely on military tactics involving the threat or use of coercive force in world politics. One of the tragedies of international development has been the gradual decline of diplomatic techniques and the rise of military ones.

DIPLOMACY AND THE FUTURE

Two modestly positive developments may improve this situation in the future. The first is that ideology has declined as a guide to foreign policy formation. As the world moves into a quintipolar or multipolar context ideologies turn out to be very imprecise guides to policy. Who is the enemy? Which powers are friends? The fluidity of multipolarity makes answers to these questions vague, and shifting. The major rival at one time period may turn out to be an ally at the next. Thus the rigidities which ideologies impose on the conduct of policy are much reduced, and ideologies themselves cannot be relied on.

The second hope lies in the development of direct leader-to-leader diplomacy. If the centralization of decision making paralyzes diplomatic agents, the only way in which the flexibility of diplomacy can be partly restored is through direct contacts between heads of regime. Even here, the limitations of nationalism and popular sentiment will greatly circumscribe the agreements that can be reached. Still, leaders have more latitude than agents; they have more authority than diplomatic representatives. In one sense, too, the establishment of personal contact between heads of state provides one link with eighteenth-century practice. Personal feelings and characteristics can enter into the diplomatic process. Moral relationships can have a limited role. This does not mean that such relationships can overwhelm those factors of national interest and perspective, but they tincture them.

In the latter part of the Second World War, the personal relationships between Stalin and Roosevelt began to erode as the cold war developed. The demands of domestic publics and conflicting ideologies took precedence. In the future, however, it is less clear that ideologies will decisively constrain relations among heads of state. Personal factors could take on a new dimension of importance. If so, even the present age of nationalism could yet see a greater cooperation among states.

NOTES

1 See Figure 4-2, p. 71, chap. 4.
2 Thomas Schelling, *The Strategy of Conflict* (New York: Oxford University Press, 1960), pp. 22, 24.
3 Immanuel Kant, *Perpetual Peace*, trans. Lewis W. Beck (New York: Liberal Arts Press, 1957), p. 13.
4 H.J. Morgenthau, *Politics among Nations*, 4th ed. (New York: Knopf, 1967), p. 241.

CHAPTER SEVENTEEN

Military Techniques

DIPLOMACY AND MILITARY FORCE

While diplomacy and military force are only two among several national techniques, they often bear an inverse relationship to one another. The failure of military arts or their incapacity greatly heightens diplomacy; the failure of diplomacy greatly increases the use of military measures. In one sense the transformation of strategic into tactical diplomacy has represented the growing feebleness of diplomatic techniques overall. Thus it is obvious that modern history has witnessed an increase in the importance of military techniques. In the eighteenth century military variables were not especially significant; certainly they were not decisive. They did not permit the destruction of one state by another. Armies were not numerous enough; they were not well enough led; they had pitifully inadequate armaments; they were not fighting for their nation, but rather for pay; they would not go to great lengths to conquer other states. The international soldiery and generalship of all European armies restrained conflict in a context of European cosmopolitanism.

Since the eighteenth century, however, the fusty and antiquated militarism of the old regime has given way to patriotic citizen armies, to technologically advanced armaments, and to the possibility and actuality of wholesale destruction of civilian populations. Thus, as we have seen, while security was not in question in the eighteenth century, it is very much in question in the contemporary world. It is by no means certain that security for all or most nations will be achieved. Increasingly, diplomacy among conflicting parties tends to be used today only when the resource to militarism has been exhausted. After nations have threatened to or actually used force, after the participants have been able to see the possible consequences of further military combat, then diplomacy can have a role. Among contending powers, however, one may have to go to the brink of war and sometimes beyond before a diplomatic accommodation can be worked out. As one of a number of examples, diplomacy may be successful in producing an agreement between Israel and the Arab states only after military force on both sides has reached a dead end. Only after each party has much to lose in a renewal of the fighting will diplomatic outcomes be possible. While military arts used to be the *ultima ratio*, they are now in a sense the *prima ratio*.

THE EVOLUTION OF MILITARY TECHNIQUES

It is not necessary to recapitulate the role of military techniques through the ages. At some point in the later nineteenth century military variables became exceedingly important, for security began to depend upon seizing the offensive in any war that might break out. Planning for that offensive, *la guerre à outrance,* meant depriving diplomatic officials of their role when a crisis unrolled. If mobilization schedules were not met, if railway timetables were not adhered to, the enemy might assume the offensive, and this would spell disaster. Getting in the first blow became crucial.

After World War I, when the primacy of defense had presumably been established, continental powers like France expected a war of fortification and attrition, not unlike World War I. The Maginot Line, the machine gun, and artillery, it was thought, would neutralize the new offensive threat posed by the armored tank. The Germans believed otherwise and were ready to rely on the lightning war of the panzer division. British military theorists also partly foresaw the role of the strategic bomber and the possible need to preempt the enemy's initiative by attacking his bomber bases before his planes could be sent on their deadly missions. Where there was such offensive primacy, stability could be achieved only if retaliation could be guaranteed. An early British student of air power pointed out: "Deadly mutual menaces are more likely to deter attack in proportion as neither side is reasonably sure of getting in first with a crushing offensive and making retaliation impossible."[1]

MILITARY STRATEGY IN THE CONTEMPORARY AGE

After World War II a doctrine of nuclear deterrence, building upon earlier British notions, began to take shape. Essentially this concept accepted the unreliability or impossibility of defense against nuclear attack. If aggressors were to be deterred, it was not to be by the prospect of defeat in their offensive ambitions or a blunting of their attack; rather, they would hesitate because of the retaliatory damage that their opponent could do to them.

If this were true, it became critically important to protect the power of retaliation, for only the threat of retaliation might stay a potential aggressor's hand. Strangely, then, at some point in the 1950s the emphasis shifted from protection of populations against attack to making sure that the retaliatory power could survive an attack and remain capable of a devastating counter-assault.

The first generation carriers of this strategic force were bombers laid down in World War II. Eventually new bombers were developed and still later the intercontinental ballistic missile. In 1956 it was believed that the intercontinental missile would be essentially invulnerable on the ground because missile accuracies could not be improved to the point where one missile could hit another at a 5,000 mile range. By the early 1960s, however, it had become clear that missiles on the ground would only be invulnerable if measures were taken to protect them. Initially these took the form of hardened underground sites capable of resisting blasts of several hundred overpressures per square inch. By the late 1960s even this degree of protection was not sufficient against large, accurate enemy warheads. Various solutions were proposed. One was to protect offensive missiles with antiballistic missiles; another was further hardening to make existing implacements more resistant to blast effects.

These measures would not be likely to cope with future accuracies and with the new ability to place ten or more independently targetable warheads within a single missile envelope. These multiple, independently targetable reentry vehicles (MIRVs) made possible the launching of many warheads against a single missile site. The ABMs protecting that site would have to shoot at each warhead separately rather than destroying them in a cluster. Therefore, if individual MIRVs became cheaper than individual ABMs and associated radars, the offensive warhead would have the edge.

In the early 1970s it seemed merely a matter of time until all fixed, land-based missiles became vulnerable to more numerous and more accurate warheads that an enemy would be capable of launching. More and more, therefore, solutions to the problem of the vulnerability of strategic forces was being sought in terms of submarine launched missiles. Both Polaris and Poseidon provided this type of system. Polaris warheads are fired from missile submarines up to distances of 2,000 miles. Poseidon warheads have a greater range; in addition, the Poseidon permits ten independently targetable reentry vehicles (MIRVs) to be carried in one missile envelope. The proposed undersea long-range missile system (ULMS), now called Trident, would have the additional advantage that its far greater range would permit basing in a much larger area of the ocean, reducing its vulnerability. ULMS would sanction

TABLE 17-1 Guerrilla Wars Since 1945

Location	Period	Winner
China	46-49	G (Guerrillas)
Indonesia	45-49	G
Indochina	45-54	G
Philippines	46-54	I (Incumbent)
Malaya	48-60	I
Tibet	59-	I
South Vietnam	58-	?
Greece	46-49	I
Cyprus	54-59	G?
Algeria	54-62	G
Israel	45-49	G
Iraq	61-66	G?
Yemen	62-	?
Kenya	52-56	I
Congo	64-65	I
Angola	61-	I
Colombia	48-58	I
Cuba	56-59	G
Venezuela	59-66	I
Guatemala	63-	?

John Mueller, *Approaches to Measurement in International Relations* (New York: Appleton-Century-Crofts, 1969), p. 8.

submarine basing directly off the United States coasts where American submarines could be protected against hostile attack by extremely intensive antisubmarine warfare measures. A higher percentage of the force could be kept "on station" at all times. Using these and other techniques, it appears likely that the vulnerability of major strategic forces can be reduced, so that no aggressor would be likely to assume that he could eliminate so large a proportion of his opponent's force that he would be willing to accept retaliation from the remaining part.

If this is true, it may be that the use of such forces becomes unthinkable. And if this in turn is true, one may be tempted to wonder how the present age can place such great emphasis upon the resort to military force, and how there can have been a relative decline of diplomatic techniques. The answer, of course, is that the inability to use weapons of mass destruction has not prevented states from making recourse to weapons of limited war, both conventional and guerilla. Nuclear weapons have not been used in war since the Hiroshima and Nagasaki bombs of August 6 and 9, 1945. But the number of limited wars between 1945 and 1965 is one of the largest over such a period since 1820. More important, the severity and magnitude of the wars in the period 1945-1965 exceeds that of any twenty-year period in modern history, with the exception of the period which includes both World War I and World War II.[2] These conclusions, moreover, are for international wars only and exclude guerilla and civil wars and also the war in Vietnam. If these were to be included at least twenty additional conflicts would have to be listed in the period since 1945. (See Table 17-1.)

Employing a still more inclusive definition of "internationally significant violence" Robert McNamara concludes:

In the eight years through late 1966 alone there were no less than 164 internationally significant outbreaks of violence, each of them specifically designed as a serious challenge to the authority of the very existence of the government in question. Eighty-two different governments were directly involved, and what is striking is that only 15 of these 164 significant resorts to violence were military conflicts between two states, and not a single one of the 164 conflicts was a formally declared war. Indeed, there has not been a formal declaration of war anywhere in the world since World War II.[3]

He also believes the situation is growing worse:

The planet is becoming a more dangerous place to live on not merely because of a potential nuclear holocaust but also because of the large number of *de facto* conflicts and because the trend of such conflicts is growing rather than diminishing. At the beginning of 1958 there were 23 prolonged insurgencies going on around the world. As of February, 1966, there were 40. Further, the total number of outbreaks of violence has increased each year: in 1958 there were 34; in 1965 there were 58.[4]

LIMITED AND UNLIMITED VIOLENCE

Thus while nuclear deterrence has been successful in that there have been no nuclear detonations in war since 1945, conventional and limited war deterrence has been very unsuccessful. The reasons for this have to do partly with the decline of diplomatic effectiveness. Beyond this, the stability of the thermonuclear balance has made possible a wide range of conflicts below this threshold of violence. This has been true from two points of view. From the standpoint of major nuclear powers, the choice between inaction and Armageddon was an unsatisfactory one. Thus from 1956 on, they labored to develop doctrines and forces for limited warfare, of both an external and internal type. The major powers saw themselves as facing challenges. If they had nothing but nuclear capabilities to use in responding to such challenges, they would either plunge the world over the abyss or they would permit the challenging power to gain a local success. In the American case under the

Kennedy Administration, forces were developed that would permit the United States to intervene in conflicts with less than unlimited force. In the Soviet case under Brezhnev and Kosygin, strong theatre forces were developed which might permit intervention in local conflicts in either the Middle East or the Indian Ocean. Once these forces were developed and doctrines were formulated to go with them, it was not surprising that policy makers strove to put them to use. In the American intervention in Vietnam under presidents Kennedy and Johnson, planners were not willing to overlook what they regarded as a communist and Chinese challenge to the United States position in Southeast Asia.[5] Limited-war notions sanctioned limited intervention when neither of the two extreme alternatives seemed appropriate. In part, therefore, the massive American presence in Vietnam was a tribute to its adherence to limited-war doctrines. In this case, moreover, intervention was easier because outside of Europe the United States limited-war forces were far stronger than those of any adversary. North Vietnam could be coerced because she could not be expected to stand up to the limited-war strength of the United States.

Limited-war doctrines, however, were not the only reason for the rather continual recourse to limited violence in the period since 1945. With the development of conventional war strategies and weapons, it was in many ways harder to deter conventional and guerilla attacks than to deter thermonuclear attacks. In the past it has been assumed that ground warfare favored the defense with ratios of up to 3 to 1. In land warfare the defensive power would be operating with interior lines of communication. His defensive fortifications could be well prepared. He could position himself for an attack, taking all the advantages of the terrain. The power wielding the offensive, however, would have to encounter his foe in locations not of his own choosing. His communications lines would likely be longer and more exposed to enemy interdiction. All these factors combined to give defensive land warfare an advantage.

Recent developments in ground-war strategy, however, question past assumptions of defensive superiority. If conventional land warfare takes place between opponents who also possess tactical nuclear weapons, the prepared, entrenched position loses much of its attractiveness. Both adversaries will have to be prepared for a sudden introduction of nuclear force and will therefore want to avoid concentrating forces in a manner that would present a tempting nuclear target. Entrenched defensive positions would offer such a target, as would the massing of troops necessary for an offensive breakthrough. In neither case would one want to defend or attack from fixed line formations. Conventional wars will be mobile, involving dispersion of mobile units over large ranges of territory. Offensive and defensive forces will be interpenetrated and intermingled. In the process most of the advantages accruing to the defense will be cancelled.

Even in wars in which nuclear weapons were not possessed by the participants, defensive advantages were less real than they had been historically. Given the potency of even conventional air forces, victory in land battle would be greatly affected by command of the air. In the first hours of a major conventional conflict, one could expect strikes upon bomber and fighter bases, seeking to achieve this objective. The side which achieved command of the air would have great advantages in the ensuing land campaign. It thus appears that surprise raids on conventional air capabilities will become more and more likely as a diplomatic crisis unfolds. The advantages will be likely to lie with the preemptive attacker.

On the ground, unless terrain presents special difficulties, offensive deployment of armor will be equally important. The North German plain, the Rann of Kutch, the Sinai desert—these and many other battlefields give significant advantages to the side with superior tank forces and also to the side gaining tactical surprise. The defense no longer has any intrinsic edge. Indeed, it even might be said that the considerations governing outcomes are becoming similar to classic Lanchester Square Law predictions. Where all firing units could be employed simultaneously, F.W. Lanchester reasoned that relative expected losses might increase in the ratio of the square of the number of units engaged on each side.[6] If, for example, in a naval encounter, seven capital ships confronted seven capital ships, their losses would be approximately equal. If one side were able to increase its number to ten, however, relative losses would be in a ratio of $(10)^2$ to $(7)^2$ or more than twice as much for the power with the smaller force. Small numerical advantages in firing units, therefore, would translate into far greater military effectiveness. Not only do such considerations take primacy from the defense, they enormously enhance the position of the numerically superior aggressor.

For similar reasons conventional arms races may be much more destabilizing than nuclear arms races. If thermonuclear retaliatory forces can be adequately protected against attack, a fairly small force can offer reliable deterrence against a large potential aggressor. In conventional terms, however, the slightest inferiority, uncompensated by advantages of terrain and fortification, may mean a failure to deter. Thus as conventional rearmament proceeds, instability develops. In conventional arms each power may insist on a small numerical superiority. If this is true, instability exists at all levels short of complete disarmament on both sides.

INTERNAL WARFARE

The calculations that make preemptive or offensive conventional warfare advantageous and therefore likely are magnified when one comes to internal war. Here even very inferior forces numerically can present a substantial challenge to governing authorities. Two investigators liken the problem of authority contending with rebellion to that of defense against air attack. "The defender does not know where an attack may come. Hence, even if he is able to keep an advantage by maintaining a high-level alert at each of the targets, there are so many targets to defend that the aggregate force ratio becomes much larger than that of the attacking force."[7] Aside from the relatively small forces needed to present a challenge to authority, these forces can gain great success if the authority resorts to undifferentiated but still not crushing measures of violence. Ted Gurr offers the curvilinear relationship depicted in Figure 17-1. In the initial stages of trying to repress a rebellion or guerilla war, the authority's use of violence (sanctions) is counterproductive, actually leading to a decline in coercive control. Only after very severe sanctions are undertaken does the regime regain control.

Amounts of regime violence are not the only factors in charting regime control. Undifferentiated violence tends to be ineffective unless it is over-whelming. Guerillas selectively use violence to damage those unsympathetic to their cause. The response to revolutionary violence, however, may be wholesale destruction of villages or leveling of the countryside. Since these tactics make no distinction between those who are sympathetic and those who are unsympathetic to the revolutionaries, this generalized form of violence may produce revulsion among those who were not initially against

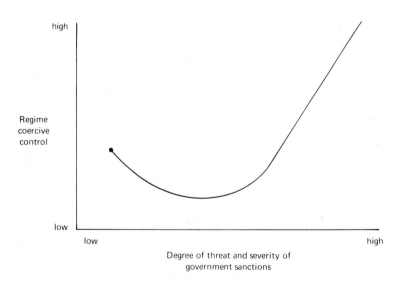

Figure 17-1 CONTROL AND SANCTIONS

the regime. On college campuses, the indiscriminate use of police tactics of tear-gassing, harassment, and intimidation may strengthen the revolutionary cause. This is particularly because police tactics do not distinguish bystanders from those who are active supporters of revolutionary change. Ted Gurr argues:

> Faced with hostile demonstrators or rioters, police are likely to seize the participants and bystanders closest to hand, beat or arrest some, release others, and ignore the majority who were able to get away. The description applies with some accuracy to the American police response to many ghetto riots and antiwar demonstrations, to the reactions of French, Spanish, and Italian riot police to student demonstrations, to South African, Malayan and Venezuelan response to some workers' protests, and to hundreds of other cases. Military forces committed to the control of insurgency may shoot or capture a few of the dissidents and many of their supposed sympathizers, decimate suspect rural areas, shoot some captives on the spot, send others to rehabilitation centers or resettlement camps, let some escape. The contemporary examples are legion: Algeria, Angola, South Vietnam, Cuba under the Batista regime, the Congo during the wars of the "second independence," Guatemala, the Kurdish areas of northern Iraq, Tibet under Chinese rule. The more inconsistent the use of force in response to political violence in any respect, the greater the anger and, often, the lower the apparent risk, for the affected survivors, and consequently the less effective the coercive control exercised by the regime that uses such policies.[9]

The difficulties of coping with revolutionary violence, however, do not necessarily lead to the conclusion that revolutionary movements are normally successful. If one looks at the record of guerilla wars since 1945, more than half have been terminated with victory for the incumbent regime.[10] In most cases where revolutionary movements were successful, they had substantial outside assistance. Where the incumbent regime failed, it was often unable to muster sufficient outside aid. It is therefore by no means clear that revolutionary war is a simple or a straightforward path to victory. Revolutionaries usually do not win in the end. What does seem to be true, however, is that revolutionary challenges to incumbent authority cannot easily be deterred. Challenges to a regime (which may not yet succeed in deposing it) can relatively easily be offered. Initial regime responses to the revolutionary challenge, moreover, often strengthen the revolutionary camp. As a means of pressure and even as a means of extracting concessions from a regime, revolutionary violence is by no means counterproductive. It is therefore very difficult to prevent.

The net conclusion must be that it is much more difficult in the contemporary age to deter conventional or internal uses of force than it is to deter thermonuclear uses. Conventional and unconventional conflicts have burgeoned at what appears to be high or increasing rates while nuclear weapons have been employed at a zero rate. This is a surprising result. One might have anticipated that the danger of all-out war would have put a damper on limited conflicts because of the possibility of escalation.

THE PROBLEM OF ESCALATION

In 1954 American Secretary of State Dulles enunciated a doctrine of "massive retaliation" against aggressors at times and places of United States choosing. If this doctrine could be implemented, it would not be necessary to develop large land or sea forces. In response to a ground attack anywhere in the world, the United States could retaliate massively on Moscow or Peking. In other words, the United States was seeking to pose the threat of escalation of every conflict to nuclear war. If aggressors wished to avoid that kind of conflict, they should refrain from engaging even in limited military operations.

As long as the United States was the sole possessor of major strategic force, this doctrine could be risked without great threat to American interests. After the Soviets had developed major nuclear retaliatory capbilities of their own, however, it was no longer operable. If the United States threatened nuclear force on Moscow in response to a limited military move anywhere in the world, the Soviets could counterthreaten the devastation of the United States. In these circumstances, it was doubtful that the American threat could be carried out. Thus if the United States wished to limit the dangers of escalation, it had to develop forces which would resist the incursion locally and more or less in its own terms. This was the rationale for limited war and counterinsurgency forces.

Even given this situation, however, it is still surprising that so many conventional and insurgent conflicts could proceed, largely without reference to the overpowering nuclear force possessed in ample quantities by the Soviet Union and the United States, and in growing strength by China, Britain, and France. Even if great powers would not themselves deliberately escalate a limited conflict, was there not the danger of miscalculation where local actions could bring about a thermonuclear crisis? The Cuban missile crisis, after all, was of this type. Soviet miscalculation of American intentions led them to implace missiles in Cuba. America, in response, was clearly willing to escalate the crisis to get the missiles out. United States willingness to provoke a crisis which might eventually have led the Soviets to take action against Berlin was not deterred by Soviet nuclear capacities. Indeed, at the time of Cuba, Soviet retaliatory capacities could probably have taken a toll of thirty to forty million American lives. Yet the United States did not hesitate.

In European strategy also, the United States has pledged to resort to nuclear weapons rather than accept a Soviet conventional conquest of

Western Europe. Such a threatened use should also have been deterred by Soviet nuclear capabilities. In 1972 Soviet nuclear capabilities probably could guarantee an excess of 100 million Americans killed, even after an American strategic strike on Soviet missile and bomber bases. How then could the United States threaten to employ nuclear weapons against the Soviet Union in response to a Soviet conventional attack on Europe?

In the case of Vietnam, the United States probably relied upon North Vietnamese fears that the United States might be willing to escalate the conflict, just as it had done in Cuba. Even if the United States would actually not do so, the North Vietnamese presumably could not be sure that it would not, and therefore might have been willing to reach a satisfactory compromise. Yet, as we know, American involvement in Vietnam did not deter the pursuit of a revolutionary strategy in the south or the supply of aid from the north. If anything, the American intervention drastically increased the flow of soldiers and material assistance from the north. Hanoi was thus not impressed by the threat of escalation. Its estimates, moreover, turned out to be correct.

There remains, therefore, a major disjunction between limited war strategies on the one hand, and all-out war strategies on the other. The threat of the former usually does not raise the probability of the latter. Even in Vietnam where American pilots were shooting at Soviet technicians manning North Vietnamese air defense missiles, the fact of Americans acting against Russians in conventional combat operations did not raise the danger of escalation. In the Middle East, the presence of Soviet and American theatre forces has not appreciably raised the risk of escalation. In the Jordanian crisis of 1970 the Soviets were not willing to strongly support Syria against the Jordanian Army. The United States gave the impression that it was willing to support Jordan but its military maneuvers were apparently a bluff. The Jordanians defeated the Syrian tank invaders without outside help. This outcome reinforced the point that possible threats of escalation from either side did not affect the result. It was the strength of the conventional antagonists which decided the issue.

As time goes on, it seems more and more likely that respective limited-war strengths will tell the tale. The United States will be less and less willing to back its commitments with the threat of escalation as the cold war recedes and world politics takes on a multipolar form. To this point, the Soviets and the Chinese have been even more conservative and circumspect in their strategic doctrine and behavior than has the United States. Aside from Cuba, neither of the great powers has been willing to risk major escalation of a conflict against his opposite number since World War II. It does not appear that this willingness will increase in the future.

If this is true, limited and unlimited strategies will remain in separate compartments. The danger of all-out war will not noticeably restrain recourse to limited and sub-limited war. Nuclear deterrence will not reinforce conventional deterrence

MILITARY FACTORS AND THE SEARCH FOR AGREEMENT

Given the fact that limited conflicts are not deterred under contemporary military strategic conditions, it is not surprising that so many disputes involve a recourse to limited force. Many if not most of the decolonization episodes have involved some resort to violence. Colonial powers were not always ready to take nationalist demands seriously until they were backed by force. Disputes among new nationalist states have often witnessed use of military measures. To compromise ideological or territorial issues with an enemy might be to sacrifice the new basis of national unity and cohesion. To moderate one's claims against an ideological opponent might be to overthrow the national ethos. In this connection it is not clear how far Arab states can go in accepting the existence of Israel without putting their own regimes in jeopardy. The general rule seems to be—use military pressure first; only if this fails should one consider diplomatic solutions.

In general terms, the more nationalistic the state, the more likely it is to resort to military means. Only in Western Europe, where the old nationalist urges have been gradually transcended, have diplomatic and cooperative techniques been used successfully. Thus the rebirth of nationalism in the extra-European areas of the world holds the promise of a continuing resort to force in the settlement of disputes. It is not yet certain, but military take-overs in a variety of third world contexts may increase this tendency. As we have said before, diplomacy works when statesmen have considerable latitude in seeking solutions to their differences. When nationalized populations limit their freedom of action, militarism is likely to follow.

MILITARY TECHNIQUES AND STABILITY

We can examine the interaction of militarism and stability by looking at the question more formally.[11] Suppose we assume that each of two protagonists attach values to peace—V_p and U_p; to their own first strike against an opponent—V_{fs} and U_{fs}; and to their second strike (assuming their opponent has already struck them)—V_{ss} and U_{ss}.

A's utilities are: V_p V_{fs} V_{ss}
B's utilities are: U_p U_{fs} U_{ss}

Under normal circumstances the utility of peace exceeds the utility of the first strike which in turn exceeds the utility of the second strike (being struck) or:

A $V_p > V_{fs} > V_{ss}$
B $U_p > U_{fs} > U_{ss}$

In short, nations normally prefer peace to striking another power. But if war is to come, they prefer to have the advantage of the first strike. They would rather strike first than be struck.

In addition, nations may make assessments of the probability of their opponent striking them:

A's estimate of the probability that B will strike = q

A's estimate of the probability that B will *not* strike = 1-q

B's estimate of the probability that A will strike = p

B's estimate of the probability that A will *not* strike = 1-p

The calculations give rise to the utility matrix shown in Table 17-2.

A

		A waits	A strikes (p)
B	waits	V_p, U_p	V_{fs}, U_{ss}
B	strikes (q)	V_{ss}, U_{fs}	✕

TABLE 17-2 Deterrence Utility Matrix

(The fourth cell in the matrix is ruled out on grounds that precisely simultaneous strikes do not take place. One state or the other will get the advantage of a first strike.) Let us now look at the expectation that A would derive from waiting as compared to the expectation he would derive from striking. For deterrence to obtain, the value of waiting must be greater than the value of striking. On the basis of the utility matrix it is possible to calculate the values that A would attach to waiting or striking. If A waits, he may get either peace (V_p) or he may be struck (V_{ss}). A assumes that B will strike with a probability of q. Thus he will expect to get V_{ss} with a probability of q and V_p with a probability of 1-q. Thus the total expectation of waiting for A is:

$$(1-q)V_p + q(V_{ss})$$

The value of striking for A is V_{fs}. A can decide whether or not he wishes to strike first. If he wishes to take this option, he can make its probability equivalent to certainty or 1. Thus the expectation of striking for A is:

$$1 \times V_{fs}$$

For deterrence to obtain the expectation of waiting must be greater than the expectation of striking. Thus

$$(1-q)V_p + qV_{ss} \text{ must be greater than } V_{fs} \text{ or:}$$

$$\underbrace{[(1-q)V_p + qV_{ss}]}_{\textstyle ①} - \underbrace{V_{fs}}_{\textstyle ②} > 0$$

It is now possible to calculate changes in the variables which will help to reinforce deterrence (to reinforce the difference in value between waiting and striking). If we call the relationships within the brackets the first term of the equation and V_{fs} the second term, we wish to increase the first term and decrease the second term of the equation to increase deterrence. The results may be summarized as shown by Table 17-3.

Variable	Variable change to strengthen deterrence
V_p	Increase V_p
V_{fs}	Decrease V_{fs}
V_{ss}	Increase V_{ss}
q	Decrease q

TABLE 17-3 Variable Change to Strengthen Deterrence (Monadic Case)

Analysis

Increase V_p   In the equation it can easily be seen that if V_p increases, the first term of the equation rises relative to the second term. This strengthens deterrence.

Decrease V_{fs}   Since V_{fs} is the second term in the equation, any decrease in V_{fs} will magnify the difference between the value of waiting and the value of striking. It will therefore enhance deterrence.

Increase V_{ss}   Any increase in V_{ss} will increase the value of the first term relative to the second and therefore increase deterrence.

Decrease q   As long as V_p exceeds V_{ss}, q should decrease for greater deterrent stability. This condition is not hard to meet since peace is almost always likely to be better than being struck.

The calculations we have just given refer only to the question of improving A's peaceful incentives (deterrence of his attack). If A is to wait rather than strike, the changes in variables should be in the direction indicated. A similar result is reached when B's incentives are calculated. *Mutatis mutandis*, the expectation of waiting and the expectation of striking for B should be:

$$[(1 - p)U_p + pU_{ss}] \quad - \quad U_{fs} > 0$$
$$\qquad\quad \textcircled{1} \qquad\qquad\qquad \textcircled{2}$$

The total change in the variables which one would wish to bring about greater mutual stability of deterrence would be as shown in Table 17-4.

TABLE 17-4 Variable Change to Strengthen Deterrence (Dyadic Case)

Variable	Variable change to strengthen deterrence
V_p	Increase V_p
U_p	Increase U_p
V_{fs}	Decrease V_{fs}
U_{fs}	Decrease U_{fs}
V_{ss}	Increase V_{ss}
U_{ss}	Increase U_{ss}
q	Decrease q
p	Decrease p

MILITARY TECHNIQUES AND STABILITY: APPLICATIONS

These calculations apply to either conventional or nuclear warfare. To show their applications we shall take several examples.

The Suez War: June 1967

In May 1967 the Israelis were faced with the closure of the Straits of Tiran by Egypt and the enforced withdrawal of the United Nations Emergency Force.

Following intelligence warnings from the Russians, the Egyptians had moved forces and armor into the Sinai peninsula. The United States had made ineffectual protests to Cairo about the need to keep open the Gulf of Aqaba to Israeli shipping, but was counseling caution and moderation on Israel's part. As early as May 20, Egypt called up the reserves and moved forces into the Sinai. Israel went through measures of partial mobilization on the same day. On May 28, President Nasser proclaimed: "We plan to open a general assault on Israel. This will be total war. Our basic aim is the destruction of Israel."[12] From the Israeli point of view the most important single act was clearly the exclusion of Israeli ships from the Strait of Tiran. Prime Minister Levi Eshkol in return branded the blockade an act of aggression. When it became clear that the Western powers and the United States in particular were unwilling or unable to reopen the Gulf of Aqaba, Israel attacked on the morning of June 5.

The Israeli calculations can be usefully summarized in terms of

$$V_p, V_{fs}, V_{ss}, \text{ and } q.$$

V_p

The opening of the Gulf of Aqaba to Israeli shipping had been the only tangible gain to Tel Aviv from the Suez war of 1956. When it was closed, the Israelis became fundamentally dissatisfied with the status quo. The Egyptians, on the other hand, had only to hold on to what they had to win a prestige and political triumph. The decline in the value of the Israeli V_p made a first strike relatively more attractive.

V_{fs} and V_{ss}

Once it was clear that war would likely come between Israel and Egypt, any delay would have been dangerous to the Israeli cause. Egypt was beginning to airlift troops and matériel to Jordan where they would be poised for an attack. Iraqi forces were also entering Jordan.[13] If Israel had been forced to begin the war after these Arab arms buildups were complete, her first-strike outcomes would have been worse. If Egypt attacked at that time, the Israeli second-strike outcomes might have been disastrous. Israel, in return, could not keep its army mobilized indefinitely without action. If it did not act soon, its own defensive posture would deteriorate. A first strike was even more necessary to the Israelis because it would be necessary to eliminate the Egyptian air force in order to win command of the air. This in turn could only be fully accomplished if Tel Aviv had the advantage of surprise. Thus as military preparations were made, the first-strike option increased in importance, while the second-strike option became less and less desirable.

It is not known whether the Egyptians were planning an attack on Israel, having already made important gains. It seemed unlikely, however, that Egypt could keep its troops in the Sinai for an extended period. It would therefore either have to attack or withdraw. Their very presence, therefore, made an

Egyptian attack more likely than it had been before the crisis. Since a second strike was much less attractive to Israel than a first strike, any increase in the probability of an Egyptian attack would cause Israel to try to preempt it.

The respective movement of the deterrent variables made war certain. V_p had drastically decreased so that a first strike was more attractive than the status quo. Second-strike outcomes were worsening, so that if war came, it should be at the Israeli initiative. Deterrence is assured if the value of peace is much greater than the value of the first strike, if the value of the second strike closely approximates the value of the first strike, and if the probability of an opponent's strike is low. In June 1967, however, the value of the first strike was even preferable to the deteriorating conditions of peace; the value of the first strike was much greater than the values of the second strike (being struck). Further, the probability of an opponent's strike was high. In at least one respect, the Israeli calculations were like those of the Austrians in 1914 and the Japanese in 1941: The status quo had become so undesirable that military action seemed preferable. Unlike the Japanese case, however, Tel Aviv did not enter the war with negligible long-term military prospects. They had a plan which promised (and delivered) victory.

Nuclear Arms Balances 1960 to 1972

Deterrent variables can also be used to depict stabilizing and destabilizing changes in arms technology over the past decade. For deterrent stability, it is desirable that V_p greatly exceed V_{fs} and that V_{ss} approximate V_{fs} as closely as possible. Increases in V_{fs} will be destabilizing; increases in V_{ss} will be stabilizing.

Example (a): Hardening of Nuclear Forces

Imagine two unprotected nuclear missile forces possessed by A and B. A now decides to harden his force, that is, to put his missiles in underground, reinforced concrete implacements. What is the impact upon stability? We shall consider the impact upon:

A: V_{fs} V_{ss}
B: U_{fs} U_{ss}

V_{ss}
Clearly V_{ss} must increase because it is now less likely that B can execute a surprise nuclear attack on A's missile bases and hope to knock them out. More hardened missiles would survive such an attack than soft missiles. Thus A would have more left to retaliate against B with.

U_{fs}
For the same reasons U_{fs} must decline. There is now less chance of B launching a successful first strike against A's missiles than before. Thus if B did attack he would expect to receive a much more devastating blow in retaliation. Thus his utility of a first strike must fall.

V_{fs} and U_{ss}

A's first strike utilities will *not* increase. While his force is better protected than before, it is not numerically larger and thus could not be expected to have any greater effect on B's forces. The retaliation that A would receive on his cities would therefore be of the same magnitude as before. For the same reason, U_{ss} would not decline.

The net effect of changes in the four cases is clearly *stabilizing*. First-strike incentives are not increased, while second-strike outcomes either increase or remain the same. It should now be clear to the alert student that V_{ss} and U_{fs} are reciprocally related and that V_{fs} and U_{ss} are reciprocally related.

Example (*b*): *City-oriented Anti Ballistic Missiles*

In this example A builds a city-oriented ABM to protect his population against B's attack. What is the impact upon stability?

V_{fs} and U_{ss}

If A decides to launch a first strike against B, his missiles will not be any more effective against B's sites than before. On the other hand, B's retaliation will now be much less effective, since part of it will be blunted by A's ABM shield. Thus the net first-strike calculation for A will increase. He can do better by striking first. The effect of his ABM system is equivalent to knocking out a certain additional number of B's missiles. For similar reasons B's second-strike outcome must deteriorate. His retaliation will now have less effect on A than before; thus A is less surely deterred from launching a first strike.

V_{ss} and U_{fs}

A's ABM shield will not make it any easier for him to retaliate against an attack by B. He will be able to hit the same number of city targets in B since B does not have ABM. For the same reasons B's first-strike outcomes do not decrease.

The net impact of changes in these four variables is *destabilizing*. A's first-strike incentives are increased and B's second-strike values reduced. The other utilities are left unchanged.

Example (*c*): *More Accurate Warheads*

In this example A's warheads attain higher accuracies. What is the impact upon stability?

V_{fs} and U_{ss}

Missile warheads already have excellent accuracies against city targets. A further improvement in accuracy will give them greater counterforce capability, a better capability against the enemy's missiles. If warheads are inaccurate, it may be necessary to send a large number against one enemy missile in order to assure a high probability kill. If they become more accurate, therefore, fewer warheads need be sent against one to knock it out.

This means that more enemy missiles can be reliably knocked out. Hence an improvement in missile accuracies of A must increase V_{fs}. They can now destroy more enemy missiles; enemy retaliation will therefore be reduced. For the same reason U_{ss} must decline.

V_{ss} and U_{fs}

A's capabilities against B's cities, however, will not be increased for A's missiles were already accurate enough to hit cities. Thus V_{ss} will not increase. Nor will U_{fs} be affected. After a first strike by B, A could expect to do the same amount of city damage to B as before.

The net result of these changes is clearly *destabilizing*. A's first-strike outcome goes up and B's second-strike outcome goes down. This makes deterrence less stable.

Example (d): More Mobility for the Strategic Force

If A's strategic force gains greater mobility, what is the impact upon stability?

V_{fs} and U_{ss}

Assuming that A's strategic force is already capable of reaching targets in B's homeland, improvements in its mobility will not facilitate a first strike. They will also not reduce B's second-strike potential.

V_{ss} and U_{fs}

A more mobile force, on the other hand, greatly facilitates A's second strike. Since the force is mobile, a smaller proportion of it can be knocked out in any single strategic strike by B. This means that a larger proportion of it remains for retaliatory purposes. Thus one would expect V_{ss} to increase and U_{fs} to decline.

The net impact of these changes is *stabilizing*. B's first-strike outcome declines and A's second-strike outcome increases. Deterrence is more stable.

Example (e): A Numerically Larger Strategic Force

In this example, A's strategic force grows in number. What is the impact upon stability?

V_{fs} and U_{ss}

As A's strategic force grows, it will be capable of launching a larger and more effective attack on B's missile sites, thus V_{fs} must increase. B will therefore be able to retaliate with fewer missiles, reducing U_{ss}.

V_{ss} and U_{fs}

With a numerically larger force, A will also be better off on second strike. Even after absorbing an attack by B, A will be able to launch a larger number of retaliatory missiles. Hence V_{ss} must increase. For similar reasons U_{fs} must decrease. A's retaliation after B's first strike will now be more effective than it was previously.

In this instance, there are two destabilizing changes and two stabilizing changes. The decrease in U_{fs} and the increase in V_{ss} are stabilizing. The increase in V_{fs} and the decrease in U_{ss} are destabilizing. Unless the changes are of greater magnitude in the one case than in the other, the results cancel each other out, and the situation is left as before. This may be a difficult conclusion to understand and accept, because it has resulted from a one-sided increase in strategic forces. Even though A's force has grown with respect to B's, it does not follow that A will be more likely to strike. If A's first-strike incentives have increased, so have his second-strike incentives. The margin between waiting and striking for A, therefore, may well be unchanged. This reasoning helps to explain why simple arms-race models do not always apply to nuclear armories. Even one-sided increases are not necessarily destabilizing so long as they are held within tolerable limits. From 1961 to 1966, the United States went through a major strategic arms buildup. For at least the first part of that period, the Soviet Union did not engage in a crash program to catch up. It was willing to wait to procure second-generation missile systems to compete with the United States. From 1965 to 1972, the Soviets have rearmed rapidly. The United States, however, did not build new missile launchers in response, contenting itself with more warheads per missile (multiple warheads and MIRV warheads). Neither side seemed to be greatly dismayed by large numerical increases by the other side for at least a short-term period.

Of course, if the missile force of one side increased to the point where it could deny the other side a retaliatory capability, the decline in U_{ss} and the increase in V_{fs} would become much larger than the stabilizing changes in V_{ss} and U_{fs}. Then instability would clearly result.

We can see from the previous examples that some techniques that major powers have employed are stabilizing; some, however, clearly are not. In the contemporary period large numbers of accurate warheads conjoined with city-oriented ABM present perhaps the greatest challenge to stability. If these weapons were introduced suddenly by one power, his opposite number might find that a greater proportion of his strategic force could be knocked out. If the rearming power had a large ABM defense of cities, the smaller retaliation by his opponent could perhaps be blunted by ABM, leaving one power supreme. The first nation would then possess a first-strike capability. In the Strategic Arms Limitation Talks of 1970-1971, culminating in the SALT Agreement of May, 1972, special emphasis was placed on an agreement on the limitation of ABMs. This agreement will hold ABM launchers down to the point where neither superpower could assume that it could knock out so much of the retaliatory force of its opponent that its ABM could handle the retaliation from the remaining part. This arrangement should greatly facilitate nuclear and deterrent stability.

MILITARY TECHNIQUES AND STABILITY: FUTURE QUESTIONS

It is interesting to note that neither the United States nor the Soviet Union has sought to manipulate the entire range of deterrent variables to produce a greater world stability.[14] If A is the United States and B the Soviet Union, the United States has clearly sought to reduce the Soviet U_{fs} and to increase its own V_{ss}. In recent years at least the Soviets have sought to reduce V_{fs} and to increase their own U_{ss}. Neither power, however, has sought to reduce its own first-strike outcomes. The Soviet SS-9 missile will pose a considerable threat to American Minuteman sites. American Minuteman III and Poseidon capabilities have some hard target capabilities against Soviet missiles. The improvement of missile accuracies on both sides will clearly reach the point where all fixed-base missiles will be vulnerable, regardless of their hardening. More important perhaps, while neither side (at least until the SALT negotiations) has concentrated on assuring his adversary of a secure retaliatory capability, nothing has been done to improve the respective V_p and U_p positions. In the longer run, if nuclear war is to be avoided, it will be because the Soviet Union, the United States, China, and other nuclear powers are satisfied enough with their status quo positions that they do not have to consider desperate expedients to improve their lot. Several wars in the past, including the Japanese attack on Pearl Harbor and the Austrian demand in 1914 to humiliate Serbia no matter what the cost, have been brought on by a perceived decline in the value of peace. Means must be found of satisfying the major nuclear powers simultaneously if thermonuclear war is to be avoided in the long run.

NOTES

1 Jonathan Griffin, *Glass Houses and Modern War* (London: Chatto and Windus, 1938), p. 62; quoted in George Quester, *Deterrence before Hiroshima* (New York: Wiley, 1966), p. 89.
2 See J. David Singer and Melvin Small, *The Wages of War* (Ann Arbor, Mich.: University of Michigan Press, 1970), Chap. 4.
3 Robert McNamara, *The Essence of Security* (New York: Harper & Row, 1968), p. 145.
4 Ibid.
5 See the documents reprinted in *The New York Times*, June 13-15, 1971.
6 See F.W. Lanchester, *Aircraft in Warfare* (London: Constable, 1916); A.L. Burns, "From Balance to Deterrence: A Theoretical Analysis," *World Politics*, July 1957; and Malcolm W. Hoag, "Stability in Deterrent Races," *World Politics*, July 1961.
7 N. Leites and C. Wolfe, Jr., *Rebellion and Authority* (Chicago: Markham, 1970), p. 86.
8 Ted Gurr, *Why Men Rebel* (Princeton: Princeton University Press, 1970), p. 240. The curve has been redrawn here because Gurr's axes are inversely labelled.

9 Ibid., pp. 255-256.

10 See J.E. Muller, *Approaches to Measurement in International Relations* (New York: Appleton-Century-Crofts, 1969), pp. 8-9.

11 The analysis which follows is based on Daniel Ellsberg's, "The Crude Analysis of Strategic Choices," (RAND Corporation P-2183, 1960).

12 Quoted, J.B. Bell, *The Long War* (Englewood Cliffs, N.J.: Prentice-Hall, 1969), p. 411.

13 See N. Safran, *From War to War* (New York: Pegasus, 1969), p. 315.

14 For a more complete analysis of these points see Richard Rosecrance (ed.), *The Future of the International Strategic System* (San Francisco: Chandler, 1972), chap. 8-11.

CHAPTER EIGHTEEN

Economic Statecraft

HISTORICAL DEVELOPMENT OF
THE INTERNATIONAL ECONOMIC SYSTEM

While military techniques have unquestionably increased in importance as diplomatic instruments have declined over the past century, the situation with respect to economic means is less clear. Even during the nineteenth century, economic factors were of great significance in world politics, though economic policies were not always self-consciously used to advance political objectives. The London money market held sway over the financial and credit needs of the major powers. Along with gold, the pound sterling provided the reserve currency for the world. Changes in the London bank rate (rate of interest) would produce vast inflows or outflows of foreign funds and gold. Countries or commercial enterprises which wished to obtain loans through London credit facilities had to submit themselves to the informal discipline of the English money managers. Great Britain was the leading trading country in the world. Its primacy in commercial and financial terms was much greater during most of the nineteenth century than that of the United States after 1945. London was the center for world trade and finance to a degree that New York never approached.[1] Indeed, the very order and international hegemony which London provided in the economic field made tolerable the divisions among states on political and nationalist grounds. There was a world economy even though there was no world polity.

After World War I the world economy was smashed. No power emerged to serve as economic regulator of the system as Britain had done during the nineteenth century. Britain was now weakened; the United States would not take leadership, and in any event the free trading mechanism of the nineteenth century had been supplanted by national economies, protected by tariffs, exchange controls, and competitive devaluations. Economic nationalism was furthered by the worldwide impact of the Great Depression.

Since 1945 there has been a painstaking attempt to recreate the world economy of the nineteenth century with relatively free trade and international access to capital markets. American hegemony, however, has not succeeded the previous British hegemony. Rather, all nations have been subject to a new economic multilateralism in which international agencies like the International Monetary Fund, the World Bank, the International Development Association, the "Paris Club," and the "Basle Club" have had important roles. While the American dollar attained an important status as a reserve currency along with gold, sterling, and the newly-created SDRs (Special Drawing Rights apportioned to members of the International Monetary Fund), its influence was never as decisive as that of the pound sterling in the nineteenth century. For various reasons nations were less willing to hold dollars than they had been to hold sterling. In some sense, therefore, the present international economic system is run more multilaterally than the nineteenth-century system. Before important departures can be made in international financial and economic affairs, the Common Market (including Britain), Japan, and the United States must agree. No nation or grouping holds paramount economic power.

THE USE OF ECONOMIC TOOLS

Historically nations have often used economic measures to influence the policy of other states. The techniques which states have at their disposal include: raising or lowering tariffs against another country or countries; controlling the import of commodities through quotas or other quantitative restrictions; depreciating one's currency against the currencies of other states; embargoes on trade with other states, or even a blockade against all trade with a particular country. In addition states have recently used foreign and military aid as a lever to influence the policy of other countries.

Tariffs and Quotas

Tariffs and quotas have been a traditional means of governing the access of foreign states to one's domestic market. Lower tariffs increase imports into one's country; they are therefore likely to hurt inefficient domestic producers of the same goods. If the exporting country also lowers its tariffs or reduces its quotas, however, one's own country can make up for any loss by expanding its own exports. In terms of general international welfare, free trade is most beneficial to the world as a whole because consumers from all countries may then purchase goods from the lowest cost source.

There are many examples of the use of tariffs or quotas to insulate the domestic market from foreign competition. In the United States inefficient domestic production of beef, textiles, shoes, and steel has led to the establishment of quotas on the admission of these products from other countries. Domestic producers cannot compete with their foreign competitors and have petitioned Congress and the President to set a physical limit on the amounts of these items imported per year. When limits have not been fixed legislatively, often there has been an informal agreement with the foreign supplier not to export more than specific quantities of a good. In the cases mentioned, the foreign states most affected (and hurt) by United States restrictions have been New Zealand, Australia, and Japan.

In other cases, domestic suppliers have been able to compete with foreign exporters, but only with certain tariff advantages. Articles that come into a country over a tariff pay a tax on their value at the border. The amount of this tax is the amount of advantage which domestic suppliers have in their own market. When the United States was striving to develop its manufacturing industries against the threat of foreign competition during the nineteenth century, American tariffs on industrial goods were high. This prevented British and continental manufacturers from invading the United States marketplace before American industries could become established. Today many of the developing countries of Africa, Asia, the Middle East, and Latin America are in similar positions. They desire to have an access to developed markets for their agricultural goods (which they produce efficiently) but they do not wish to withstand the full force of foreign competition in the industrial sector. Many of them, therefore, have high tariffs on the importation of industrial goods. When their own industries are established, they will gradually be able to lower their tariffs, as the United States did after a considerable delay.

Tariff arrangements, of course, can have great political effect. When nations lower their tariffs they sometimes do so on a preferential basis. The nations of the Common Market, for example, have given African states formerly associated with France preferential tariff concessions in selling within the Common Market. The United States has recently proposed that special tariff concessions be given to all developing countries in the markets of the developed states. These particular concessions, if fully realized, would be very important in the pattern of friendship and antagonism among states. It is not surprising that those nations which have benefited from a preferential tariff arrangement have stronger economic and political stakes in the maintenance of their connection than otherwise would be the case. Imperial preference arrangements within the British Commonwealth of Nations have allowed many Commonwealth countries to sell in the British market with special concessions on tariffs. Most important of all, perhaps, the Common Market itself is a preferential tariff arrangement where the formerly six (now ten) nations of the Common Market have internal free trade among themselves and a common external tariff with outsiders. The creation and maintenance of this arrangement has unquestionably improved political ties among the participating members. Other similar arrangements in East Africa and Central America could have similar effects. The granting of tariff concessions, therefore, is an unmitigatedly political act, and its consequences will be political as well as economic. Nations which benefit from such concessions are receiving a reward or a reinforcement of their policy in international politics. Conversely, raising tariffs may have deleterious effects on the relations between countries.

Depreciation

Another economic instrument is the exchange rate. The exchange rate for dollars into pounds, for example, will influence the trade between the United States and Britain. If dollars are high priced relative to pounds, the export of American goods will be hampered; they will be expensive relative to British goods in the British market. British goods, however, will be able to compete much more effectively in the American market. Recent movements are in the opposite direction. With the recent changes in international exchange rates the value of the pound initially increased from $2.40 to about $2.64. This is a 10 percent increase, and it meant that the price of British goods in the United States would be 10 percent higher. It also meant that the price of American goods in Britain would be 10 percent lower. It therefore stimulated American exports to Britain and depressed British exports to the United States. Since the United States was running a record deficit in its balance of payments, an increase in United States exports and a decrease in imports into the United States helped it regain a balance.

Nations have often used a change in their exchange rates to gain equilibrium in their balance of payments. If a nation wishes to reduce imports and increase its exports, it may devalue its currency relative to others. Whether the devaluation will have the intended effect, however, depends upon what other countries do. Just as nations can have tariff wars, with a tariff increase by one nation leading to an increase by others, so competitive devaluations also can occur. In the postwar period, for example, if the United States had retaliated in 1949 when the British devalued sterling from £1 = $4 to £1 = $2.80, the advantage to the British might have been cancelled. The United States could have reduced the value of its own currency proportionately to the British devaluation leaving the £1 = $4 rate unchanged. In the 1930s in fact, that is what happened. The British, the French, and the Americans devalued their currencies within a few years, and no nation improved its position. After World War II, however, with the reconsolidation of the international trading and financial system, a more international perspective prevailed. Nations that were in financial trouble were permitted to devalue without retaliation. Thus British and French devaluations in the early years did not provoke response. Later when it was the United States' turn in 1971, the other developed countries did not try to prevent the Americans from gaining the benefits of stimulus to their export trade. Today, it is very nearly true that devaluation by a major trading country has become an international act which requires the assent of all other major trading partners if it is to succeed. This is another indication of the degree to which economic internationalism has triumphed over the economic nationalism of the 1930s.

Embargoes and Blockades

Embargoes and blockades are much more severe measures. When the United States was trying to prevent British depredations upon its commerce and ships in 1807, it declared an embargo on trade with Britain. This meant that Americans could not send goods to Britain. As it turned out, however, the embargo hurt American exporters more than it did the British. Napoleon I made use of an opposite device: in his "continental system" of 1806 he sought to prevent the importation of British goods not only into France but into all the other parts of Europe which he controlled. If British exports were denied markets, Napoleon reasoned, Britain would be brought to her knees. But there were loopholes in the "continental system" and British goods did find certain European markets. Britain also had the rest of the world as a preserve for its exports.

In the years after World War II there were Western embargoes on strategic trade with China and Russia, and the United States cut off all trade with China until very recently. Because of its racial policies the United Nations General Assembly has called for an embargo on trade with Rhodesia; many countries have violated this ban, however, particularly South Africa. And the United States itself moved in 1972 to import Rhodesian chromium.

In these instances embargoes and blockades have not worked very efficiently. There are cases, however, where they have had great effect. One salient example is the allied blockade of Japan during World War II. More than the conventional or nuclear bombing campaign, the effectiveness of the blockade forced Japan to submit. It remains true, however, that blockades and embargoes are not effective unless all nations are willing to apply them vigorously. They are also ineffective if states can generate most of their needed raw materials and industrial goods from domestic production. Even a well-enforced blockade would, for these reasons, put less pressure on the Russians than a similar blockade would put on the British. The British are much more dependent upon foreign sources for many of their essential foodstuffs and raw materials.

Foreign and Military Aid

If nations have often tried to influence other states by economic threats and punishments, they have also used the rewards of foreign assistance and loans. The United States has given hundreds of billions of dollars in foreign and military aid since World War II. It is unquestionably true that foreign aid has had a desirable though small redistributive effect on world wealth. It is less clear that foreign aid leads to direct political influence upon the recipient country. This is particularly true where the aid given by one country is offset by aid given by another. But even where one country is the sole source of another's foreign assistance, it still does not uniformly follow that the recipient country will follow the lead of the donor country in foreign affairs. Britain has been a major contributor to Commonwealth countries over the years, but these have often diverged from British policy, notably on Rhodesia. The United States contributed large amounts of assistance to Greece, India, Pakistan, South Korea, South Vietnam, Taiwan, and Turkey, but these political systems have not always adhered to the United States line in foreign policy. Private aid to Israel has been very high, but this has not meant that America could dictate Israeli policy. Indeed, the greatest long-term effect of foreign aid is probably not gratitude or regard toward the donor country, but rather domestic stability. If a country wishes to support another's political system, aid may help. It is much more difficult to get countries to change their political systems or policies in response to foreign assistance.[2]

NATIONAL AND INTERNATIONAL ECONOMIC TECHNIQUES IN THE PRESENT ERA

The current international trading mechanism is one in which no single nation or regional group of nations holds predominant power. A multilateral decision-making framework has emerged. Given this situation, much of the independence which previously attached to national economic policy has been lost.[3] In the 1930s, no country would have hesitated to put on a tariff, to levy exchange controls or quantitative restrictions, or to devalue its currency because of the impact on the system. President Franklin Roosevelt, among other national leaders, was quite willing to hurt the international trading system in order to halt the depression in the United States. "Beggar thy neighbor" policies were indulged in by many states as they strove to raise domestic production and employment.

As a result, national use of economic techniques to gain national objectives was unfettered in the interwar period. After World War II, however, a more enlightened point of view prevailed. If worldwide depression of trade, employment, and production were to be avoided in the future, nations had to think not only of their own narrow national interests, but also of the long-run impacts of their policies. Unquestionably, tariff wars, competitive devaluations, and quantitative restrictions may have helped the short-run position of their initiators, but in the long run most countries ended up worse off, and the depression was prolonged. If states could not rely on their neighbors to seek to maintain relatively open economies and convertible currencies, international trade and commerce would be restricted, limiting the wealth of all. Since much of present-day international prosperity rests on the belief that nations will not return to the economic nationalism of the thirties, states which are tempted to use such policies risk a collapse of confidence in which their own long-term futures would be much affected.

States, therefore, have hesitated to devalue their currencies, to put on exchange controls, or to levy tariffs, and often have done so only as a last resort. Britain, as one classic example, deferred the devaluation of sterling to the point where much of its beneficial effect on exports and the domestic economy had already been lost. If nations postpone such readjustments to the point where the economic system makes them mandatory, they lose much of their effect. Devaluations must take place from a position of some strength, not universally acknowledged weakness. The delays in making such changes, however, were partly due to the general belief that the international financial system had to be maintained with minimum recourse to purely national policies designed to regain payments equilibrium and to foster domestic growth. For years Britain imposed domestic economic stagnation upon itself in a vain effort to maintain the international value of the pound sterling.

Partly because so few nationalistic measures have been employed by debtor states, creditors on the whole have been understanding of their plight. While the creditor nations of Germany and Switzerland might have responded to the French and British devaluations with devaluations of their own currencies, they did not do so, preferring to contribute to British and French financial health. Devaluing countries, moreover, have usually tried to keep the changes in their exchange rates within relatively narrow bounds. Thus there has been less need for others to resort to countermeasures.

This result has been strengthened by the network of economic consultation in the present world. The creditor nations are aware of the difficulties of debtor states; they know that very drastic efforts by debtors to regain their financial positions could topple the edifice of general economic cooperation. If there is some multilateral way in which needed adjustments can be made, these are seen as preferable to nationalistic measures. Thus the Special Drawing Rights of the International Monetary Fund were created to increase the reserves of the international financial system, and to make it easier for debtor states to safeguard their positions without drastic action.

The resolution of the dollar crisis of August to December 1971 indicates the truly multilateral nature of financial decision making. On August 15,

1971 the United States suspended the convertibility of the dollar into gold and put on a temporary import surcharge (equivalent to a tariff on all imports) of 10 percent. At first the United States appeared to insist that the best means for settlement of the crisis was through upward valuations of European and Japanese currencies, while the dollar's par value remained unchanged. This would have made it more difficult for the Europeans and Japanese to export their now more highly priced goods to the United States. It would also have meant that the United States would have had special advantages in selling its own goods in the European and Japanese markets. Since the dollar was not at first to be devalued, however, the United States would not obtain similar advantages in its trade with other countries—namely the less developed countries of Asia, Africa, Latin America, and the Middle East. In the course of the negotiations, however, the Europeans insisted that the United States should formally devalue the American dollar, and in a compromise reached at the Smithsonian Institution in Washington in December 1971, the United States agreed to devalue the dollar 10 percent while the Europeans and Japanese revalued their currencies upward by varying amounts. The import surcharge was removed. Neither initial position prevailed in the final settlement. The Smithsonian Agreement represents the first general revaluation of currency exchange rates since the Bretton Woods accords of 1944.

Most important perhaps, the critical differences between the United States and the Europeans were not over the question of whether or not exchange rates should be changed to permit the United States to remove its balance of payments deficit. They were over the best means by which rates should be changed and the deficit eliminated. No country was thinking of retaliating against the United States, as might have been the expected reaction in the context of economic nationalism of the 1930s.

The result is that although nations have formal economic sovereignty— they can devalue, put on tariffs, levy exchange controls, or establish quantitative restrictions on trade—the exercise of sovereignty has been greatly limited in recent years. Since all nations wish to avoid the national and international depression of the 1930s they are careful to tailor their national measures to those which are consonant with overall confidence and cooperation.

Oddly enough, this places the subtle nation in a very favorable position to take advantage of Prisoner's Dilemma aspects of the negotiating situation. Neither party may wish to see the general atmosphere of confidence and openness interrupted; but if one party is willing to cooperate and to express understanding of the financial problems of the other, then the other has considerable negotiating scope. If one can rely on the cooperation of an opposite number, one is tempted to limit one's own cooperation. It is far from clear whether there will be new competitions between trading countries and blocs that reflect this asymmetry. But it is possible that a united European trading bloc and a Japanese bloc might seek to maintain or to increase their access to the American market while radically reducing or failing to expand their markets to American products and investment. In the longer term this could give rise to a very severe trading crisis. It could disrupt the progress made since World War II.

ECONOMIC DEVELOPMENT AND PEACE

Through the centuries economic remedies have been proposed to prevent war. Immanuel Kant believed that war was incompatible with the "spirit of commerce" and that sooner or later it would disappear. Marx foresaw a socialist world commonwealth in which there would be no conflict among nations.[4] More recently, a variety of statesmen have contended that the causes of war lie in poverty, pestilence, and disease. If these could be eradicated, the roots of war would wither and die. Economic development would then be the key to prosperity and peace. Much doubt was cast on this theory by the behavior of Japan and Germany in the late nineteenth and early twentieth centuries. Surely these two nations offer the greatest success stories of rapid economic development and progress in modern times. But the political and international aspects of German and Japanese industrialization do not give grounds for optimism. Rapid economic development was associated with extreme international and domestic policies, and with a much more warlike demeanor on the part of both powers. Further, one sociologist found a correlation between very rapid development and domestic political extremism. Citing the cases of Russia, Germany, and Scandinavia, S.M. Lipset concludes that rapid industrial change is likely to be politically destabilizing.[5] Considering a wider range of cases, Michael Haas reaches similar conclusions.[6]

Recently, two observers have offered new versions of the old theme. Robert McNamara, U.S. Secretary of Defense in the Kennedy and Johnson administrations, noted a relationship between poverty and violence. From 1958 to 1966 he recorded 164 internationally significant outbreaks of violence, violence which affected the very existence of the governments involved. Fifteen of these involved military conflicts between two states; the others were wholly or partly domestic in origin. In 1958 there were twenty-three major insurgencies in progress; in 1966 there were forty. Further, the total number of outbreaks of violence has increased every year since 1958. "What is most significant of all is that there is a direct and constant relationship between the incidence of violence and the economic status of the countries afflicted."[7] Dividing nations into four categories—rich, middle-income, poor, and very poor—McNamara found that only one of the twenty-seven rich nations had suffered a major internal upheaval on its territory since 1958. Among the thirty-eight poor nations, on the other hand, thirty-two had experienced significant conflicts. Since 1958, 87 percent of the very poor nations, 69 percent of the poor nations, and 48 percent of the middle-income nations have undergone serious violence. "There can be no question but that there is a relationship between violence and economic backwardness, and the trend of such violence is up, not down."[8] McNamara concluded that in a modernizing society security means development, and that without development there could be no security.

If one looks a little more carefully at this argument, however, it fails to show that international violence declines with increasing economic development. Over 90 percent of the cases were those where violence was primarily internal. It does not appear that in these cases violence automatically spilled over into the international orbit. Indeed, with the exception of China and Indochina, the classic guerilla episodes since 1945 were not associated with international wars. At the same time, the major participants in conflicts around the globe were not less developed nations, but rather developed states like the United States, the Soviet Union, Britain, France, Holland, and Portugal. Nor does it appear that high indices of development are an indicator of high domestic stability and peace. Since 1966 when the McNamara study was completed, there have been significant episodes of domestic violence in France, the United States, Belgium, West Germany, and Japan. It may even be hazarded that there may be a curvilinear relationship between development and internal violence (Figure 18-1). The paradox of affluence may be that with very high living standards, certain sectors of the community, less versed in technological and communication skills, may be left out of the development process and become relatively deprived in status and economic terms.[9] This in turn may form the basis for renewed civil strife. In international relations a similar curvilinear function may exist, relating

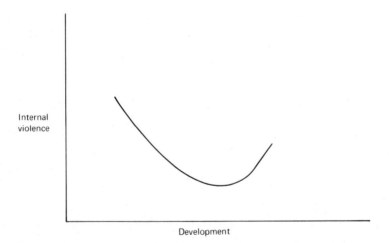

Figure 18-1 RELATIONSHIP BETWEEN INTERNAL VIOLENCE AND DEVELOP-
MENT

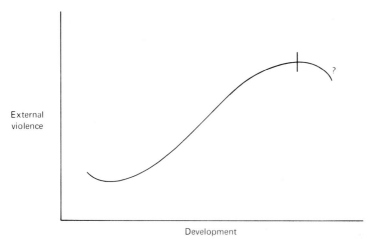

Figure 18-2 RELATIONSHIP BETWEEN EXTERNAL VIOLENCE AND DEVELOP-
MENT

external violence with development (Figure 18-2). Such a curve hypothesizes
that external violence may actually increase with development, at least until a
stage is reached in which the quality of domestic life takes precedence over
international entanglements. Scandinavia appears to have reached this stage at
the beginning of the twentieth century. Western Europe approached it after
World War II. It is still too early to tell whether Japan, the United States, and
the Soviet Union are reaching such a threshold. At the very least, however, it
is clear that the simple equation, security = development, does not hold for
international relations. Oddly enough, if peace were to be the only value and
welfare entirely disregarded, there would be a case for extremely low levels of
economic development. Nations which are on the verge of starvation, and
which possess preindustrial economies, are not in a position to wage large-
scale war against their neighbors.

The second theme linking economic development and peace has been
offered by Karl Deutsch. Deutsch, a long-time student of nationalism, is not
optimistic that the present nation-state can be eliminated. Communications
barriers will prevent the full integration of mankind.

As long as there are any substantial effects of unevenness and distance
upon communication, the splitting up of very large networks of communicators into smaller subgroups with their communication codes, languages,
cultures, or variations of ideology is highly probable. It becomes more
probable with increasing number of communicators, with increasing
frequency of communication, with increasing risk of communication over-
load and sharper competition among messages, and with increasing un-

evenness or variance in the distribution of communications. This process of splitting will stop, according to this reasoning, at those group sizes where local and translocal communications will be equally frequent and salient, but these equilibrium points are likely to fall short of all mankind.[10]

He does believe, however, that communications differences can be mitigated and that peace among nation-states is possible. The argument goes as follows: at the present time the average annual per capita income in the world is about $600. Even if this average were approximated in all nations, there would still be war for at this low level, "a marginal addition of another $100 would seem large enough and desirable enough to many people to risk or initiate violence or war . . . to get it." If the theory of marginal utility is true, however, there should be some level of income at which the extra utility of additional amounts of income would be so low that nations would not be willing to use violence to gain them. In Figure 18-3 the increasing utility of income is portrayed against the increasing disutility of effort required to get it. At the level of $600, the marginal utility of extra income is high and the marginal disutility of the effort to obtain it low. At the level of $4,800, the marginal utility of extra income is low and the marginal disutility of the effort to obtain it high. Deutsch is not sure what a "peace level" of income might be in international relations. But he notes that in the 1930s when the per capita

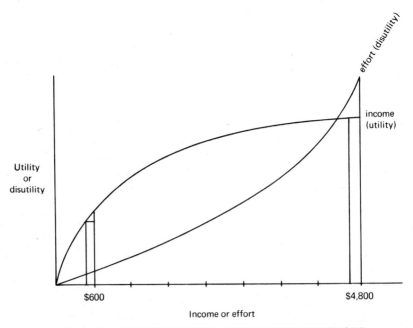

Figure 18-3 UTILITY OF INCREASING INCOME AND EFFORT

income in the United States was below $1,500 in current money values, "there was still frequent loss of life in labor conflicts." [12]

> Today at an average income level of $3,000, wage disputes have ceased to be a killing matter, although fear for real estate values in half-poor neighborhoods—but not in rich ones—sometimes still reinforces the propensity to bloodshed. It seems not implausible, however, that much of the economic drive to nationalism, racism, and violence would abate at an average world-income level 50 or 60 percent above that of the United States today. The higher of these figures would suggest a world-income level of $4,800 per capita, or eight times the present-day amount.
>
> This potential peace level could be reached in about seventy-two years, by means of a net annual economic growth rate of per capita income of about 3 percent, which is almost exactly the average economic growth of sixty-eight countries in the 1950s. [13]

Hence in seventy-two years it is possible that some of the major motivations for international conflict will be eliminated.

This line of analysis, however, is subject to a number of criticisms. First, it obscures the degree to which human motivations relate to relative status and economic welfare rather than absolute status and welfare. Poverty has increasingly become a relative term. Jealousies among peoples and states might be tolerable even if average per capita income were low, assuming that inequalities were not great. If, however, average per capita income were high, but disparities between people and/or nations great, the less advantaged might be willing to resort to violence to improve their lot. Since their concern would be relative, rather than absolute, they might derive a good deal of utility from further efforts to improve their position. Today, the gap between rich and poor nations is not closing. [14] When the world achieves an average per capita income of $4,800, the disparity may be even greater. Thus the relative incentive to violence may not only remain high; it may increase.

Secondly, in order for the argument to be effective, it presumes that economic goals are critically important factors in international politics. Attaining these goals, then, makes for relatively peaceful behavior. As the record of developed states tends to show, peace does not necessarily obtain among the most highly developed powers. And the process of that development may be very destabilizing. Taking the entire record of modern history, the more developed commercial states have been more involved in war than the less developed nations. It is therefore by no means generally true that economic development is a means to peace. It may, for important periods of the development process, lead to war.

The most that one can say is that economic development offers one path to those goals that wars have often been fought over. The outpouring of European imperialism at the end of the nineteenth century certainly had some economic roots in the drive for raw materials and markets. The

Japanese decision to launch the Pacific war in 1941 was prompted by the need to gain access to the raw materials of Southeast Asia. If more highly developed economies could have offered new skills and new technologies, and these in turn created new markets, the demand for external expansion might have been less. In certain favorable circumstances the processes of internal development and change may obviate the need for concern with political control externally. But these circumstances are not usually approximated; throughout history high rates of economic development have probably been more often associated with war than with peace.

ECONOMIC TRENDS: TOWARD NATIONALIZATION OR INTERNATIONALIZATION?

The net effect of the proliferation of modern technology, industry, and communications is difficult to discern. On the one hand, technology has contributed greatly to international forces. Information processing, scientific experiment, and even production are no longer national in scope. There is a global community of cosmopolites in technology, industry, and intellectual life who communicate more with each other than with non-cosmopolites of their own national group. The nation-state can no longer provide for many of the essential needs of its citizens, including security from the threat of national or international violence. In economic terms, national economies cannot insulate themselves from the impact of foreign production, distribution, and innovation. Even more clearly, in the information field, people are beginning to rely less on national and more on international sources of information. Whatever national manipulations may permit, they do not apparently succeed in cutting whole societies off from communication with the outside world. Further, it might be suggested that these trends are likely to increase as the global exchange of information and the communications revolution proceed.

In the fields of production and distribution the new multinational corporation is becoming a fact of life. Partially outside the control of the political jurisdictions in which they operate, these corporations are creating networks of economic decision making that transcend national perspectives and boundaries. While American concerns have the largest single share of overseas investment and operate the most powerful multinational corporations, there is an important countermovement by European and Japanese firms. By 1970, outside assets under American business control were nearing $200 billion. At the same time, European and Japanese holdings in the United States alone were approaching $100 billion.[15] If American multinational firms influence economic outcomes in Europe, Japanese and European firms help to shape the American economic context. In the future the penetration of national markets and production centers will be likely to increase. Individual states, even the United States, will find it harder to control the proliferation of international economic activities which take place within their frontiers.

But while economics and technology have surely contributed to a greater internationalization of information, production, and distribution, the nation-state has not been outmoded by the new developments. In some ways it has even been strengthened. The multinational corporation has evoked a partly negative political reaction in Europe. The Japanese role in the United States market has created a political reaction of some force. While the enlargement of the Common Market to include Britain and other states may increase trade and development within the community, the relatively high common tariff may inhibit the growth of United States exports and lead to greater political and economic tension. Indeed, as regional consolidations proceed, one may anticipate greater interregional conflict. Economic internationalism may ultimately cause a resurgence of political nationalism.

Beyond this, however, it does not appear that new international institutions and movements can serve as foci of loyalty for individual citizens. Loyalty is in part a reflection of personal and social contact in in-group–out-group situations. Identity may require a consciousness of what is foreign. The new international forces of the modern age have blurred this distinction, and in part this is responsible for feelings of anomie, powerlessness, psychic alienation. As international images compete with national ones, the we-feeling of national identity declines. But the result is not the substitution of international for national loyalties. International foci remain disembodied and functional. National and local loyalties are still personal and social. It is possible, therefore, that the ultimate result of economic, technological, and communications internationalism may be a desperate, psychic search for new symbols and units of identification. Z. Brzezinski argues:

> Because he finds himself living in a congested, overlapping, confusing and impersonal environment, man seeks solace in restricted and familiar intimacy. The national community is the obvious one to turn to, and a definition of what a national community is may well become more restrictive as broader transnational cooperation develops.[16]

> As the nation-state is gradually yielding its sovereignty, the psychological importance of the national community is rising, and the attempt to establish an equilibrium between the imperatives of the new internationalism and the need for a more intimate national community is the source of frictions and conflicts.[17]

Moreover, the net trend of economic and political mobilization of the populace in many countries has been to strengthen the state as the source of satisfaction of personal and national needs and the purveyor of essential services. The role of national government in the solution of the problems of the city, race, education, employment, and ecology is now crucial. Lesser jurisdictions cannot possibly handle the problems. Even those who most categorically reject a given political basis for the state, plan to utilize it to accomplish alternative political purposes. National foci are by no means in discard, and they may even be strengthened by nationalist reactions to international influences. One has the impression that nations and peoples today are looking for new national leadership which will interpret the issues and concerns of the age in terms that are politically relevant and can be understood. Internationally oriented technocratic leadership may be incapable of accomplishing this task. As one possibly significant indication of this feeling, the votes for German and Italian authoritarian and nationalist parties have increased substantially in recent years.

On balance, therefore, it is not clear that the ultimate result of new economic and technological forces will be an increasing internationalism. While the state cannot cope with all the needs of its citizens, it may be able to satisfy, or to appear to satisfy, their most physically relevant needs. This could give it a new lease on life.

ECONOMIC TECHNIQUES IN THE PRESENT ERA

Generally speaking, states have tended to foreswear the economic nationalism of the 1930s. They have used economic instruments in such a way as to protect the multilateral and international economy. Desiring to maintain the climate of economic confidence, creditor nations have on the whole been remarkably understanding about the plight of their debtor colleagues. At this juncture it is unthinkable that the world could be plunged into another welter of "beggar thy neighbor" policies like those of the Depression. At the same time, it may be that less cooperative economic policies will be adopted by trading blocs as major industrial or integrated groupings strive to protect themselves from the impact of foreign competition. A greater use of nationalist measures such as exchange controls and quotas could then be forecast.

NOTES

1 See E.H. Carr, *Nationalism and After* (London: Macmillan, 1945), pp. 11-16.
2 On this point see particularly, E.B. Haas, "Multilateral Incentives for Limiting International Violence," in R. Rosecrance (ed.), *The Future of the International Strategic System* (San Francisco: Chandler, 1972).
3 See R.L. Vernon, "Economic Sovereignty at Bay," *Foreign Affairs,* October 1968.
4 See Elliot R. Goodman, *The Soviet Design for a World State* (New York: Columbia University Press, 1960).
5 See S.M. Lipset, *Political Man* (Garden City, N.Y.: Doubleday, 1960), pp. 68-72.
6 See Michael Haas, "Social Change and National Aggressiveness, 1900-1960," in J.D. Singer (ed.), *Quantitative International Politics* (New York: Free Press, 1968), pp. 221-222, 230-231.
7 McNamara, *The Essence of Security* (New York: Harper & Row, 1968), p. 145.
8 Ibid., p. 146.

9 See G. DiPalma, *Apathy and Participation* (New York: Free Press, 1970).

10 Deutsch, "Nation and World," in Ithiel Pool (ed.), *Contemporary Political Science* (New York: McGraw-Hill, 1967), pp. 214-215.

11 Ibid., p. 219.

12 Ibid.

13 Deutsch, op. cit., p. 219.

14 See Theodore Caplow, "Are the Poor Countries Getting Poorer?" *Foreign Policy,* Summer 1971.

15 See Raymond Vernon, "Multinational Enterprise and National Security," *Adelphi Papers,* no. 74, p. 1, Institute for Strategic Studies, London, January 1971.

16 Z. Brzezinski, *Between Two Ages* (New York: Viking Press, 1970), p. 54.

17 Ibid., p. 56.

5

Contemporary
International Systems

We have reviewed international systems, objectives, and techniques. The present international system is in flux, changing from a past bipolarity to tripolarity and then perhaps to multipolarity. While the post-World War II system contained conflict relatively well between the two superpowers, it is not so certain that military conflict between multipolar nuclear powers will be so easily deterred or contained. Two different forms of future international systems are discussed. In one, conflict will be even more widespread than it has been in the past. In the other, cooperation will be more likely.

CHAPTER NINETEEN

The Present
International System

THE AFTERMATH OF WORLD WAR II

In retrospect, the intensity of apprehension in the immediate post-World War II generation that bipolar tensions would lead to major war is surprising. Some observers believed that the Soviet Union was as bent on territorial expansion as Hitler's Germany, and that nothing short of Western employment of force would put a stop to these ambitions. Some other students were convinced that American imperialism would cause conflagration: the United States would extend "manifest destiny" to world politics and would seek major new gains. Both sets of scholars were wrong. The Soviet Union was essentially a conservative power in international political terms and was certainly not willing to risk all the achievements of the Russian Revolution and three decades of internal construction in a futile attempt to dominate the world. The United States, for her part, was an irresolute imperialist: sometimes she would extend doctrines of containment and liberation to ridiculous lengths; on other occasions she would overlook changes that materially affected her real national interests. After 1964 she ceased trying to direct the affairs of Western Europe. In 1972 it is possible that she is retrenching on a wide range of previous international obligations.

The reasons for relative quiescence in both cases, however, are worth pondering. First, the Soviets were far too weak to risk war with the capitalist states in 1917-1920. After World War II they were relatively much stronger, but they now had much more to lose. The original ideological élan had faded with the unfolding of Communist bureaucracy in the twenties and thirties. Those who succeeded in the system were less radical ideologues than skillful managers and power wielders.[1] Moreover, internal Communist rule was secure enough that its continuance was in no sense dependent upon a succession of foreign victories. The Soviets were also as conscious of the evils of unrestrained conflict as were Western leaders, having suffered greatly from World War II. Unlike the French revolutionaries, the Soviets were weakest when the Revolution reached its peak. They could not carry the Revolution to Europe and the rest of the world. In this respect the Russians in 1945 were not completely unlike the French in 1830: both nations were very strong, but far from dominant on the international scene: both already had internal and external achievements to their credit. The need to push further was less, the danger of pushing further was greater.

In the United States case, the American role in world affairs had to be legitimized in semimoral terms. The United States could undertake a "crusade" to rehabilitate Europe or to "stop Communism." When the moral issues became blurred, however, American policy began to lose its missionary quality. Europe soon proved that it could stand on its own feet, and even compete with America. The Communists were not able to maintain a united front against the West. In various areas, several communist nations were willing to seek a *détente*. One began to wonder whether new communist "victories" would be regarded in Moscow or Peking as triumphs or as contributions to chronic indigestion. In these ambiguous circumstances, United States policy faltered. It no longer had a moral *raison d'être*.

Thus the first major postwar tension, that between the Communist and the Capitalist worlds, was less serious than once believed. Of perhaps greater long-term importance was the further development of nationalist conflicts in the Third World. One of the unanswered questions of historical international politics is whether nationalist conflicts are self-generating. The argument for their continual regeneration supposes a cyclical pattern. In the first stage, a nationalist state breaks away from imperial rule. After consolidation of its own domestic position, a nationalist regime may seek to expand into adjacent territories, winning greater influence for itself on the world scene. Sooner or later, however, the territories which it has acquired will seek independence on their own and revolt. This starts the nationalist process again. Clearly some areas of the world have been able to avoid such constant strife; since 1945 Western Europe has been in the process of becoming a "security community" in which wars among participating state units are effectively ruled out.[2] The admission of Britain and three other states to the Common Market will further extend this grouping.

In other areas of the globe, however, peaceful unification and reconciliation are far from being the typical pattern. In the Middle East, Arab and Israeli nationalisms have been fanned by three wars in twenty years. Nationalist tensions between India and Pakistan have led to renewed war over Bangladesh. Given the heterogeneous intermixture of populations in several areas of the world, it is not clear how self-determination can ever result in wholly satisfactory boundaries. In Southeast and South Asia, and in Africa there is a chronic potential for irredentism. There is even such a potential in Central and Eastern Europe, but the European political context has thus far damped such possibilities.

INCHOATE TRIPOLARITY

It is uncertain whether such nationalist conflicts will continue indefinitely. By the mid-1950s, however, it was at least clear that there were more than two groupings in world politics. The period 1956-1961 was one of incipient tripolarity, with the United States and the Soviet Union seeking to advance their political and ideological causes through additional adherents among the nonaligned states. This gave the Third World great influence in the previously bipolar competition. For a time it seemed possible that the neutralist-nationalist camp would consolidate itself as a balancer between the two major blocs, following the policy traditionally imputed to Britain in the nineteenth century. By 1961, however, it was clear that the nonaligned countries would not form a bloc, and that they would not seek to create a balance against the extremist behavior of either of the two superpowers. Rather, it appeared that the nationalist-neutralist group conceived of its position as an approximate mid-point between contending camps. Thus, if one of the two prior blocs engaged in reckless or aggressive behavior, the nonaligned camp did not chastize it or lean toward the other side. Instead, the neutralists moved toward the offending party so that they would still occupy the midpoint of the East-West international continuum. This pattern of behavior is shown diagrammatically in Figure 19-1.

When, during the Belgrade Conference of nonaligned states in September 1961, the Soviet Union resumed atmospheric nuclear testing, the Conference

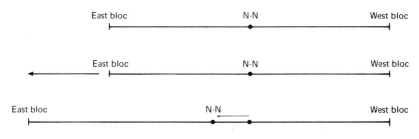

Figure 19-1 NEUTRALIST BALANCING BEHAVIOR

could not bring itself to condemn the Soviet action and instead adjusted to it. When in October 1962, the Soviets placed offensive missiles in Cuba and the United States precipitated a world crisis in response, the neutralists did not proclaim a "plague on both your houses." Even the war in Vietnam has not produced a major neutralist reaction against the United States. Gradually the two superpowers came to consider the neutralists as dependent variables in world politics. Far from having to adjust their policies to neutralist requirements, the Big Two were able to alter neutralist policy. At this point the superpowers greatly moderated their effects to curry favor with the nonaligned group.

THE RELATION BETWEEN LOCAL AND CENTRAL CONFLICT

While this meant that the Third World would no longer have major influence in world politics as a group, it did not produce a dissociation in the United States and the Soviet Union from smaller, less developed nations. The United States remained heavily involved in Southeast Asia. The Soviet Union was becoming more and more involved in the Middle East. Each major power had minor clients to support and protect. There remains the possibility, very real in the Middle East, that major powers will become embroiled in the conflicts of their client states. This means that there is some relationship between the probabilities of local and central conflict. Since the mid-1960s there has been a rapprochement between the United States and the Soviet Union on nuclear proliferation, arms control, European, and other issues. It is possible that both powers now believe that their understandings are durable enough so that they would not be fundamentally interrupted by a small power crisis. This provides reassurance only insofar as neither power attempts to capitalize on the understanding or the forbearance of the other.

One could imagine a scenario, however, in which each power, relying upon the other's abstention, would commit itself to a course of action which could end in major war. Believing in the restraint of the other, one power could make irrevocable commitments to an area or a country. Once one power had made such commitments, however, the other might be forced to respond. Such a situation would be not unlike that which prevailed prior to World War I. By June 1914 allies had failed to come to each other's assistance so often, that alliances failed to deter. But when the July crisis came, alliances did not deter; they merely broadened a local conflict in the Balkans into World War I. If it had been certain beforehand that Germany would come in to support Austria and that Russia would be supported by France, both sides might have hesitated, knowing that the war would engulf all of Europe. Deterrence might have worked. In this sense, the most dangerous situation is intermediate: where there is not enough concrete military opposition to deter war; and where there is not enough cooperation to obviate it.

If there were total dissociation of the major powers from local conflicts among client or allied states, there would be no relationship between local and international war. The probability of the first could be high, while that of the second could be very low. Under contemporary circumstances, however, total dissociation by either major power is unlikely. This means ultimately that the greater the local violence, the greater the danger of a central clash. In the longer run, therefore, the potential for violence among nationalist or lesser nations may hold a threat to the general peace.

THE QUESTION OF THE DISTRIBUTION OF WEALTH

Another issue that may cause conflict in the future is that of maldistribution of wealth in the world. We have already seen that in the present world status, influence, and access to resources are very unevenly distributed. The nations with greatest influence also have greatest access to resources. In one sense, this should not present an untenable situation because, though resources are unevenly distributed, it will be very difficult for those without resources to get them by threatening military force. The national elites at the top should be able to keep their privileged positions.

Yet the demand for a more even distribution of wealth is likely to grow with time. It is likely to be accentuated if it turns out that there is an upper limit of growth, which for reasons of ecology the world should not exceed. Then all the efforts of the southern half of the world will be turned toward effecting a redistribution. As nuclear weapons spread, it may even be that nations or groups in the Southern Hemisphere will resort to desperate expedients to speed redistribution. These efforts may be attempted in part because the expansion of international trade, investment, and monetary adjustments has greatly benefited the Europeans, the United States, and Japan without correlative benefit for the less developed countries.

A NEW TRIPOLARITY?

One of the imponderables of the immediate future is whether the emergence of China on the world scene will lead to a new version of tripolarity. In years past, and particularly when she was convulsed by the Cultural Revolution, China played a minor role in world affairs. She either had not developed a worldwide pattern of interests, or that pattern was not a stable one. To say nothing of European and new nationalist powers, her relations with the United States and the Soviet Union have been inconstant and undependable. After the Communist victory in China, 1948-1949, the tripolar relationship appeared relatively stable (Figure 19-2). By the later 1950s, however, the

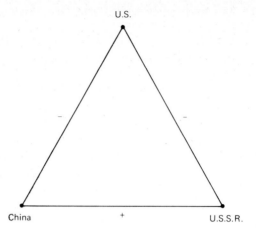

(−) negative or hostile relationship
(+) positive or friendly relationship

Figure 19-2 TRIPOLAR RELATIONSHIP–1949

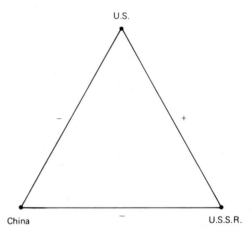

Figure 19-3 TRIPOLAR RELATIONSHIP–1964

negative valence of the relationship between the Soviet Union and the United States was moving in a more positive direction. At the same time, the positive valence for Sino-Soviet relations had been replaced by a negative one (Figure 19-3). While it is difficult to say which change came first[3] they clearly reinforced one another. If three negative valences had obtained, there would have been a temptation on the part of one power to improve its relations with at least one other on the postulate, "The enemy of my enemy is my friend."[4] If two positive valences coexisted with one negative valence, there would be a tendency either to move to a tripolar alliance or to substitute one negative valence for a positive valence on the theory that one cannot be a friend to a friend of an enemy.

Of greatest interest in 1972 is the tentative rapprochement between the United States and China, thereby introducing another element of instability in the structure of world relations (Figure 19-4). Such a situation is unlikely to continue in a triangular relationship. There is pressure on the Soviet-American relationship to become more hostile or on the Sino-Soviet relationship to become more friendly. Alternatively, and perhaps most probably, the Sino-American rapprochement may not be of great scope or duration. Much depends upon whether the Sino-Soviet split is the fundamental point of reference for the rest of the system. If it is fundamental, then it would seem unlikely that the United States could maintain equal and stable friendships with both the Soviets and the Chinese. One or the other would have important incentives to improve its relations with the United States.

A NEW QUADRIPOLARITY?

Additional quandaries are presented when one adds the complication of Japan. In the mid-1950s the relationship between the four countries—the United States, the Soviet Union, China, and Japan—was balanced and stable as Figure 19-5 indicates. It offered fundamentally a bipolar arrangement with the United States and Japan siding against China and the Soviet Union. The

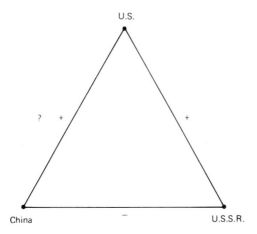

Figure 19-4 TRIPOLAR RELATIONSHIP–1972

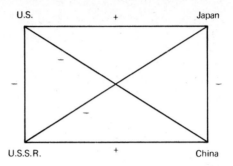

Figure 19-5 QUADRILATERAL RELATIONSHIP–1955

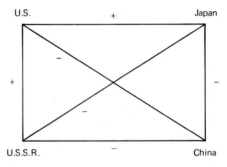

Figure 19-6 QUADRILATERAL RELATIONSHIP–1964

development of a rapprochement between the United States and Russia and the opening of the Sino-Soviet split, however, led to imbalance, as we see in Figure 19-6. Here two cycles are unbalanced: U.S.–Japan–U.S.S.R. and U.S.S.R.–China–Japan. But this imbalance was nothing compared to that introduced by the rapprochement between China and the United States (Figure 19-7). With President Nixon's visit to China the following cycles become unbalanced:

> US–China–U.S.S.R.
> US–Japan–China
> Japan–U.S.S.R.–China
> Japan–US–U.S.S.R.

If balance reasserts itself in the form of a new bipolarity, it might do so in either of two ways. The Japanese might become very discontent with United States policy, switching instead to a link with the Soviet Union, and the United States might reverse its previous favorable attitude toward the Soviets (Figure 19-8). Alternatively, and more likely, a bipolarity could develop with

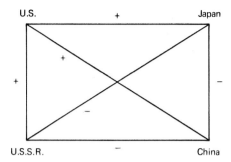

Figure 19-7 QUADRILATERAL RELATIONSHIP–1972

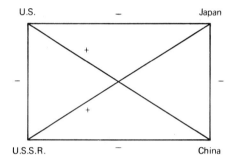

Figure 19-8 POSSIBLE QUADRILATERAL RELATIONSHIP

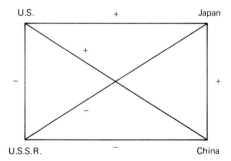

Figure 19-9 POSSIBLE QUADRILATERAL RELATIONSHIP

the United States, Japan, and China all aligned against the Soviet Union (Figure 19-9). That the Soviet Union is quite worried about just such a relationship developing is indicated by its recent attempts to woo Japan and to settle outstanding territorial questions between the two countries. Since the American-Japanese tie and the Sino-Soviet split are the most strongly developed valences among the four states, the Japanese may have a crucial influence on United States policy, helping to determine how far the Soviet-American and the Sino-American rappochements will proceed. The Japanese seem quite likely to change their traditional policy of hostility to both China and Russia in the next year or so. The power they select as a possible friend will also have great impact on American choices. If China is chosen by Japan, the world might move to a three against one bipolarity in the East Asia region.

The types of possible changes indicated in these valence relationships show once again that the future of international politics is likely to be more fluid and unpredictable than the past bipolar system of international relations. The number of major actors has already risen to three or four, and with the emergence of a united Western Europe a fifth pole may be added. The Chinese influence in world affairs is already beginning to affect outcomes in Europe, dampening further moves of rapprochement between the Europeans and the Soviet Union. It appears likely that the consolidation of a quintipolar world will provide for shifting friendships and antagonisms, not totally unlike the shifts in the eighteenth-century balance of power. This prospect could in general, theoretical terms be a welcome one, but nuclear balancing may be more difficult to accomplish than traditional power balancing. Uncertainties of nuclear strategy raise a quandary that may require new methods of stabilizing the future international system.

NOTES

1 See Barrington Moore, Jr., *Terror and Progress: USSR* (Cambridge, Mass.: Harvard University Press, 1954).

2 See Deutsch et al., *Political Community and the North Atlantic Area* (Princeton: Princeton University Press, 1957).

3 See Sophia Peterson, "Conflict, Communication and Mutual Threat in Soviet-American and Sino-Soviet Relations: A Statistical Examination of Interrelationships" (UCLA, 1968).

4 See also for a more formal statement, Harary, Cartright, and Norman, *Structural Models* (New York: Wiley, 1965).

CHAPTER TWENTY

Two Future
International Systems

In this chapter we shall examine two purely hypothetical international systems. The first is an extreme model of nuclear strategic multipolarity, with nuclear weapon capacities in the hands of a substantial number of states. In this model it is presumed that strategic and military considerations are dominant, and that nations will attack one another when deterrent conditions are absent. This model shows by exaggeration some of the logic of a future military strategic system. Other considerations are deliberately neglected. The second model is a highly cooperative model of economic interpenetration in which foreign trade and investment proceed to the point where each major nation in the system is constrained economically to avoid politically disruptive policies. Nations have mutual leverage within each other's domestic economies and do not dare undercut each other's markets.

A MILITARY MODEL[1]

Deterrence and Bipolarity

In order to observe the problems presented in a multipolar deterrent world, it may be best to commence with the rational difficulties of deterrence in a bipolar framework. Clearly, for deterrence to succeed, the negative payoffs to an aggressor must be much higher than the positive payoffs. The expectation of attack (of striking) must be negative, certainly as compared with the *status quo ante*. If a potential aggressor faces a high probability of large negative payoffs and only a small probability of large positive payoffs, he may hesitate. But while these payoffs are the ones we wish to offer to a potential aggressor, they are not always easy to arrange. Indeed, there is a central tension in two-party deterrence theory. On the one hand, *ex ante* one must assure high probabilities of a devastating response to any aggression in case hostile action takes place. On the other hand, *ex post* one may or *may not* want to make a devastating response if hostile action does take place. There is thus a major difference between *ex ante* and *ex post* incentives.

To see why this is true, let us take a few examples. In Europe it has been the traditional policy of the United States and NATO to refuse to rule out the use of nuclear weapons if the Soviets turn their conventional arms strength against Berlin or West Germany. To assure deterrence of an attack in central Europe or an absorption of Berlin one may even want to pledge that one will retaliate with all the force at one's command upon an enemy if he should make such an attack. These are the *ex ante* incentives before an attack takes place.

If an attack actually does take place, on the other hand, one may very well not want to carry out one's declared policy. If the United States hits the Soviet Union massively with nuclear weapons, it presumably will not be able to prevent Soviet retaliation upon American or European cities with nuclear bombs. Thus the automatic recourse to an *ex ante* policy brings about a very undesirable chain of events for one's own side. What one says one would do before the event is not what one necessarily wants to do once the event occurs.

Somewhat similar quandaries are involved in assuring reliable deterrence of an attack on the United States. To reinforce deterrence of such an attack one may want to pledge in advance that American forces will wreak the most terrible vengeance upon the homeland of an attacker. These are the *ex ante* incentives. Yet in most instances of possible Soviet attacks on the United States, the United States would not want to retaliate in unlimited fashion upon Soviet population centers. Probable Soviet attacks would concentrate on hitting American strategic forces, missile and bomber bases. If American policy makers were then to decide to retaliate massively on Soviet cities, America would be inviting Soviet forces to stage second-wave massive attacks on American cities, attacks which until that point were by no means inevitable. Once again, *ex post* incentives are very different from *ex ante* incentives. In this instance, the carrying out of the deterrent threat actually disadvantages oneself as much as it harms the attacker.

Even in the case where an initial Soviet nuclear attack had been directed primarily at American cities, it is by no means certain that the revenge motive would lead to a spasm retaliation upon Soviet urban populations. This point is reinforced by the Soviet-American agreement at the Strategic Arms Limitation Talks to consult over the "hot line" in the event of a discharge of nuclear weapons on either side. Whether United States leaders would be tempted to indulge in this massive retaliation would depend upon their perceptions of the best means of war termination. If it were presumed that the final political shape of the world would be determined in negotiations with the U.S.S.R., America might decide to retain its large, unimpaired strategic nuclear capability (presuming it could do so) to prevent further attacks and to influence the course of the bargaining. In this bargaining process, ratios of surviving missile stocks could be of great significance. Once again, *ex ante* and *ex post* incentives are in conflict. Thus one may even state: the success of deterrence as a prewar policy may depend upon convincing the enemy that one would do things that it was not in one's interest to do, if an attack actually occurred. If this is true, the requirements of deterrence are difficult to meet even in dyadic or bipolar conditions. They are even more difficult to attain under conditions of multipolarity.

Deterrence and Multipolarity

The dyadic case is simpler in that there are only two central nuclear countries. Each protagonist measures itself against the other. It is relatively easy to estimate the minimum requirements for necessary force. There is no difficulty in knowing whom to retaliate against. If there is a nuclear attack, it must have been staged by the opponent. Both of these problems are complicated in a multipolar order.

In the first place, it is not clear how much force one needs. Should one plan to retaliate against all members of the strategic system, against some, or only against one? Since one cannot be sure how much force he needs, the arms race is likely to be accelerated. Some aspects of this problem can be seen even today. The United States maintains capabilities large enough to cope with the Chinese and the Russians, and it must have enough left over to deal with each, no matter what the other does. The Russians have allocated their forces in the same way. But the two-power arms race between the United States and the Soviet Union may be speeded because the capabilities that each thinks in terms of using against the third power may be viewed by the principal opponent as destined for himself. Thus in the presence of third powers, bilateral arms races may increase in intensity.

In the second place, in strategic multipolarity there may be the question of whom to retaliate against. There is the possibility of the spread of mobile or concealed capabilities, for example submarine-launched missiles. The miniaturization of weapons will make possible suitcase bombs which might be clandestinely introduced into the cities of an important power. Even fishing boats in major port cities could be used to transport and hide nuclear weapons.

Two possible problems are presented here. First, there are dangers of anonymous delivery in which a state merely wants to attack another state and avoid retaliation. Second, there is the threat of catalytic war in which a state seeks to simulate an attack by some third power, inducing the victim to retaliate upon the innocent party.

Anonymous delivery is certainly not consistent with attempts to threaten or coerce another power. Any such threats would reveal the potential attacker before the world. But a state might seek to use punishment even if it did not thereby induce, persuade, or compel a nation to perform a desired act. There might be motives of retribution, revenge, or hatred which did not require specific compliant actions on the part of the target state. A state might wish to eliminate another as a competitor. Various Arab nations might like to bring about the destruction of Israel. If one Arab state could anonymously attack Israel and get away with it, it might be difficult to resist the temptation. At a hypothetical extreme it is conceivable that some outraged nation might wish to punish the United States for its past behavior in Southeast Asia or the Soviet Union for its actions in Eastern Europe.

Catalytic war would be more difficult to arrange than anonymous delivery, but cannot be ruled out as a multipolar stratagem in a crisis. Suppose, for example, that the Chinese had had a missile-launching submarine on station off Cuba in October 1962. At that time President Kennedy said that he would regard a missile launched from Cuba upon any nation in the Western Hemisphere as an attack by the Soviet Union, justifying a full retaliatory response on Russia. The Chinese might have been able to exploit that situation. It is not inconceivable that they might have simulated a Cuban missile attack on New York, Washington, or Miami. Not many Chinese weapons in these circumstances would have been needed to trigger an American assault on the Soviet Union. Such possibilities increase with the spread of multipolar strategic capabilities.[2]

If in these two respects a multipolar order could display greater instabilities than a dyadic bipolar system, there is at least one respect in which strategic problems will be easier to solve. Multilateral strategic systems present the "dilemma of the victor's inheritance" in a way that bilateral systems do not. In a two-power strategic world, after eliminating the major opponent, one does not encounter other strategic opposition. In a multipolar context this is not true. After an attack on the United States, the Soviets would have to consider whether their expenditure of missiles against the United States made them vulnerable to the Chinese. If Chinese capabilities were large, Soviet unilateral aggression would be much less likely.

But if unilateral aggression is much less likely in a multipolar context, multilateral aggression is much more feasible. Let us assume for a moment that there is some critical ratio c which represents the ratio of superiority which an aggressive state must achieve in terms of numbers of missiles and warheads before it can successfully launch a preemptive blow against a particular state. In a dyadic system before the age of MIRV (multiple independently-targetable reentry vehicles), c ratios for land-based missiles were always greater than 1. c ratios for warheads remain above 1, and c ratios for all strategic launchers are still greater than 1. Presuming states with equivalent strategic capacities, the criterion for stability in a system is:

$$c > n - 1 \text{ (where } n = \text{the number of states in the system)}$$

In the dyadic case, $n = 2$ so that a c ratio which is greater than one assures stability.

It is quite possible to imagine circumstances in a multipolar strategic environment, however, in which c is not greater than $n - 1$, and in which, as a result, the other members of the strategic system may gang up on a single power. If $c = 2$ and there are three powers in the system, the system is unstable, for two can successfully attack and eliminate the third. If one power now raises his arms position slightly so as to avoid vulnerability, the other two powers will become even more vulnerable.

The major difficulty, however, of multipolar strategic systems is that probable technological and political tendencies move inversely to stability. As time goes on, more and more nations will become nuclear strategic powers, thus n will rise. But the countries joining the nuclear system are not likely to have capacities as invulnerable as those possessed by the two charter members of the nuclear club. Thus as n rises, c is likely to fall. Both tendencies are destabilizing.

As states fall below the minimum deterrent threshold in an expanding nuclear world, they may be tempted to use their capabilities while they still possess credibility. If they fall beneath the minimum technological deterrent threshold on an overt basis, they may have to place more stress upon covert methods. The greater the number of strategic powers, the greater the anonymity any one state can achieve. It may not be able to retaliate against another power after absorbing an attack. It may, however, be capable of launching a clandestine attack, hoping to escape retaliation. If its opponent is involved in a crisis with some third power, a catalytic attack may become possible.

One is led to the rather horrific conclusion that signature retaliatory capabilities may be inadequate for quite a number of powers in a multipolar strategic world. More emphasis, therefore, may be placed upon covert—anonymous or catalytic—capabilities. Preemption may be more likely.

The problem of deterring such attacks under conditions of strategic multipolarity is complex. A state might develop the doctrine of hitting all other nuclear powers in case it is attacked by one. But such notions would not have political or internal credibility. Moreover, they might be counter-deterred by other nations' adoption of a doctrine of automatically destroying an antagonist which shot nuclear broadsides at the rest of the world. Alternatively, a power might employ a statistical strategy of randomly retaliating, so that an aggressor would have a .1 or .2 chance of being hit. But the innocent power which was attacked would be likely also to seek vengeance, thus there would be some doubt whether a statistical strategy actually would be carried out. It is possible that a nuclear victim, before retaliating, would ask to examine the condition of nuclear forces in each of his colleague's countries to see which had been recently fired. It would be likely that a number of countries (even though innocent) would refuse such inspection, however, for fear of revealing the vulnerable points in their strategic arsenals. If clandestine devices had been detonated in the cities of the victim, moreover, how would inspection of homebased strategic weapons reveal the attacker?

One means of remedying this unstable situation might be to use defensive alliances. Indeed, if it is assumed that instabilities flow from nuclear ganging-up, perhaps restabilization can be found in defensive combinations. Initially, let us assume a world of five equal nuclear powers. Among these powers, equal capabilities would deter an attack launched by a single state. Alliances among groups of powers, however, could change this outcome. If the c ratio is 3 (that is, that three powers attacking together can eliminate the nuclear force of one defending state) then any alliance of two states would be purely defensive. Such an alliance could be used to prevent three other powers from combining against one, but it could not be used for offensive purposes. An alliance of four powers, on the other hand, could only be aggressive. Since superiorities of 4 to 1 would not be needed for assured retaliation, any four-power coalition could only be for the purpose of knocking out the remaining state. An alliance of five powers would confer general peace, and would be tantamount to universal arms control at the strategic level.

If the critical ratio, $c,$ were 2, the situation would be ambiguous. An alliance of two powers might be formed to attack one of the remaining states, or it might be designed to prevent two other powers from attacking one of the two remaining states. Under these conditions the normal alliance configuration would be 2 to 2 to 1. This would permit either of the two alliance pairs to attack the single remaining power, but not each other. If one of the alliance combinations desired to help protect the remaining power, they might include it in the alliance, giving rise to a stable 3 to 2 combination.

If $c = 4$, any alliance of four would clearly be aggressive, and any alliance of two or three purely defensive. If $c = 1$, an alliance of two powers could be either defensive or aggressive. An alliance of two could protect against an attack by one power, but could not deter attacks by two or three powers. Under such conditions, defense = aggression. Any power which is sure it cannot be attacked must be in an alliance which is capable of knocking out other states. No alliance combinations can stabilize such a system. If c were 5, on the other hand, stability would exist for all states, without recourse to alliance. In the examples above, c ratios of 2 and 1 generate conditions in which alliances can be either aggressive or defensive. Uncertainty and tension would be very high in such systems.

The situation worsens if five lesser and unequal states are added to the system of five equal great powers. c ratios and alliance systems which would be stabilizing among the big five would be destabilizing in respect of the five lesser nuclear states. Alliances among the lesser states might be stabilizing, but any alliance blocs among the five larger powers would be likely to undercut the deterrent viability of some of the lesser five.

As a general rule it would appear that as states fail to get over the orthodox deterrent threshold, the more likely they will be to resort to unorthodox means of nuclear delivery and retaliation. This in turn would greatly contribute to the tension, uncertainty, and insecurity of the nuclear supergame. The only way in which stability might be maintained in such circumstances would be for some of the big five powers to ally with some of the little five, forging perhaps two or three giant blocs. This would be by no means a certain outcome, however, for the big five powers would be seeking alliances among themselves to guard their own security. Some of these alliances or blocs among the big five would be likely to be capable of major and successful attacks upon one or more members of the little five.

In sum it appears that there is even greater difficulty applying deterrence theory in a multipolar than in a bipolar context. The minimum technological conditions are less likely to be met, putting a premium upon unorthodox solutions, some of which are very destabilizing. The *ex ante* and *ex post* incentives jibe even less than in dyadic systems for there is the additional problem of whom to retaliate against. If it is difficult enough to develop a political focus on Russia or China as presumptive foes justifying reliance upon massive retaliatory sanctions, it will be even more difficult to prime the electorate to be ready to spring upon any one of ten to twenty foes in case it should misbehave. Part of the credibility of retaliation in the two-party context was supplied by the cold war and public hostility to communism and the Soviet Union. In a world of many nuclear powers, notions of external threat will be much more diffuse; they will be analytical rather than personified. It is difficult to muster citizens to justify retaliating against or countering an analytical threat. Thus the rationale for a deterrent posture based upon the threat of retaliation loses even more force in a multipolar environment.

Beyond Deterrence

Thus one is forced to conclude that there are difficulties in the dyadic deterrence model and that these difficulties are compounded in a multipolar environment. This does not mean that deterrent forces and mechanisms should be entirely rejected, though they have clearly been shown to be inadequate. While there can be no certainty of deterrent retaliatory punishment in either bipolar or multipolar worlds, there is at least uncertainty. A nation with weapons might use them; it might be irrational; it might not calculate its utilities correctly. An aggressor cannot be sure that he will get away with it. There are grounds for hesitation. But insofar as we have thought that a defender would have rational grounds for massive retaliation, these are largely nonexistent. Rational incentives would lead powers to adopt strategies on *ex post* grounds which would not offer deterrence *ex ante*. The uncertainties are biased against deterrence. Moreover, whatever advantages the specter of deterrent thinking offers, it does not solve the problem of producing stability in the future. It may therefore be useful to have deterrents to attack, but it would be a gross mistake to rely upon them totally.

One of the strange outcomes of post-World War II strategic deliberation has been the almost exclusive concentration upon the threat of punishment as the major equilibrator of the international system. Even the most traditional learning theorists in the field of psychology argue that behavior is as direct a function of reward as it is of punishment. But while an entire literature has grown up since 1945 focusing upon manipulations of the punishment structure in world politics, virtually nothing has been said or written about manipulations of the reward structure. The reasons for this are not hard to understand. Since the appeasement efforts of the 1930s stressed rewards as incentives and failed, states have been disposed to look elsewhere for international stability. But the failure of appeasement is not a reason for considering rewards an inappropriate subject for investigation or employment. Appeasement does not work under conditions of the constant-sum game. If there are two major international protagonists, A and B, and the sum of their positions is a constant, *k,* rewards cannot be used. Any attempt to enhance the position of B only succeeds at the expense of A. Thus resort to reward as an instrument of international stability depends on finding relationships among states which are not strictly constant-sum, where two nations may increase their positions simultaneously. Increasing or variable-sum games are ideal subjects for reward structure manipulation. Economic realms clearly show variable-sum outcomes, even if territorial ones do not. Most important for the future, therefore, would be the definition of realms in which constant-sum results do not hold. If it were possible to enhance the positions of two potential adversary states simultaneously, both would be less likely to engage in disruptive military actions in order to alter those positions. If states experience high status quo utilities, they are less likely to find war an attractive outcome.

AN ECONOMIC INTERPENETRATION MODEL

The military model of future multipolarity poses serious problems. Conflict may conceivably be more endemic in such a system than it has been under the bipolar conditions of recent years. The military model, however, is only one possible outcome of present tendencies. Even if nuclear weapons continue spreading, other factors may help to mitigate the acerbities of pure strategic calculation. One set of factors which may push in a different direction is that of economic interpenetration. In the years since World War II the economies of developed states have become increasingly interpenetrated and interlinked. While Communist regimes have been largely unaffected by this phenomenon, it is possible that trade and other relationships will reduce Communist economic isolation in the future. If Communist nations need access to world currencies in order to finance burgeoning trade, they may even develop an indirect relationship with the International Monetary Fund.[3] In any event, the rest of the developed nations are likely to intensify their economic relationships over time.

If tariffs are low and quantitative restrictions on currencies and goods at a minimum, nations may develop markets and fields of investment that range far beyond their frontiers. Indeed, in the nineteenth century at least, one major incentive to imperialism and political-military conflict was the shutting off of international trade by the gradual development of tariff protectionism. If nations could not trade freely with all nations and territories of the world, they each had to have their own enclaves or empires which they could protect for their own market and for supplies of raw materials. High German and French tariffs forced the British after 1880 into a movement for political imperialism, carving up Africa, Asia, and the Near East. Today, if tariffs remain relatively low and foreign investment relatively unrestricted, the economies of the developed states will become even more interpenetrated than they are at the moment. Indeed, it is no longer possible to speak of economic progress for many countries without considering the development of international trade. In this degree, Japan's own internal economic position is partly, even largely, dependent on what she can sell in the United States. Economic stagnation in the United States can only be avoided by markets in Europe and by a return on foreign investment. The great development of the consumer market in Europe not only provides a stimulus to European industries, but also to American and Japanese industries. In raw materials terms, nations are less self-sufficient than they were; they are more dependent on foreign sources. An open international economic system facilitates the development of mutual interdependence. In so doing it intertwines the political interests of two states in fundamental ways. If national actions in foreign policy seem likely to hurt markets, they will be eschewed.

To be sure, the mere existence of a relatively open international economy does not guarantee that the economy will remain open. The international economy of Europe collapsed with World War I. The economic nationalism of the thirties followed. The process might be repeated. Whether economic openness will be preserved depends upon each major trading nation exercising a degree of restraint in pressing for a greater share of resources. It also certainly depends upon greater economic stability internally. No nation can ask its colleagues or the International Monetary Fund to make an unlimited series of adjustments which are required simply because that nation has not tried to control its own domestic inflation. Thus if an open trading system is to continue, it must depend upon states keeping their financial houses in order and making genuine efforts to respond to the criticisms of their colleagues.

Even then, open economic systems are by no means a guarantee of peace. The British-regulated international trading system of the nineteenth century did not prevent World War I. But, as we have seen, the nations which entered into World War I did so without the slightest knowledge of the probable effect of the war on international relations, trade, or the domestic economy. They did not believe that war would require them to give up the benefits of the trading system; the mid-century wars had not interfered with them. Thus they could have both economic strength and war; no choice was required. Today such naive notions could hardly be entertained. Major conflict sharpens nationalism, and nationalism puts an end to internationalism.

If breakdown is avoided, the interpenetration of economic systems gives each power great leverage upon the others. Indeed, in certain respects economic interpenetration means that economic man is held hostage, just as military deterrence means that military man is held hostage. Economic retaliation, moreover, may even be more credible than military retaliation. Thus one nation is unlikely to retaliate massively against the markets which other countries develop within its borders because it is afraid of counter-retaliation against its own overseas markets. Markets are held as hostages for the safety and security of each other. In turn, therefore, there must be a very finely tuned and orchestrated political relationship. Politics and military strategy, if pressed forward without attention to their probable consequences, could jeopardize economics. This, after all, was what happened when World War I occurred. Nations will try very hard to avoid its occurring again.

The economic interpenetration model, however, even if it operates within a given sphere, does not solve all problems of international conflict. It limits conflict among developed states. It may, as markets and trade are opened, even have a slight desirable effect on the policy of Communist countries. It is by no means sure, however, that interpenetration will have a similar desirable effect on the political connections between developed and less developed worlds. The developed world can cut off access to its own markets for developing economies, without worrying greatly about the retaliation that the developing countries may take against the markets possessed by developed countries within their borders. Thus economic interpenetration by no means insures that there will not be conflict and tension between developed and developing states. It does not even greatly limit conflicts between the communist and non-communist worlds; the stakes of the participants are pretty minimal compared to those in the huge trade among developed non-communist countries. Economic penetration serves, if at all, to limit conflict which might otherwise have broken out as nuclear multipolarity emerges among Europe, America, and Japan.

CONCLUSION

In this chapter we have looked at two extreme models of future international politics. The one confined itself to military variables and speculated on the prospects of stability in a world in which nuclear weapons were widely disseminated. Instabilities at the purely military strategic level were seen to exist, requiring the use of other methods besides traditional deterrence. The model of economic interpenetration clearly does not have any greater application than the model of strategic multipolarity. While some movements have been made in the direction of interpenetration of markets, the world as a whole does not manifest such tendencies. The Communist countries, to this point at least, have been unaffected by the burgeoning crest of international trade. They have not permitted outsiders to gain markets, nor have they secured special access to the markets of developed countries. External economic influences on their policies has been minimal. Nor have developing countries been able to develop economic leverage in developed markets. The leverage has been all one way. Even among certain developed countries, there are major deviations from this model. Japan's position in the developed economic sector is asymmetrical. Japan has greatly benefited from a one-sided penetration of American and European markets. She has not allowed Europeans and Americans to develop a similar position in the Japanese home market. Thus Japan is particularly vulnerable to European and American pressure because she has no hostage markets to curtail in return.

Neither strictly military-deterrent nor strictly economic factors are likely to predominate in the future. The international system will see an amalgam of economic and military factors. It will remain a complex combination of nationalism and internationalism, of the threat of punishment together with the occasional use of reward. It is difficult to tell which tendency will predominate in each case, but the next chapter speculates on the overall direction the world appears to have chosen.

NOTES

1 These issues are treated in more detail in Rosecrance (ed.), *The Future of the International Strategic System* (San Francisco: Chandler, 1972), chap. 8.
2 This scenario has been discussed by Donald G. Brennan in R. Rosecrance (ed.), *The Future of the International Strategic System* (San Francisco: Chandler, 1972), chap. 2.
3 See Richard N. Gardner "International Organization and Reward: Potentialities and Limitations," in Rosecrance (ed.), *The Future of the International Strategic System* (San Francisco: Chandler, 1972), chap. 9.

6

Prospects for Harmony?

The previous two chapters have examined the portents of conflict in future international relations. The concluding chapter seeks to draw a trial balance on conflict and cooperation and to suggest techniques for the maintenance of peace based upon the empirical conclusions from the preceding pages. First a propositional inventory is offered. Then the results of that inventory are applied first to the question of trends toward nationalism or internationalism, and second to means of equilibrating the system—the use of reward and punishment strategies.

CHAPTER TWENTY-ONE

The Problem of Peace:
Nationalism versus Internationalism
Punishment versus Reward

A PROPOSITIONAL INVENTORY AND SUMMARY

A number of propositions have been advanced in this study which afford modest guidelines in striving to reach a more peaceful world.

1. It was suggested that formal and informal regulation have different strengths and weaknesses in holding outcomes within stable limits. Formal regulation is likely to be much less powerful than informal regulation, but it is also less likely to be animated by a sectarian political purpose. Formal regulation is more likely to respond to the interests of all states in devising international restraints.

2. A conclusion was reached that economic regulation is more likely to be successful than political regulation. The international economic organizations which exist are more potent than their political counterparts. Further, there is a greater agreement on international economic matters, at least among developed states, than there is on international political matters.

3. It is possible that there is a relatively greater reliance upon self-restraint than upon regulation in the present international system. Objectives of states have been more limited than they were formerly. The threat of thermonuclear destruction has made states more cautious and perhaps less ambitious in world politics.

4. The degree of stratification in influence and access to resources may affect the regulative capacity of the system. A system which is uniformly

stratified may be easy to regulate; one which is uniformly equalitarian may not require regulation. The difficulties are intermediate, i.e., where the system is equalitarian on one dimension and stratified on another.

5. Neither multipolar nor bipolar systems are likely to be easy to regulate. In bipolar systems, regulative coalitions will not be strong enough to contain a major power disruptor. In multipolar systems, regulative coalitions will be strong enough, but the participants will be less likely to form them. It is possible, but by no means certain, that a quintipolar or septipolar order would be better on both counts. Regulative coalitions would be easier to form than under conditions of multipolarity; they would be more successful than under conditions of bipolarity.

6. Neither balances nor imbalances of power appear to contribute to stability by and of themselves. It would appear, however, that when a single coalition possesses the greatest power, there are greater chances for peace than when a single power is paramount.

7. Other things being equal, systems which are homogeneous on political and ideological grounds are more likely to be stable and are easier to regulate than heterogeneous systems.

8. A nation's geographic involvements in world politics are likely to affect its participation in war. The greater the degree of geographic and political commitment, the more wars a nation is likely to be involved in.

9. Social or cultural distance appears to have a two-edged impact upon the likelihood of war. Social differentiation is probably a stimulus to war in that linguistic, cultural, religious, and ethnic differences often beget misunderstanding which may in turn breed war. At the same time, social distance is also a deterrent to the waging of war, for nations of one cultural type will face great difficulties in permanently subduing nations of another cultural type. It therefore offers disincentives to war.

10. While the growth of international transactions has been significant in recent years, it may have been overshadowed by an even greater growth in intranational transactions. If this is so, the nation-state remains far from obsolete.

11. Two variables which seem to affect the degree of cooperation among states are contact and interdependence. Contact refers to communications and transactions links. Interdependence refers to relationships of interest. Nations which have low contact may be brought together by positive relationships of interest. Nations which have few ties of mutual interest may find cooperation through greater contact. Nations which either have (1) high positive relations of interest and high contact; or (2) low relationships of interest and low contact will not go to war. Where contact is low, but relationships of interest are strong and negative, conflict is likely. Where contact is high, but relationships of interest are unfocused or unclear, a state may not see its underlying interdependency of interests with other states, and would likely cause hostile reactions on the part of others. In relations among

developed states today, one possible negative feature is the presence of high positive interdependence with low net contact. In relations between developed and less developed societies, one undesirable aspect is the presence of a certain minimum of real, though possibly negative, interdependence, but low net contact.

12. In history, states began with diffuse objectives and later developed fused objectives. Fused objectives, implying a fixed hierarchy of superordination and subordination of goals, are harder to change than diffuse objectives.

13. One of the quandaries of present international politics may be the development of an intermediate level of cooperation. This cooperation is sufficiently high so that antisocial action is the exception rather than the rule. Nations, therefore, become in a measure habituated to the expectation of cooperative behavior on the part of others. On the other hand, in such a system the non-cooperator will almost always improve his payoffs. Thus intermediate cooperation directly presents the conditions for the operation of the "prisoner's dilemma."

14. The extension of the international system since the nineteenth century has probably in a measure constitutionalized the behavior of Western and also of non-Western nations. The legal equality of mankind has made it more difficult to rationalize imperialist or atavistic activity. This partly helps to explain the outcry over the war in Indochina. It has by no means, however, eradicated such behavior.

15. Since the eighteenth century states have had to find new means of solving the security problem. This has meant, paradoxically, both more cooperation and more conflict in the system. Preemptive war is one means of seeking to gain security. Alliance with other states is another.

16. There appear to be important relationships between domestic and international security. These are, however, by no means one to one. Domestic insecurity or revolution does not necessarily spill over into the international orbit. War does not uniformly cause domestic change or revolution. The impact on the international system of the French and Russian revolutions was very different. It appears that revolutions which sap basic internal social and economic strength may not project themselves into international relations. Revolutions which are only superficial do not call forth basic new social forces and therefore do not generate a demand for the revision of international relationships. Intermediate cases, however, like the French Revolution, may have substantial impact upon international events.

17. The relationship between internal and external political resources may well be curvilinear. That is, up to a point any increase in the domestic resource position enhances the international position and vice versa. After that point, however, further attempts to increase one's international position may reduce domestic resources; further attempts to increase one's domestic resources may impinge upon one's international position. At this point, decision makers face a real choice of the value they wish to maximize.

18. Throughout history states have typically aimed at material, ideological, and security goals.

19. At least at certain periods, these goals could be conceived as layers of an onion of objectives, with material goals the outermost and least important layer, ideological objectives as the middle layer, and security goals as the core of the onion. In general, material objectives were pursued when other, more fundamental, objectives were not challenged. As the more central goals came into question, however, states tended to forget about material objectives and to concentrate their attention on gaining their more central ends. Among developed states at least, there has been a peeling of the onion of objectives. States now tend to pursue the most central core, security, and to relegate material and ideological goals to a lesser status. As long as security questions remain important, this will be likely to continue.

20. At least two forms of diplomacy have been employed by states: strategic diplomacy and tactical diplomacy. In the eighteenth century, strategic diplomacy was used. Diplomatists were able to change the objectives or the priorities of other states and to reach agreement. After the development of tactical diplomacy, however, objectives could not be changed or reordered. Diplomacy was limited to trying to find ways in which fixed objectives of states might be accommodated in some degree.

21. In the post-1945 period, nuclear deterrence soon emerged as one of the stabilizing features of the system. However, there has been no counterpart to nuclear deterrence in the conventional and subconventional field. If the nuclear aggressor would hazard great risks in attacking, the conventional or subconventional aggressor faced no such risks. Preemptive surprise attacks in the conventional field now seem to be much more successful than those in the nuclear field. This helps to explain why such attacks have so often been made.

22. In the future, it is even possible that there will be instabilities in central nuclear relationships. This is partly because there have been unrecognized inconsistencies in deterrence doctrine which are only now coming to the fore. It is partly because multipolar deterrence is much more difficult to attain than bipolar deterrence. A world of many nuclear powers may be very unstable.

INTERRELATIONS OF PROPOSITIONS

Each of the propositions formulated above has been stated in terms of a univariate relation between peace and the particular variable. Actually, some of the propositions incorporate variables that are causally linked. For example, the development of security objectives in the nineteenth century stressed two different means of achieving the goal: preemptive war against an opponent, and alliance with like-minded states. Thus security goals may lead to alliances. Alliances, as we have seen in proposition eight, however, may increase the geographic and political commitments of nations and make involvement in war more likely. If alliances are not to have this effect they must be of a restricted nature. An ally must not be asked to defend more than the contours of narrowly defined national interests that he would have defended in the absence of the alliance. It is clear that some alliances are of this type. American alliances in the post-World War II period, however, tended to extend the periphery of United States' interests far beyond its previous extent. Many allies in Asia, Africa, and the Near East were not strictly necessary for the defense of the continental United States. In addition, the alliance was one-sided; it added American efforts to the defense of these countries, but contributed little to the defense of the United States. Alliances with major European nations, however, were more central to narrowly defined United States interests. The United States, regarding Europe as a vital area, would have fought for Europe with or without alliance arrangements with European states. The common allied effort contributed to American security.

A second interlinkage may be seen in propositions seven and nine. We concluded that a homogeneous international system, in which states were of the same cultural and political form, would probably be more peaceful than a heterogeneous international system. At that same time proposition nine indicates that social and cultural differentiation may sometimes be a deterrent to aggression and therefore a bulwark of peace. Here one must distinguish between incentives and capabilities. The incentive to warfare in a heterogeneous international system is likely to be greater than in a homogeneous system. Misunderstandings and failures of communication are more likely when cultural and ethnic characteristics differ. On the other hand, successful aggrandizement of differing cultural and linguistic groups is harder than expansion within a common cultural and ethnic area. Thus the capabilities for expansion may be lower where there is substantial differentiation. Ideally, if all nations shared similar communications and cultural patterns and had high and continuous contact with one another, the very intensity of communication should rule out war. The United States and Canada, Norway and Sweden and a few other countries have attained this status with respect to each other. If such a common basis of communications and high contact cannot be attained, however (and it appears that it cannot), a second-best strategy may be to educate nations to the truth that one nation cannot successfully rule another of a different cultural and political type. In each case one strives for a combination of low incentives and low capabilities. If incentives are not low enough, capabilities have to be lower still.

It is also possible that there are some repetitive interactive processes involved in the various propositions. For example, one could imagine a multipolar international system in which various states became insecure. They then sought allies to bulwark their security; the patterns of alliance could well be bipolar, thus transforming the system, and perhaps leading to further insecurity. It would also be possible to conceive of the following sequence:

war→ decreased involvement→ power vacuums→ increased involvement→ war

Indeed, one of the tragedies of western international history has been that this cycle has been repeated time and time again. If the cycle is to be broken, nations have to find patterns of involvement which are diminished beyond their current extents, but which do not lead to power vacuums. This may be very difficult to do.

FUTURE EVOLUTIONS

Some of the propositions sketched above offer optimistic prognoses for future international relations; some are more pessimistic. Nations, confronting the prospect of nuclear war, may be more willing to restrain themselves today than at any previous time. Certainly, among developed states, ideological objectives appear to be on the wane. On the other hand, conventional deterrents to war are not sufficient. Deterrents to nuclear war in the multipolar future may be inadequate. Nationalism and patriotism are far stronger today than they were during the eighteenth century, but there seem to be some limits on their extent. In Western Europe, narrow economic and political nationalism is being transcended as the Common Market admits new members. Even among developed states as a whole, economic relationships are now being handled with greater reciprocity and respect for mutual interests than they were in the 1930s. This very reciprocity and mutuality, however, offers benefits to non-cooperators.

Such trends do not apply to the less developed, nationalist sphere of the world. Self-restraint is not clearly evidenced in the bilateral conflicts which have divided India and Pakistan, Israel and Egypt. Political nationalisms are still very much in the process of working themselves out in the nations of Southeast Asia. Africa and Latin America are being partly transformed by new political leadership; their future orientations are unclear. As new and modernizing leaders take control, however, it does not appear that their international policies will be quiescent. Active and even interventionist policies will be entertained. The nationalist fires which are now burning low in Europe may be rekindled in other areas of the globe. As these nationalisms in some instances will be endowed with substantial military capabilities, there are grounds for repetitive patterns of conflict. The two halves of the world, in short, appear to be moving in different rhythms and following different scores. Trends in one part do not mirror those in the other.

Tensions between the two halves of the world, moreover, may be on the increase. Demands for redistribution of the world's wealth are growing apace in the Third World. The developed nations, however, are reluctant to grant such demands, nor do their populaces wish to sacrifice their high standards of living. It may be true that for many years the developing world will not be in a position to force a redistribution, but equity will not be achieved. Tensions will continue.

NATIONALISM AND INTERNATIONALISM

As far as the developed world is concerned, there is a growing enfeeblement of doctrine. Previous foci of loyalty appear to be breaking down. The nation no longer compels respect as the core of ultimate allegiance. The revolution in communications and technology has provided the denizens of the developed world with myriad images and few clear reference points. Television tends to blur the distinction between national and international events. But while the national focus has dimmed, there is no well-defined alternative focus. In economics, in professional life, and in the urban ghetto the patterns of communications are likely to be larger or smaller than the national unit. Indeed, it is surprising that the national focus should have held primacy so long. If we look at an individual's concentric circles of loyalty (Figure 21-1), it seems difficult to understand why his national ties were singled out as those of such great importance as to take precedence even over family or primary group loyalties. With five possible foci of loyalty besides himself, why should an individual have tended for so long to concentrate on the fourth ring? The answer may be that messages from the inner rings were downgraded as societies modernized and developed economically and because messages from the fifth ring were traditionally blocked, muted, or distorted. Although distortion still continues, messages from outside the nation are no longer blocked, or they are not so easily blocked. The image of events inconsistent with a sectarian national focus thus reduces the importance of the fourth ring, but it does not erect a single alternative to it.

Indeed, the flow of messages may make loyalties to any sectarian doctrine impossible. For doctrine to compel belief, messages must be circumscribed and limited in flow. If the flow of information becomes a torrent, individuals cannot make sense of what is being presented to them; their impressions are kaleidoscopic and fragmentary. Information is not doctrinal or systematic; individuals receive it in bits. Moreover, they cannot comprehend what they take in; they cannot impose a unity or uniformity on what they know. Thus, each particular ethos fades. The failure of previous doctrine tends to produce a bifurcation of orientation. On the one hand, there is the reversion to technology and information processing as a "solution" to the problem. On the other hand, there is the formulation of new attitudes, prejudices, and orientations which are less than doctrine but which might afford a guide to action. The first solution is predicated on the assumption that only information processing machines can make sense out of the welter of facts, and draw the necessary conclusions. But machines do not draw conclusions; they only offer correlations and relationships. Human beings still have to decide how to

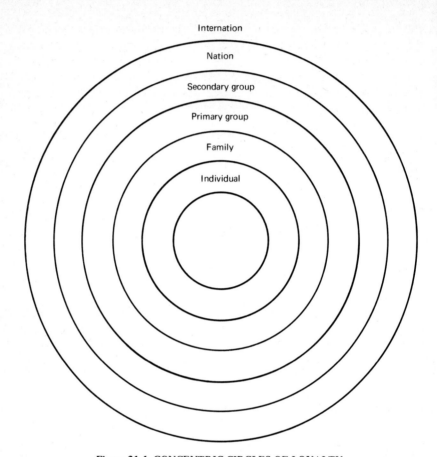

Figure 21-1 CONCENTRIC CIRCLES OF LOYALTY

use the statistical relations which the machine helps find. The area of ethics is untouched. Science does not decide value. The other orientation gives opposite results. It highlights the areas of value, ethical concern, and action to redress grievances. But beyond the most rudimentary sort of goals and theories it fails to offer a logically integrated doctrine or a scientific account of how society operates. It does not make sense of the information with which we are deluged. Thus even the commitment to action which the new activist orientation represents is partially undermined by the vagueness and lack of clarity of its theories. In the end, liberalism, Marxism, and populism become discredited in the wake of nationalism and patriotism.

But the question remains: where does that leave us? Is internationalism the more likely because of the at least theoretical demise of nationalism? Is internationalism possible when it still remains true that individuals turn to the state for the satisfaction of most of their wants? The intensification of intranational transactions makes it impossible for international transactions to gain the day. In the world at present, moreover, one of the most undesirable portents is the surplus of intranational over international messages in a context of great mutual interdependence. The interests of states are very closely interlinked factually, but the intensification of intranational communications may fail to make all publics aware of it. The nation-state remains as the necessary reference point for policy decision making even though it is no longer the exclusive, or perhaps even the primary, focus of loyalty.

Globalism

One solution to the problem of political nationalism in decision making might be sought through a transformation of the system into global world government. A globalist world would be, formally at least, a regulated world. While nation-states would continue to exist, federalist power in the system would be transferred to central institutions. Major elements of military power would be possessed by the federal (world) government. Perhaps only the federal government would have access to weapons capable of causing mass destruction. The difficulties with a globalist solution to the problem of nationalism and internationalism, however, are two.

First, it is not likely that such a government could be created, given current international trends and portents. Herman Kahn, the prophet of apocalypse, has argued that world government will certainly be easily installed, but only after the next nuclear war. One tends to agree with him, but to argue that the remedy is not worth the cost. Short of such a war, the trends in international politics are as much centrifugal as centripetal. Nation building has not been completed in many regions of the globe. In this gradual process of construction existing units may be broken down or rearranged. While the central issues of the day have to do with the success of domestic governance, it seems that few if any nations would be willing to focus so centrally on the problems of international relations as to resign their sovereignties in the creation of world government. The periods in which greater international consolidation has been possible have been those in which nations have been totally preoccupied with the international problem. Catastrophic war has fostered such an awareness. But such a consciousness does not exist at present. The contemporary problem is seen as government within society, not between societies. Even among the developed nations, it is inconceivable that Japan, Germany, or United States would consider grants of sovereignty to international agencies. In several respects, each of these states is now benefiting from a reduction of the previous more general level of cooperation in economic and political spheres. It may, therefore, pursue a policy which more directly benefits its own population. Until the problem of domestic governance is solved, it is highly unlikely that nations will devote their attention to a radical reconsolidation of politics at the international or supranational level.

The second difficulty with the globalist solution is that under current conditions, it would be unlikely to cope with the real political tensions in the world. Since 1945 there have been fewer than ten major international military conflicts. Domestic military civil war or prolonged insurgency, however, has been two or three times as frequent. The creation of a world government might merely have the effect of redefining the categories of conflict. What had previously been *international* would now become *civil,* but the incidence and significance of conflict might not be reduced. In one sense a world government would be akin to the traditional empires of the nineteenth century. Since 1945, one after another, these have collapsed. Rule from a distance and across cultural frontiers has proved too difficult to accomplish. A similar fate might await world government. If the federalist government threatened to use nuclear weapons against dissidents and did so, the use of federal police power would be worse than any war since 1945. Indeed, if the same number of civil and internal political conflicts were to occur under a federal world regime, the only effect of world government might be to escalate the means that would be used in fighting such conflicts. This would represent a more violent order than the one it replaced.

Regionalism

A second mode of limiting nationalism might be sought in the development of regional polities. At least within their separate jurisdictions, nationalism might be held within narrow limits. Further, the one doctrine which has not yet been discredited by modern technology, information, and communications has been the doctrine of regionalist supranationalism. In Europe at least, this doctrine appears to be gaining adherents. In some other areas, Latin America and perhaps Africa, the future of regionalist movements remains uncertain. It is possible that new consolidations lie ahead, though at present they appear unlikely.

Two difficulties, however, lie athwart the regionalist path to a reduction of nationalism and conflict. The first is that regionalism in many areas of the globe appears to be the least likely arena for future cooperation. Regionalism is defined in geographic terms. But national interests and capabilities are not determined by the regions in which states reside. Japan is much more a member of the functionalist sphere of developed polities than she is of the East Asian international system. United States concerns are not confined to the Western Hemisphere nor are Russia's to Central Asia. Perhaps oddly, some of the most significant ties among states have been those functional clusters which have violated regional limitations. If we look at certain specific regions like the Middle East, South Asia, or Southeast Asia, it appears that regional consolidations will be the last movement of integration to occur. Intra-regional conflicts are in many instances much more intense and of longer duration than extraregional conflicts. If regionalism is to be the prescription for the future, many areas of the globe will be excluded from participation in the theoretical panacea, at least for generations.

The second problem with regionalist approaches is that they fail to cope with relationships among the newly consolidated regions (even if the latter could be set up). Of course, it is possible that relationships among regions could be benign, and that we would have a relationship among four or five major regions of the world similar to the relationships among the four or five great powers of the nineteenth century. If quintipolarity and septipolarity have some advantages over bipolar or multipolar extremes, could these not be realized in a regionalist world system? The answer, of course, is that theoreti-cally they could. The difficulty with regionalism does not lie in the pattern of relationships that would exist in such a world. Rather, the problem occurs in the working out of regionalism in local contexts. The type of polity that regionalism currently suggests is not that of a United States of Europe, or Central America, or Africa. Rather, individual states retain foreign policy and defense autonomy while granting certain limited powers to economic instrumentalities. Even in the economic area, crucial decisions are made in diplomatic instrumentalities like the Council of Ministers where no major state can be outvoted. Essentially, therefore, even in matters where regionalist unions have been most successful, as in the Common Market, individual states retain crucial powers of decision. Perhaps paradoxically, the great success of the Common Market has not been due to its supranational features, but to the high degree of consensus among governments which then made interna-tionalism work. Thus even in the most successful unions, one cannot expect that a truly supranational entity will emerge with contours like that of a national state. If this is true, most of the energies of members of such a regionalist grouping will be spent on accommodating and harmonizing policies *within* the union. Little enough time and decision-making capacity will be left over to deal with nations and problems outside the community. Regionalism, then, may have an intrinsic introverting effect. If this is true, the problems that would beset a regionalist international system would not be altogether different from those that would occur in a globalist system. The problem of domestic (in this case regional) governance would be crucial. Major attention would be concentrated in this realm with possible neglect of external problems. Relations among regionalist units might then be like relations among the European empires of the nineteenth century. Because of preoccupation with domestic problems, Austria, Turkey, and Russia could only focus episodically on solving the problems of European diplomacy. When they did concentrate on Europe, their policies tended to be utopian or millenarian. By 1914 the Austrians had come to believe that their empire could survive only if Serbia were eliminated. They tended to embrace ad hoc and erroneous solutions. Once tension within the empire had risen to a certain point, international enemies would be designated as the source of trouble. Even when such radical solutions were not entertained, preoccupations within the empire could lead to sudden shifts from international quiescence to activity. During most of the 1890s, the Russians neglected affairs in Europe because they were bent on extending their empire in the Far East. When they returned to European concerns after 1905, they had to find solutions which would assist them domestically. Thus, if regional groupings are to focus major attention on relations within, they may slight relations without. Thus far, the evidence offered by history does not suggest that the most peaceful practitioners of external relations are those who have to decide their external policy wholly on the basis of internal policy.

The problem which a regionalist international order would present can also be seen from the perspective of decision theory. The expectation of conflict among national states is of course equal to the probabilities of conflict multiplied by the consequences if conflict should occur. It seems likely that the probabilities of conflict would decrease if an international order of nation-states were succeeded by an international order of regional groupings. Fewer points of interest would exist to be accommodated. The consequences of conflict among regional groupings, however, would surely be much more disastrous for the international system than the consequences of conflict among national states. Hence the result might not afford a better expectation than one would derive from the present international system.

$$E = \downarrow P_c \times \uparrow C_c$$

Inhibition and Enmeshment

A third strategy for reducing the excesses of nationalism might be sought in a greater degree of national caution and restraint. If formal integration of a regionalist variety might not succeed in tying up all nations in a web of interdependence, perhaps something short of full integration could be aimed at. Ernst Haas has recently noted that nations like the United States are enmeshed in a web of commitments to international organizations and alliance structures. These enmeshments do not prevent the United States from taking action, but like the strings binding the sleeping Gulliver they limit action unless the nation-state is willing to make a great effort to burst its bonds. While these constraints have limited American foreign choices, however, it does not follow that enmeshment is a kind of indirect constitution-alization of United States behavior. In some areas, as Haas admits, enmeshment has imposed undesirable alliance limitations upon American foreign policy freedom. In some cases the United States has become more involved in the interests of its allies than it should have been. In other areas, foreign entanglements have led the United States to espouse UN doctrines that it would not have supported on their own merits. Indeed, in some cases enmeshment and inhibition have been inverse quantities. Enmeshed in alliance relationships and a variety of international obligations and commitments, the United States has engaged in actions which certainly have not uniformly reflected national self-limitation, restraint, or inhibition. Just because a nation is enmeshed with others in a variety of international organizational and alliance relationships, one should not expect pacific or nonnationalist behavior. Alliance ties, as in the period before World War I, have often served to enlarge the scope of war.

The problem is to develop restraints on national policy through enmeshment, instead of greater assertion through enmeshment. In the aftermath of World War II, the United States was induced, largely at the urging of its friends and allies, to make a series of commitments. At some point in the 1950s, however, the initiative changed hands. The United States began to urge friends and neutrals to make commitments to it and to forge a series of collective defense alliances. This was the so-called pactomania of Secretary of State John Foster Dulles. These new pacts served not so much to limit and inhibit American behavior as to draw lines of commitment and deterrence against the communist world. This enmeshment was inconsistent with inhibition and self-restraint. Once these commitments had been made, it was a foregone conclusion that some of them would be challenged. If the United States were to respond with limited force at each point of challenge, it would become involved in a series of limited conflicts all over the globe. If a few United States responses had been sufficient to guarantee the credibility of response and therefore to bulwark deterrence, they might have been justified. But the difficulty was that blocs were no longer controlled from Washington or Moscow. There were also many independent centers of action outside the blocs. United States participation in the Vietnam conflict did not reinforce deterrence against Moscow or Peking, because the decisions in North Vietnam were not being made by the Chinese or the Russians. The drawing of a wide range of commitment-deterrence lines ended up being an attempt to confine international change to a Procrustean bed. Since this attempt could only fail, its impact was to produce United States involvement in conflicts which it could not prevent, and which it had no interest in contending.

The drawing of commitment-deterrence lines also reflected different and less politically mobilized phases of the international system. In the late 1940s and early 1950s, one could think of the need for containment or for alliance situations of strength because the political lives of many countries, both internationally and domestically, had been transformed by the war. Nations were dazed by the bloodshed and destruction of World War II. They might be willing to accept domestic political transformations, even those they did not like, if war could be avoided. Hence, there was a period in which Russia and the United States could successfully treat other countries as pawns, on the assumption that their domestic political systems were so unformed or so paralyzed by the impact of war that international relations could determine the domestic outcome. Since the 1950s, however, perhaps the most salient characteristic of the international system has been the refurbishing of competent domestic polities and the remobilization of the domestic electorate. Polities that the Soviets and the Americans used to treat as permeable turned out to have hard shells. The new knights and bishops were much harder to capture than the previous pawns. As Deutsch has aptly phrased it, there came to be a "rising cost of foreign intervention." Domestic impulsions turned out to be much more dominant than international pressures. Even in Eastern Europe, the most extreme current case, the Soviets cannot simply determine internal politics by the threat of Czechoslovak-style invasions. The Rumanians have not bent to the Soviet will, and the Poles have had to respond much more sensitively and rapidly to popular demands. In all East European countries, foreign influences appear to be waxing. The ability of either the Soviet or local regimes to entirely prevent such influences is limited.

If these trends continue, the need for commitment-deterrence lines will decrease with time. This will not be because such lines and such deterrence have succeeded. It will be because there is coming to be a naturally operating deterrence in the system that strengthens, and in some ways outmodes, national deterrent doctrine and policy. Within the community of developed nations, the major restraint upon aggressors is not solely or even particularly deterrence of one superpower by the other. It is the dilemma of the victor's inheritance. Once one has conquered another state, what then? How can one manage to organize or govern it? When one intrudes into a fully mobilized polity, one cannot expect to be able to bend the populace to one's will. Thus the problem of domestic governance is compounded by external aggression. Aggression does not solve the problem; it makes it worse. Could Europe be digested by either of the two major powers, or would an attempt to assimilate it be self-defeating?

The rationale even applies to the superpowers themselves. Suppose a successful nuclear attack by one power on the other. What then? Would the victor then strive to occupy his defeated foe? Could he succeed in doing so? How long could the occupation last? Even if a regime of similar ideological coloration were set up in the conquered foe's territory, how long would it take direction from the victorious aggressor? Soviet conquest of Germany or, even more unrealistically, of the United States would not solve Russian problems. It might even accentuate them. There is, in short, an amount of self-operating deterrence in the system which makes it less and less necessary for nations to draw commitment-deterrence lines all around the globe. The point which is important, however, is that nations come to recognize the operation of this natural deterrence, and that they consider what their situation might be even after a victorious war. If they do, aggression among the developed nations seems less and less likely for any rationally calculating power.

In the less developed world, the conclusions cannot be so sanguine. Limited war is effective in changing political relationships and even shifting territory back and forth. Where populations are still inert, and where their political directions still have to be established, military victory or defeat can help chart the course of nation building. There is very little self-operating deterrence in the system. Still, the amount of such natural deterrence is growing. With the mobilization even of less developed polities, the dilemma of the victor's inheritance is presented. In this context it is worth asking whether Israel could rule and assimilate five to ten million Arabs, entirely changing their political loyalties and religious and national orientations? Could India or Pakistan take large sections of each other's territory and govern them stably? The same question has to be posed even for the militantly nationalist North Vietnamese. Could Hanoi hope eventually to subvert Thailand or Malaysia, given the entirely different national and ethnic orientations of the Thai and Malaysian peoples and given also their increasing degree of political awareness and mobilization? Even where political sentiments are unformed, aggression is facing a curve of rising costs. Since political mobilization is proceeding very rapidly in the present world, these costs will rise year by year.

Thus national inhibition is likely to be a far more successful policy, even in defense of one's own interest, than it would have been forty years ago. One loses little by inhibition, and one avoids the kind of enmeshment in alliance structures which artificially extend the range of one's interests and thus results in involvement in a large number of irrelevant national conflicts. It avoids the error which Frank Denton has ably pointed out in the overcommitment of such powers as England, France, Spain, Austria, and Holland in years past, implicating them in warfare.[1]

Of course national inhibition, as the necessary and sufficient condition of good policy, has certain drawbacks. Participation in the affairs of the system, by definition, is reduced. While it might be advantageous in some ways for international relations to return to the state of affairs which prevailed at the time of the medieval fortress, with contending forces at some remove from one another and assault unlikely to succeed against a heavily defended bastion, modern technology and communications have rendered this impossible.[2] Nations cannot contract out of world politics, and they are bound to be affected by its course. If they seek to withdraw from all participation, they can only end up worse off. Thus the question becomes that of finding a policy of national inhibition or abstention which does not have this result. Here enmeshment in multilateral or international organizations becomes important and even desirable. Such enmeshment could be confined to economic and functional realms and to those political relationships which would automatically flow from such functional ties.

These types of interrelationships seem in principle to be far more productive even than regional associations and ties. As we have seen, a nation's role in the international system is not usually determined by the geographic region in which it exists. It is an error to believe that regional uniformities are high. Where regional consolidations have been successful, they have worked because the nations of the region were similar in respects other than those of belonging to a specific geographic area. The nations of Western Europe, for instance, could combine functional and regional ties because they were highly developed nations, with similar trading, economic, and political interests. Their cultural attitudes were similar. New Zealand and Australia, however, are unlikely ever to have high regional uniformities with other nations in Southeast Asia because they are different economically, culturally, and politically. From this same point of view, both the United States and Canada share much more in common with Japan and Western Europe than they do with the rest of the Western Hemisphere. Regionalism seems to work, in short, only where it is accompanied by significant similarities on functional, economic, cultural, and political grounds.

It does seem to follow, however, that functional ties of the sort that relate the nations of the OECD, the Group of Ten, and the IMF together are extremely important. Even given the occasional fits of monetary nationalism which beset these organizations, they have been remarkably successful. There are grounds for believing, as we have previously argued, that functional regulation along the lines of action by such organizations is likely to be far more successful than political regulation in the international system today. The economic nationalism of the 1930s appears to be behind us, and a de facto whittling down of economic sovereignty has been characteristic since World War II. Thus, functional enmeshment may be much more significant in the future than it has been in the past. In some ways it may even substitute for the outmoded military enmeshment of the 1950s.

As we have seen, however, even the realm of economic, financial, and monetary affairs poses problems for the future. It is a classic arena for intermediate cooperation, and therefore for the operation of the prisoner's dilemma. The amount of economic cooperation is already so great in the international system, or at least among developed states, that a noncooperator can almost count on the cooperation of his fellows. The payoff for the noncooperating player when one partner cooperates and one does not cooperate is higher than when both cooperate. If player A, in the payoff set in Figure 21-2, assumes that B will play the cooperative strategy (1), then he is tempted to play the noncooperative strategy (2). In the classic prisoner's dilemma, each party reasons the same way, and the actual payoffs are then (1,1), with both players opting for strategy 2. This situation does not fully describe what occurs in economic negotiations among developed countries, however. Instead of both players playing uncooperative strategies, it is more likely that one will play cooperative and the other noncooperative strategies, yielding payoffs of (11,0). In a single game, such outcomes would clearly be intolerable to player 2. But economic negotiations among developed

B

	Cooperate 1	Does not cooperate 2
Cooperate 1	10, 10	0, 11
Does not cooperate 2	11, 0	1, 1

Figure 21-2 PRISONER'S DILEMMA PAYOFFS

countries form a recursive game. Thus the (11,0) payoff for player 2 is more tolerable. In fact, at the next play of the game the payoffs are likely to be (0,11), so that player 2 partly makes up for his losses due to cooperation in the previous game.

The payoff structure of this game, moreover, probably understates the reward one gets for a lack of cooperation in a developed economic context. Prisoner's dilemma incentives are equally presented by the payoff set shown in Figure 21-3. In this matrix if A thinks that B is likely to play strategy 2, he will certainly want to play strategy 2, for in this way he obtains a payoff of 1 instead of O. If player A thinks B will cooperate, he is even more resolved not to cooperate, for in this manner he gets a payoff of 21 rather than 10. Thus the structure of the game leads to the same conclusion as before, with rational players in a single game context both choosing their noncooperative strategies with payoffs to each of 1. In a recursive game, however, if we have outcomes of B_1,A_2 and then B_2,A_1, the payoffs over a series of repeated games are better than if cooperative strategies had been pursued uniformly by both. A series of (21,0)(0,21) payoffs give higher rewards than a series of (10,10) (10,10) payoffs. In the field of economic relationships among developed countries, this type of result is more characteristic than strict prisoner's dilemma outcomes. Countries will stand aside and absorb the blow when one nation devalues its currency or puts on a surcharge. They do not retaliate. In return, at a later stage, they know that other countries will equally stand aside and absorb the blow when they have to improve their payments

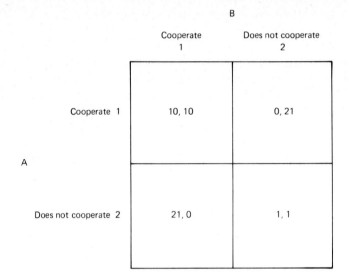

Figure 21-3 ALTERNATIVE PRISONER'S DILEMMA PAYOFFS

position. Thus, despite the structure of prisoner's dilemma payoffs, one does not get uniform noncooperation. One gets cooperation-noncooperation, followed by noncooperation-cooperation. The payoffs end up much higher than in either the strict cooperation or the strict noncooperation outcome.

This does not mean that prisoner's dilemma outcomes could never apply to the developed states. One could see a return to the monetary and commercial nationalism of the thirties if recourse to noncooperation were too frequent. At present, however, it appears that nations prefer to exchange positions of noncooperation against a background of general cooperation than to go to constant noncooperation. If so, functional relationships among states may continue and even expand in a stable framework of cooperation.

REWARD AND PUNISHMENT

Enmeshment and inhibition might be twin means of overcoming nationalism in some current contexts. Inhibition means that states will strive to keep their nationalism within bounds by avoiding overcommitment. Enmeshment means that nations will be entangled in a web of functional contacts in which cooperation is fostered and even increased. Narrow nationalism is transcended. Inhibition is a more feasible option because the international system itself provides a measure of self-operating deterrence. Thus, in one sense, the incentives to warfare are reduced in some parts of the contemporary international system.

The ability to capitalize on warlike incentives is likely to be much more widely spread in the future than it has been in the past. The spread of nuclear weapons is continuing under the auspices of the Non-Proliferation Treaty. Future technology will make bombs or bomb options available to more than a score of powers. At some time before the end of the century it is likely that an environment of strategic quintipolarity or septipolarity will have developed with major weapons capacities in the hands of Western Europe, Japan, China, India, Australia, and perhaps other states in addition to the United States and the Soviet Union. The difficulties of maintaining rational deterrence in such a system have already been illustrated.

In the extreme formulation of nuclear multipolarity tension is endemic. Anonymous delivery will be possible. It is certainly likely that deterrent requirements in 1990 will be harder to meet than those of 1970. There will be a need for enhanced capabilities to assure retaliation against all remaining members of the system at a time when the technical characteristics of forces will probably make them more vulnerable. Aggressive nuclear alliances could well destabilize the future international system. The one bright spot on the horizon is that the dilemma of the victor's inheritance may even present more problems to an aggressor in nuclear multipolarity than it does under conditions of bipolarity. Aggression by powers acting singly becomes less likely. Assured destruction capabilities against one other nation, however, may no longer serve to deter. It does not appear that this problem can be solved in strictly military ways; that is, that deterrent doctrines and capabilities will fully rule out recourse to nuclear weapons.

Of course, the measure of self-operating deterrence in the system will give an aggressor pause. Because the strategic environment will be more complex, uncertainties will be very high. Aggressors will not know the ultimate result of their policies. Populations will be obdurate to foreign direction or governance. The gains that aggressors might make will not be generally commensurate with the costs they will incur. Still, where anonymous delivery or catalytic war is possible, some nations may take the plunge, hoping to avoid retaliation or to have it visited upon some third party. The insecurity and vulnerability of some strategic forces may increase the tendency to pre-emptive war.

Psychological theorists have emphasized that reward and reinforcement facilitate the learning of new tasks as readily as the threat or use of punishment. Yet the international system since at least 1945 has focused almost entirely on the manipulation of punishment structures to ensure deterrence. Perhaps because of the unfortunate appeasement episode of the 1930s, all resort to the use of rewards has been foresworn. Yet this conclusion has been premature. It is clear that reward cannot be used where a constant-sum game obtains. If A strives to reward B in order to keep his favor and constant-sum conditions apply,

$$A + B = k \text{ (constant)}$$

A must end up worse off.

$$\downarrow A + \uparrow B = k$$

Whatever B wins, A loses. These results, however, would not apply in an increasing- or variable-sum game. In such a relationship A and B can improve their positions simultaneously, or they can suffer simultaneously. If B's position is improved, it does not follow that A's is worsened. Thus the error in deductions about the 1930s was to assume that international politics always takes the form of a constant- or zero-sum game. In the 1940s and 1950s, the applications were not entirely erroneous, for the United States and the Soviet Union in the period of strict bipolarity had important contrarieties of interest. By the 1970s, however, the range of common interests is much greater. Indeed, the range of common interests for all major powers is larger. Even a quintipolar game would not be constant-sum. Thus the usefulness of mutual and reciprocal reward as a stabilizing device has greatly increased.

Yet there are limitations and constraints upon the use of reward in the international system. Both Susan Strange and Ernst Haas point out that nations may capitalize upon rewards, but not alter their political or military behavior.[3] Haas contends that unless there is an interpenetration of policy domains, the use of rewards in the economic area might not influence outcomes in the military area.[4] Indeed, in certain circumstances miscreant nations which are heavily in debt to international creditors may be able to increase their access to reward simply because the creditors will not let them go bankrupt. The rewards that Hitler received in his trading relationships with Eastern Europe did not deter him in the days preceding World War II. They may even have given him more leverage. Thus rewards are by no means a panacea.

There are a number of ways, however, in which rewards and reinforcements may help to prevent recourse to war. First, in those parts of the international system where variable- or increasing-sum outcomes exist, rewards can improve the position of both parties simultaneously. These areas may even become more important as time goes on, since there appears to be a shift in the currency of international relations from politics to economics, from military might to economic progress. The increasing influence of West Germany and Japan in the international arena is not attributable to their military power, but rather to their economic strength. The lessening of America's position in recent years is not the result of military weakness or strategic incapacity, but rather of her vulnerable economic position. President Nixon's severing of the tie between the dollar and gold and the devaluation of the dollar clearly indicate how important economic factors have become in American foreign relations. The reaction of other countries to Nixon's new economic policy and to the import surcharge demonstrates that the American action was seen in political as well as economic terms. The fall of the dollar from its previous eminence as major reserve currency in the system is viewed as an enormous setback to the United States politically. Indeed, in the past ten years, among the developed nations at least, much more emphasis has been placed upon changing economic relationships than upon changing military relationships. The debate over missile preparedness and the possibility of first-strike capabilities on either the Russian or American side is taking on an antique flavor. To many foreign policy specialists it has become ritualistic, while the substantial issues are being centered more and more in the economic and financial realm. Thus the first point that needs to be made is that the economic arena, where variable-sum outcomes apply, is becoming increasingly important. It may even become the dominant arena in international politics. Reward structure changes then, can have great influence.

Second, if rewards were to be used coequally with the threat of punishment, they would probably have the impact of strengthening those areas of international politics where variable-sum payoffs occur. Indeed, in the past thirty years, the exclusive concentration upon the threat of punishment as an equilibrating device has probably strengthened unnecessarily those areas of international politics where constant-sum outcomes exist. Bipolarity, containment, and deterrence have all reinforced and strengthened constant-sum aspects of world relationships. If equivalent or even greater influence were given to reward manipulations, this would strengthen the elements of the system which are increasing-sum.

Third, rewards should not be used as *quid pro quo* for pacific international behavior. Nations cannot be expected to respond like laboratory animals to alternate use of the carrot and the stick. If rewards are conditioned upon correct and scrupulous behavior, they are not likely to be effective. Rather, it seems desirable to seek ways in which nations can find greater satisfactions in their relationships with others, so that they are not tempted to use military techniques to change those relationships. If one returns to the deterrent paradigm of Chapter Seventeen, one sees that peaceful behavior is reinforced if there is a large difference between the value of peace and the value of the first strike. That this difference is critical in the causation of war can be seen by looking at the Japanese example in World War II and the Austrian example in World War I. In both cases, the value of peace fell so markedly that the first strike seemed preferable. In the Japanese case, the value of peace deteriorated so much that even an undesirable first-strike option proved preferable. The Japanese attacked even though they had no realistic plans of victory if the war went beyond 1942. In the German case in 1939, an opposite mechanism was at work. Hitler's value of peace had not greatly deteriorated, but the value of the first strike had risen greatly. This was in part because Hitler was not convinced that a decision for war would result in the loss of Germany's peacetime position. The lesson to be drawn is twofold;

first, nations should have high peacetime value positions; second, they should be convinced that in war they will lose those positions. If both of these factors had obtained, neither World War I nor World War II would have occurred. While it is not sufficient merely to build peace values for nations, the higher these are, the greater risk a nation takes in deciding to wage war.

Finally, there is some evidence that building rewards and peace values may have some impact even in the less developed areas of the world. In one sense this seems doubtful because rampant nationalism and militarism are actually chronic in the less developed areas. Rewards, certainly of an economic nature, are likely to seem less important than ideological or territorial gains. Nations in a phase of ideological flood tide are not likely to make the cost-gain calculations that would be necessary to pacify the system through rewards. The question becomes one, therefore, of changing the system in ways that lessen the influence of ideological factors.

Two radically opposite alternatives might be considered. The first would be to so militarize the system that an ideological regime seems destined to suffer cataclysmic losses in its security position if it persists with its ideological expansionism. Essentially, this was the American response to Vietnam. The second is to rely more on self-operating deterrence and to permit nationalistic consolidations consistent with this deterrence. Once North Vietnam has brought about the unification of the Vietnamese people it may be a much more quiescent member of the Southeast Asian international system than it has been over the past ten years. While both the Soviet Union and China have been willing to support her unification effort with large sums of money and materiel, they may be less willing to support a program of expansion in other Southeast Asian countries once unification has been achieved. Indeed, warfare distracts attention from domestic problems. The population is mobilized for military purposes; all attention is directed to a foreign foe; questions of national governance are relegated to the background during the period of war emergency. An ending of the Vietnam war would eliminate some of these factors, and make a repetition of war less likely. If one looks at World War II, the War united the British people in a way they were not united previously or since. After the War, however, the concern for economic welfare asserted itself, and Britain adopted a much less important position in world affairs. Thus an ending of the Vietnamese war might provide a kind of peacefulness in the future which a rigorous contending of that war could not offer. A united Vietnam would have to turn to questions of internal governance; economics would take precedence over politics and ideology. Problems of domestic rulership would then come to the fore.

In one sense, as states develop politically, even if not economically, they begin to face the same problems. Masses are mobilized to political activity, but the direction of their activity cannot be controlled for all time without the presence of a foreign threat. Once a nation-state is consolidated, rulership becomes crucial. Only after a war has ended can economic currencies of power begin to replace military currencies. A united Vietnam would have to put questions of rehabilitation and reconstruction first. It would have to look at trade and economic development. Proprietors are more concerned about profit and loss than clients, customers, or burglars. Proprietor standing in international politics helps to reestablish concern with cost-gain results.

In the less developed realm of world politics, important political freedoms have already been or are in process of being won from imperial or colonial powers. But the new states are finding and will find that political independence and security mean little if they cannot be accompanied by economic independence and security. Ultimately, therefore, it appears that even the less developed world will be concerned with economic currencies, and with development and growth. This will be insisted upon by populations in those countries. The transition may well see wars, even small nuclear wars in the Asian, African, and Middle Eastern areas of the globe. But the transformation should eventually take place. When it comes, the use of rewards may have a utility in the less developed context that they are beginning to have among developed societies. As the divergence in rates of economic growth is made clearer, economic tools should become paramount as a means of bridging the gap. This in turn should depress the tendency to make recourse to militarism and nationalism the solution to all problems.

Of course, these results will not be obtained if nations believe that they will not sacrifice any of the values of peace in deciding to launch aggressive war. But war destroys value, it does not create it. If economic strength will be the measure of polarity in the future, militarism actually makes one less strong. More important, the future of international politics is in itself uncertain. With more major powers and an approximation to nuclear multipolarity, the range of possible outcomes is greatly increased. Aggression may succeed, but the dilemmas of the victor's inheritance will be more acute. In an arena of many strong players, ultimate outcomes are much harder to foresee. Thus it will be more difficult to predict whether values of peace will be maintained or not. Uncertainty dominates the calculations. If, as a result of rewards and reinforcements, the values of peace are high, they may be chosen in preference to the dark uncertainties of war.

SYSTEMS, OBJECTIVES, AND TECHNIQUES

This book began with an analysis of international systems, objectives, and techniques. In the future, the international system is likely to be easier to regulate in one sense than some of the systems of the past. Regulation of quintipolar systems is simpler and more effective than regulation of bipolar systems. Environmental supply will hold out some new vistas for realization of national goals because economics seems increasingly to be a major arena of state objectives. While economic primacy cannot be obtained by all states simultaneously, economic development and welfare can be simultaneously achieved in an expanding environment of world trade and commerce.

Objectives will shift. Security will continue to be the preeminent goal, but the means of gaining it will change. Economic security may well come to be seen as more fundamental than military security. Ideological objectives will continue in some parts of the globe, but they may eventually be transcended as economic goals assert themselves.

Techniques are the most dangerous element in the future picture. Nations will have much greater abilities to wreak destruction upon their fellows than ever before. The possession of these abilities will be much more widespread. On the other hand, the political power which military capabilities confer may well be less. Military force is not governance. As societies are rapidly mobilized by new economic and technological processes, the ability of military arts to command obedience declines. Thus one has the odd paradox that military force is stronger than ever before, but that its use brings fewer values, and may even sacrifice those previously possessed. The prognosis for the future cannot be Panglossian; but neither can it be wholly pessimistic. There remains the possibility that as nations and leaders come to recognize that militarism is not the solution to security or governance, they will develop new techniques, new mechanisms of seeking domestic stability and cooperation which will transform traditional international relations.

NOTES

1 Frank Denton, *Factors in International System Violence, 1750-1960* (RAND Corporation P-4216, October 1969).
2 See Kenneth Boulding, *Conflict and Defense* (New York: Harper, 1962).
3 Susan Strange, "The Meaning of Multilateral Surveillance," in Robert W. Cox (ed.), *International Organization: World Politics, Studies in Economic and Social Agencies* (London: Macmillan, 1969); Ernest B. Haas, "Multilateral Incentives for Limiting International Violence," in Richard Rosecrance (ed.), *The Future of the International Strategic System* (San Francisco: Chandler, 1972).
4 Haas, op. cit., pp. 158-165.

Index

Nationalism, 9, 16-17, 25, 29, 30, 33, 34,
    37, 40, 42, 43, 47, 48, 69, 125,
    126, 133, 136, 139, 140, 164, 166,
    182, 183, 203, 229, 230, 242, 254,
    257, 259, 263, 274, 291-293, 295,
    297-320
Nationalization, 266-268
Nazi Germany (*see* Germany; Hitler, Adolf)
Nazi-Soviet pact, 58
Near East (*see* Middle East)
Negative valence, 279
Negotiating (*see* Bargaining)
Nehru, J., 180
Nepal, table, 111
Netherlands, 173, 210
    table, 111
Netherlands Antilles, table, 111
Neutralist states, 276
    figure, 275
Neutrality, 92
Neutrality Acts, 181
New York Times, The, 251*n.*
New Zealand, 92, 130, 255, 312
    table, 111
Nicaragua, table, 111
Niger, table, 111
Nigeria, table, 111
Nixon, Richard, 149, 316
Nkrumah, Dr. Kwame, 95, 180
Nobility, 28
Nonalignment, 8, 91, 92, 275
Nongovernmental elite sector, 150, 158
    figures, 151-154
Norman, Robert Z., 282*n.*
North Atlantic Treaty Organization
    (NATO), 81, 284
North German Confederation, 34, 52
North German plain, 237
Norway, 301
    table, 111
Nuclear Non-Proliferation Treaty, 59, 86,
    315
Nuclear powers, 49, 251, 271
Nuclear proliferation, 276
Nuclear Test Ban Treaty, 59
Nuclear war, 3, 4, 194, 213, 240, 285, 298,
    302, 310, 319
    (*See also* War)

Nuclear weapons, 3, 25, 58, 69, 81, 119,
    130, 177, 178, 192, 194-195, 206,
    234, 236, 237, 240, 257, 275, 283-
    285
    balances, 247-250
    spread of, 48, 99, 140, 277, 293, 315

Objectives (*see* International objectives)
Old regime of 18th century, 27
Olson, Mancur, 198*n.*
Organization for Economic Cooperation
    and Development (OECD), 80, 312
Organski, A. F. K., 14*n.,* 124*n.*
Ottoman Empire (*see* Turkey)
Overcommitment, 45
    (*See also* Commitments)

Pacific Ocean, 138
Pakistan, 23, 189, 258, 275, 302, 311
    table, 111
    (*See also* Middle East)
Palmer, R. R., 59
Palmerston, H. J., 162
Panama, table, 111
Parable of the stag and the hare, 167-169
Paraguay, table, 111
Participation, 125, 126, 140
    over-, 130
    (*See also* Involvement)
Patriotism, 25, 26, 174, 224, 292, 304
    (*See also* Nationalism)
Payoffs, 99, 104, 106
    figures, 100-103
Peace, 9, 12, 46, 60, 63, 65, 66, 70, 71,
    79, 85, 119, 121, 126, 147, 161,
    215, 217, 219, 220, 297-320
    conditions of, 69
    (*See also* International stability)
Peace of Westphalia, 1648, 15
Peace level of income, 264, 265
Pearl Harbor, 58, 159, 176
Permeability, 19, 20
Personalization, 222
Peru, table, 111
Peterson, Sophia, 282
Philippines, table, 111, 234

Western Europe, 86
Western nations, 44, 45
Western powers (*see* Developed countries)
Wilhelm II, Kaiser of Germany, 41, 157
Wilkenfeld, Jonathan, 186*n*.
Wilson, Woodrow, 56, 200
Wohlstetter, Albert, 144*n*.
Wolfe, C., Jr., 251*n*.
World domination, 215
World government, 9, 11, 23, 60, 79, 305
World Trade, 63
World War I, 5-9, 16, 23, 34, 36, 39-43, 47,
    60, 64, 68, 70, 79, 81, 84, 90, 91,
    94, 98, 118-120, 122, 127, 159,
    162, 164, 171, 176, 181-184, 203,
    204, 210, 214, 232, 235, 254, 276,
    292, 309, 317, 318

World War II, 3, 6-10, 26, 41, 43, 45-47,
    58, 60, 68, 79, 81, 91, 94, 101,
    118-121, 128, 138, 158, 170, 171,
    184, 186, 204-206, 208, 209, 211,
    212, 214, 230, 232, 233, 235, 257,
    258, 261, 263, 266, 271, 273-275,
    291, 301, 309, 312, 316-318
Wright, Quincy, 7, 13*n*.

Yemen, table, 112, 234
Yugoslavia, 56, 95

Zambia, table, 112
Zanzibar and Pemba, table, 112
Zeckhauser, R., 198*n*.
Zero-sum game, 89, 105, 138, 161, 316
Zimmern, Alfred E., 39, 59, 87*n*.